Stephanie Harvey & Anne Goudvis

W9-BIQ-016

Strategies *That* Work

third edition

TEACHING
COMPREHENSION
for UNDERSTANDING,
ENGAGEMENT, *and*
BUILDING KNOWLEDGE
Grades K–8

Stenhouse Publishers
Portland, Maine

Pembroke Publishers
Markham, Ontario

Stenhouse Publishers
www.stenhouse.com

Pembroke Publishers Limited
www.pembroke.com

Credits
Page 7, Figure 1.1: From *Scaffolding the Toolkit for English Language Learners* by Anne Goudvis, Stephanie Harvey, Brad Buhrow, and Anne Upczak Garcia. Copyright © 2011. Used by permission of Heinemann.
Page 9, Figure 1.4: Figure A, Model of Reciprocity, adapted from Cervetti, Jaynes, and Heibert. Heinemann Professional Development Journal 2016/2017 (http://www.heinemann.com/PD/journal/Harvey_Goudvis_Content_Literacy.pdf). Used by permission of Heinemann.
Page 28, Figure 3.1: Comprehension Continuum. From *Content Literacy: Lessons and Texts for Comprehension Across the Curriculum* by Stephanie Harvey and Anne Goudvis. Copyright © 2016. Used by permission of Heinemann.
Page 42: "This Is Cruising" by Kevin Keating. Copyright © 1998. Hemispheres Magazine, March.
Page 60: Adapted from *Teacher's Guide: Tools for Teaching Comprehension*, from Revised Comprehension Toolkit by Stephanie Harvey and Anne Goudvis. Copyright © 2016. Used by permission of Heinemann.

Page 167: "Celebrations of Earth." Photo Essay by Stuart Franklin. *National Geographic Magazine* January 2000.
Pages 98 and 104: Polar bear photo by Steven C. Amstrup, USGS. 2005.
Page 96, Figure 7.4: From THE RED-EYED TREE FROG by Joy Cowley, photographs by Nic Bishop. Scholastic Inc./Scholastic Press. Text copyright © 1999 by Joy Cowley, photograph copyright © 1999 by Nic Bishop. Reproduced by Permission.
Page 171, Figure 10.12: From The Shocking Truth About Energy, copyright © 2010 by Loreen Leedy. All rights reserved. Used by permission of Holiday House Publishing, Inc.

Library of Congress Cataloging-in-Publication Data
Names: Harvey, Stephanie, author. | Goudvis, Anne, author.
Title: Strategies that work : teaching comprehension for understanding, engagement, and building knowledge, K–8 / Stephanie Harvey, Anne Goudvis.
Description: Third edition. | Portland, Maine : Stenhouse Publishers, [2017] | Includes biblio-graphical references and index.
Identifiers: LCCN 2017004524 | ISBN 9781625310637 (pbk.)
Subjects: LCSH: Reading comprehension. | Reading (Elementary) | Thought and thinking—Study and teaching (Elementary) | Children—Books and reading.
Classification: LCC LB1573.7 .H37 2017 | DDC 372.47—dc23 LC record available at https://lccn.loc.gov/2017004524

Cover and interior design by Martha Drury
Cover photograph by Martha Drury

Manufactured in the United States of America on acid-free paper

PRINTED ON 30% PCW
RECYCLED PAPER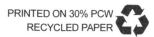

23 22 21 20 19   9 8 7 6 5 4

For P. David Pearson, whose lifelong commitment and dedication to the cause of education has inspired so many of us.

Contents

To access the online appendixes, including updated book lists for launching strategy instruction and teaching across the content areas, visit www.stenhouse.com/strats3 and enter the access code TEACH.

Appendix A: Great Books to Launch Strategy Instruction
Appendix B: Great Books for Teaching a Range of Content Areas and Subjects

Strategy Lessons in Part II

Chapter 10 Visualizing and Inferring:
Making What's Implicit Explicit 151

Chapter 12

Summarizing and Synthesizing Information:
The Evolution of Thought   211

Acknowledgments

Education is a collective and collaborative effort. This book, as well as its predecessors, is no exception. We want to take a moment to acknowledge the many people with whom we have worked over the years and who have influenced our thinking and teaching in so many ways. Our teaching careers began in the classroom, and to this day, we are teachers first and foremost. We honor all teachers. We know how hard they work, and we applaud them. And of course, kids are always our main inspiration. We are grateful every time we walk into a classroom and learn from them.

We couldn't have written this edition without the thoughtful contributions of teacher, writer, and coach extraordinaire Katie Muhtaris. Katie brought the book into the 21st century with her terrific lessons merging comprehension and technology. We are also grateful to Brad Buhrow, Jennifer Burton, Karen Halverson, and Kai Johnson, all of whom added their voices and their classrooms to this book, bringing it to life. Finally, the stunning photographs taken by Ehren Joseph and Kirsten Boyer enhance the third edition beyond measure.

For nearly twenty-five years now, we have been members of the dubious group "Usual Suspects," which includes Ellin Keene, Debbie Miller, Cris Tovani, Susan Zimmermann, Chryse Hutchins, and Sam Bennett. We remain totally grateful for the laughs, all they have taught us, and their contributions to the field. And we offer our heartfelt gratitude to Franki Sibberson, who championed the book from the day she saw the first-edition manuscript.

We are thankful to Philippa Stratton, our editor extraordinaire, who has put up with us for seventeen years and three editions. This book would not be possible without her. We are truly grateful! Also mounds of thanks to the Stenhouse crew, Erin Trainer, Jay Kilburn, Martha Drury, Grace Makley, Chandra Lowe, Drew Yemm, and Dan Tobin.

We again dedicate this book to P. David Pearson because it is grounded in his wisdom and life's work. As a researcher with a practitioner's knowledge of children—how they learn, how they think, and how they understand—David's brilliance and passion is contagious. His research context has always been real classrooms in real schools and is based on a profound respect for the contributions of teachers and kids. We are deeply indebted to David for bridging the worlds of the researcher and the classroom as we continue to learn from him.

Once again, above all, we thank our families for their encouragement as well as their welcome distractions. And we have some really big (or little) distractions this time with the addition of our precious grandchildren Esai (Anne's) and Riley (Steph's). And last but not least, we are still speaking and still high-fiving each other. No small feat after so many years and so many words!

Introduction to the Third Edition

The process of reading is not a half sleep, but, in highest sense, an exercise, a gymnast's struggle; that the reader is to do something for himself, must be on the alert, must himself or herself construct indeed the poem, argument, history, metaphysical essay—the text furnishing the hints, the clue, the start or frame-work.
                                                                    —Walt Whitman

When we wrote the prior editions of this book, we wanted to grapple with Whitman's jungle gym of thoughts, words, and ideas that make up reading. We are still following clues on the pathway to meaning and remain insatiably curious about kids' thinking. We love to hear about their reading—their questions, reactions, interpretations, opinions, inferences, arguments, and celebrations. This new edition is a reflection of our collective thinking. Books offer little without readers.

It's the teachers over the years who have come up to us to share their thinking who have really moved us to write this third edition. We never cease to be amazed at how much we learn from educators as we work side by side in their classrooms, converse in workshops, meet with study groups, correspond by email, and keep up with each other on Twitter and Facebook.

We learn from teachers for sure, but we also learn from the professional community of reading researchers and teacher educators who have contributed so much to the field of reading comprehension. We are not researchers. But we rely on research to guide our practice. So we read and study the continuing efforts of comprehension researchers who push the field further and keep us on our toes. We have spent the past twenty years attempting to translate the research into classroom practice. Classroom teachers and school-based educators are likely too busy at the end of the day to read many research studies, so we like to think of ourselves as a bridge between research and practice. The lessons and units we create here reflect our interpretation of up-to-the-minute thinking in the field.

So What's New?

Much has occurred with comprehension instruction since we wrote the first two editions of this book. Numerous books have been published on the topic. More teachers are teaching comprehension than ever before. More and more educators view comprehension strategies as tools to understanding rather than ends in themselves. Kids around the country can articulate how comprehension strategies help them understand what they read. And new research on reading comprehension abounds This edition highlights the current state of comprehension instruction. We have incorporated recent research and practices that embody this. Although many of the chapter titles remain the same, much of the book has been revised to reflect our new thinking and learning.

To access the online appendixes, including updated book lists for launching strategy instruction and teaching across the content areas, visit

www.stenhouse.com/strats3 and enter the access code TEACH.

Here's what's new:

The Title: *Strategies That Work: Teaching Comprehension for Understanding, Engagement, and Building Knowledge*

- Although the main title remains the same, once again the subtitle reflects how our thinking has evolved. Our new subtitle may be a mouthful, but this edition focuses on the idea of comprehension as a knowledge-building activity. Cervetti, Jaynes, and Hiebert (2009) point out that "knowledge building is the next frontier in reading education," so that idea permeates this edition even more than it has in the past two.

The Organization and Chapters

- A wholly new chapter in Part I titled "Comprehension at the Core: Building Knowledge Through Thinking-Intensive Reading" includes sections on current trends such as close reading, close listening, close viewing, text complexity, and critical thinking.

- A revised chapter in Part I called "Twenty-First Century Reading," which includes a focus on digital reading, with strategies for integrating comprehension and technology and ways to provide access for all by differentiating with technology.

- A new chapter in Part II titled "Instructional Practices for Teaching Comprehension" features instructional strategies and practices that we use again and again. These practices are generic in nature and can be used to create your own lessons with your own text and content. These instructional practices will surface throughout the lessons in this book.

- In Part III, we focus on comprehension across the curriculum, particularly in science and social studies. If there is one place where we really need to use comprehension strategies, it is to learn new information and challenging content. P. David Pearson and researchers at the Lawrence Hall of Science at the University of California, Berkeley, suggest that "reading and writing are tools, not goals" (2006a). We view literacy in the service of learning in the disciplines—science, history, geography and and so forth—and research backs this up.

  Two new and revised chapters in this section are Chapter 13, "Content Literacy," which shares practices for reading, writing, and researching in science and social studies, and Chapter 14, "Researcher's Workshop: Inquiry Across the Curriculum," which features three examples of classrooms—primary, intermediate, and middle—that are engaged in inquiry-based teaching and learning.

Thirty New Lessons

- We have always viewed *Strategies That Work* as a practical resource for teachers to use in their classrooms every day, and that hasn't changed. In this edition, we have added thirty new lessons and kept many of the old favorites. Although we feature the lessons throughout with specific texts, we encourage you to teach them with any text you choose that fits your purpose and the kids' needs.

  We feature new lessons in every strategy. Many include the use of technology to enhance comprehension. They also emphasize using strategies to teach content. Some show how we integrate strategies in a single lesson to better replicate what real readers do as they use strategies to understand what they read.

The bibliographies are no longer at the back of the book in appendixes, but will appear online. They include compelling picture books focused on a range of content areas and subjects, such as social studies, science, literacy, sports, and the arts. To access the online appendixes, including updated book lists for launching strategy instruction and teaching across the content areas, visit

www.stenhouse.com/strats3 and enter the access code TEACH.

We hope this third edition will give you something worth thinking about. It reflects much of the work we have been doing for the past ten years since the release of the second edition. In schools across the country, kids brim with curiosity, questions, and opinions. Schools need to be havens for thinking; classrooms, incubators for deep thought. Thinking thrives when readers connect to books and to each other. We hope kids' thinking shines through here.

Part I

The Foundation *of* Meaning

Chapter 1

Reading Is Thinking

Thirty sixth graders crowd onto a woven area rug in the reading corner. A brass floor lamp casts a warm, amber glow onto their faces. Steph takes a seat in the rocking chair in front of them. "Today, I am going to read you a picture book called *Up North at the Cabin*, by Marsha Wilson Chall. I wish I had written it. I'll tell you why. This book reminds me exactly of my own childhood. It is the story of a young girl about your age who left the city every summer to spend time in a cabin on a lake in Minnesota. Minnesota is called the Land of Ten Thousand Lakes. I grew up in the neighboring state of Wisconsin. We had our share of lakes, too," Steph tells them as she points out the location of these two upper-midwestern states on the wall map.

"Writers write best about things they know and care about," Steph says. She reads from the inside flap that the author spent her summers on northern lakes and was inspired by her own experience as a child and later on as a mother

3

when she returned to this cabin with her own children. "I was a kid who loved summer," Steph says while a dozen heads nod in agreement. "Like the young girl in the book, I spent summers on a lake where we fished, swam, water-skied, hiked, and canoed." Steph mentions how fortunate she feels that Marsha Chall wrote a book with which she identifies so closely. "Have you ever read a book that reminds you of your own life?" she asks. Hands wave wildly as kids share their favorites.

"If we connect to a book like some of you just shared, we usually can't put it down. Good readers make connections to their own life experiences. Let's try something. I am going to read you *Up North at the Cabin*. As I read the words, I am going to show you the thinking that is going on in my head. I'll use these sticky notes to jot that thinking down. I'll place the sticky note with my thoughts on the appropriate passage or picture and let it stick out of the book a little, like a bookmark, so I can find it easily if I want to come back to it later on."

Steph reads through the book page by page, sharing her thinking about waterskiing, the local bait shop, pruney fingers from too much swimming. When she comes to a page that shows the main character in an orange canvas life jacket with two white cotton closures, she laughs and stops to share a brief story. "I can't help but think of my mom when I see this orange life jacket. There were five of us kids, and we lived right on the edge of the water. When we were toddlers, my mom was racked with worry that one of us might fall into the lake and drown. Her solution: the day we started to walk, she wrapped us in those orange life jackets. We wore them everywhere. We ate our cereal in them. We watched TV in them. We looked like five little bulldozers!" Two kids in front grab the book to take a closer look at the telltale life jacket.

"How embarrassing," Josh murmurs.

"You'd better believe it. But I think my mom was on to something. We learned to swim quicker than any kids around just to get rid of those goofy life jackets!" When Steph finishes reading out loud, she encourages kids to find a book they connect with and respond to it.

Kids fall in love with books they can relate to. Find one of those books you really connect to. Unless you are one of Steph's life-jacket-bound siblings or a Wisconsin ice fisherman, it may not be *Up North at the Cabin*. Read it to your students, sharing your thoughts, connections, and reactions as you read. There is nothing more powerful than a teacher sharing her passion for reading, writing, and thinking. Passion is contagious. Kids will respond.

The Reader Writes the Story

Reading out loud and showing how readers think when they read is central to the instruction we share in this book. When we read, thoughts fill our mind. We might make connections to our own life, as Steph did. We might have a question or an inference. Strategic readers address their thinking in an inner conversation that helps them make sense of what they read. They search for the answers to their questions. The written word acts as a springboard for readers to construct meaning, starting with their own thoughts, knowledge, and experiences. The reader is part writer. The novelist E. L. Doctorow says, "Any book you pick up, if it's good, is a printed circuit for your own life to flow through—

so when you read a book, you are engaged in the events of the mind of the writer. You are bringing your own creative faculties into sync. You're imagining the words, the sounds of the words, and you are thinking of the various characters in terms of people you've known—not in terms of the writer's experience, but your own" (quoted in Plimpton 1988).

Active readers interact with the text as they read. They pay attention to their inner voice as they read, listen, and view. They develop an awareness of their thinking, learn to think strategically, and actively use the knowledge they glean. In this way, reading shapes and even changes thinking.

When we walk into classrooms, we often begin by asking kids to describe reading for us. "What is reading?" we ask. A variety of answers bursts forth, and we record these on a chart. "Figuring out the words," "sounding out the words," "knowing the letters" are common responses. Fourth grader DeCoven blurted out that "reading is thinking." He went on to explain that "when you read, you have to figure out the words and what they mean. Sometimes it's easy. Sometimes it's hard." DeCoven hit the target. Reading encompasses both decoding and meaning-making. The first entry on the word *read* in *Webster's New World Dictionary* (1991) defines reading as "getting the meaning of something written by using the eyes to interpret its characters." We're inclined to add "by using the brain" to that definition. Reading demands a two-pronged attack. It involves cracking the alphabetic code to read the words and thinking about those words to construct meaning. Consider asking your students to define *reading*. Keep a chart posted in the room with their responses. The nature of their answers may evolve as your class begins to explore thinking when reading and as you provide explicit instruction in comprehension.

Thinking-Intensive Reading

This book focuses on the meaning-making side of reading, what we have come to call "thinking-intensive reading" (Harvard College Library 2007). Our kids need to be thinking whenever they read, listen, or view, and they need to recognize that thinking is what reading is all about. A few years ago an issue of *Educational Leadership* arrived in Steph's mailbox with an article written by Arthur Costa (2008). She couldn't wait to read it, as he was near the top of her most-revered-educator list. As she scanned the article, a line in the introduction flashed like a neon sign: *"You can't teach students to think."* Her heart sank, her stomach churned. She shut the magazine instantly and tried wishing it away. She simply couldn't bring herself to read it. She and Anne had spent nearly twenty years telling teachers nothing was more important than teaching kids to think, and now this. Yikes!

When she finally mustered the nerve to read it, she understood the message. You can't teach kids to think because human beings are born thinking. It is in their DNA to think. In fact, human beings pop out of the womb thinking. They cry when they are hungry. That's comprehension. They smile broadly at three months when they see their mom. That's comprehension. And at age two, they fully comprehend the word *no* but refuse to pay a whit of attention to it. Kids are thinking from the moment they are born. Costa was right!

So because kids are already thinking, what can we actually teach them when it comes to thinking? We can and must teach them *about* their thinking.

We can teach them to do the following:

- Be aware of their thinking
- Think strategically
- Recognize the power of their own thinking

Develop Awareness

We have observed that some readers, particularly less experienced ones, may not realize that they should be thinking when they read. One afternoon Anne sat down to confer with a second grader and asked, "So what are you thinking?" The young reader looked puzzled and replied to her, "What??! I'm not thinking, I'm *reading*." Anne hid her surprise, but began to wonder how many more kids may not link reading and thinking. Often as kids read, they simply run their eyes across the page without even really thinking about the text. We share the inner conversation we have with text when we read so that kids get a sense of what experienced readers do to make sense. Awareness is the first step to becoming a thinking-intensive reader.

Become Strategic

Once readers are aware that thinking is essential for understanding, strategic reading becomes the focus of instruction. Strategic reading refers to thinking about reading in ways that enhance learning and understanding. Webster's dictionary defines *strategic* as being "important or essential to a plan of action." Having a nodding acquaintance with a few strategies is not enough. Students must know when, why, and how to use them.

When thinking of ways to help students become more strategic, we encourage what Tishman, Perkins, and Jay (1994) call "a strategic spirit—a special kind of attitude that urges students to build and use thinking strategies in response to thinking and learning challenges." We help students recognize the thinking challenges they meet when reading. We teach them strategies, such as activating background knowledge, asking questions, determining importance, drawing inferences, and synthesizing information, as tools to break through to meaning. One of the most important reasons to teach kids to become strategic readers is so they have both the "skill and will" to figure out what the text says when they are confused or meaning eludes them. Kids with a strategic spirit have the disposition to implement a plan of action no matter what they are doing.

Strategy instruction is useful only insofar as it leads kids to better understand the text, the world, and themselves so they can gain insight and do something about obstacles they encounter. Ultimately, being strategic enables us to find and solve problems and accomplish our goals. Chapter 2 delves more deeply into reading as a strategic process.

Recognize the Power of Thinking

Above all we teach kids to recognize the power of their own thinking. Too many of them, particularly those who feel marginalized (and what kid doesn't?), do not recognize the power that rests between their ears. In *Choice Words*, Peter Johnston says, "If nothing else, children should leave school with a sense that if they act, and act strategically, they can accomplish their goals" (2004). He refers to this as *agency* and notes that "the spark of agency is simply the perception that the environment is responsive to our actions." Too often our kids believe the reverse.

To help students recognize the power of their own thinking and develop a sense of agency, we emphasize the distinction between information and knowledge. Harvard professor David Perkins (1992) said the following:

> *Learning is a consequence of thinking. This sentence turns topsy turvey the conventional pattern of schooling. The conventional pattern says that first students acquire knowledge. Only then do they think with and about the knowledge they have absorbed. But it's really just the opposite: Far from thinking coming after knowledge, knowledge comes on the coattails of thinking. As we think about and with the content we are learning, we truly learn it . . . Knowledge does not just sit there, it functions richly in people's lives so they can learn about and deal with the world.*

For Anne and Steph, who attended grade school in the 1960s, knowledge did just sit there, but only long enough for Friday's quiz. Information in. Information out. To meet the challenges of an increasingly complex world, we teach comprehension strategies so our students can turn information into knowledge and actively use it.

Figure 1.1

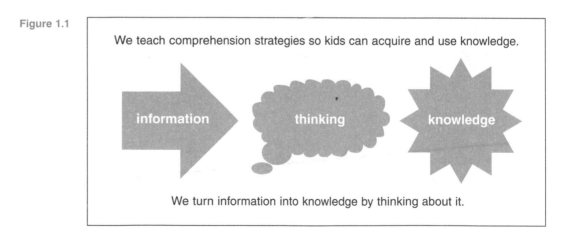

We teach comprehension strategies so kids can acquire and use knowledge.

information   thinking   knowledge

We turn information into knowledge by thinking about it.

Figure 1.1 represents a powerful notion for our kids. Few things will give them a more complete sense of agency than knowing that they have the power to turn information into knowledge. As teachers, it is our role to provide explicit instruction in strategic reading. The kids themselves must turn what they hear, see, read, write, and discuss into knowledge by thinking deeply and expansively.

Comprehension as a Means to Building Knowledge and Understanding

Comprehension means that readers think not only about what they are reading but about what they are learning. In Mary Pfau's fourth-grade classroom, student responses to a Colorado history lesson illustrate how acquiring knowledge and enhancing understanding go hand in hand. While reading a nonfiction trade book called *It Happened in Colorado* (Crutchfield 1993), Jonathan conveys a sense of astonishment and wonder when he responds to a gripping vignette on ancient buffalo hunting (see Figure 1.2). His classmate Amanda reveals both knowledge and understanding in her response to the same piece (see Figure 1.3). Amanda imagines herself in the hunt and responds in a very personal way, saying, "I feel I know what it would be like as an Indian. I painted myself in my head and made myself an Indian." Jonathan wonders, "How could have Indians thought of the ambush plan?" Both Amanda and Jonathan acquire factual information as they read.

Amanda visualizes to better understand what she is reading, while Jonathan can't resist asking piercing questions and making inferences about the entire scenario. Jonathan and Amanda use these strategies as tools to learn new information. They successfully link their strategy knowledge with their purpose for reading. By questioning, drawing inferences, and creating sensory images, Jonathan and Amanda build knowledge and enhance their understanding.

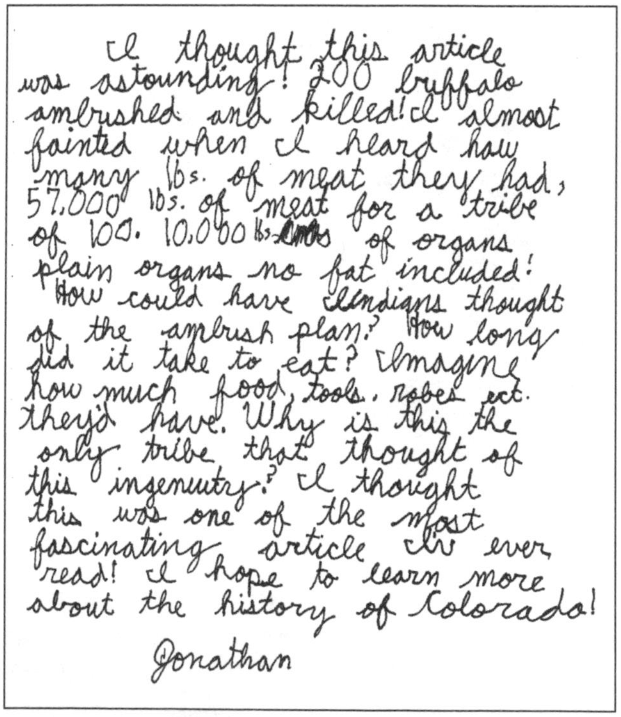
I thought this article was astounding! 200 buffalo ambushed and killed! I almost fainted when I heard how many lbs. of meat they had, 57,000 lbs. of meat for a tribe of 100. 10,000 lbs. of organs plain organs no fat included! How could have Indians thought of the ambush plan? How long did it take to eat? Imagine how much food, tools, robes ect. they'd have. Why is this the only tribe that thought of this ingenuity? I thought this was one of the most fascinating article I've ever read! I hope to learn more about the history of Colorado!

Jonathan

Figure 1.2
Jonathan's Response to "The Great Buffalo Hunt"

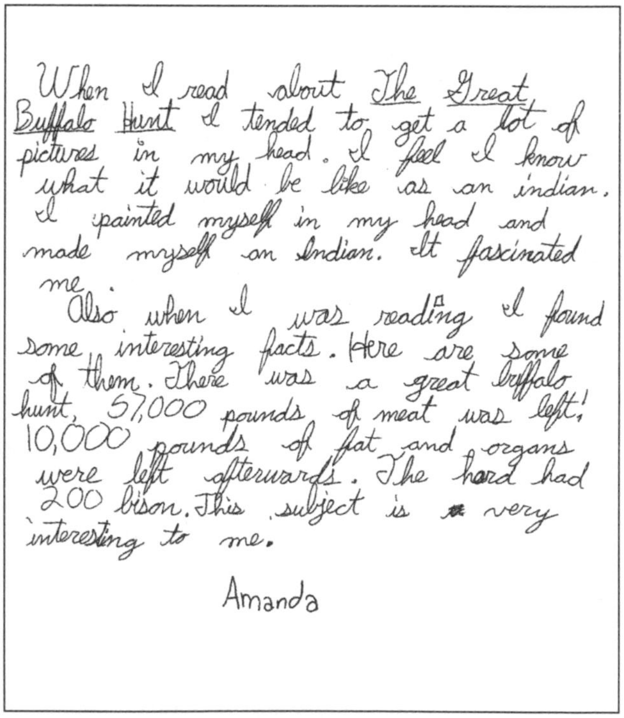
When I read about The Great Buffalo Hunt I tended to get a lot of pictures in my head. I feel I know what it would be like as an indian. I painted myself in my head and made myself an Indian. It fascinated me.

Also when I was reading I found some interesting facts. Here are some of them. There was a great buffalo hunt, 57,000 pounds of meat was left! 10,000 pounds of fat and organs were left afterwards. The hord had 200 bison. This subject is very interesting to me.

Amanda

Figure 1.3
Amanda's Response to "The Great Buffalo Hunt"

In reviews of the research, Cervetti, Jaynes, and Hiebert (2009) argue persuasively that "knowledge building is the next frontier in reading education . . . because evidence is beginning to demonstrate that reading instruction is more potent when it builds and then capitalizes upon the development of content knowledge." They suggest that this is a reciprocal process. As students build their knowledge through reading, they create a foundation that in turn supports ongoing thinking, learning, and understanding.

Cervetti, Jaynes, and Hiebert emphasize the knowledge-building side (see Figure 1.4), which underscores the idea that when we comprehend, we add to and enhance our store of knowledge. So above all, *comprehension is a knowledge-building activity*. In turn as we continue to learn about and comprehend the world, our comprehension is strengthened by existing and new knowledge.

Figure 1.4
The Reciprocal Nature of Reading Instruction
(Adapted from Cervetti, Jaynes, and Hiebert 2009.)

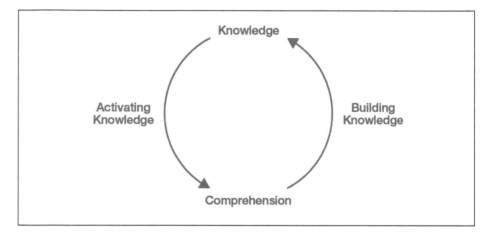

But along with knowledge must come understanding. Professor Howard Gardner, known for his theories on multiple intelligences, says simply, "The purpose of education is to enhance understanding" (1991). When readers enhance their understanding, they go beyond the literal meaning of a story or text. A reader who understands may glean the message in a folktale, form a new opinion from an editorial, develop a deeper understanding of issues when reading a feature article. Acquiring information allows us to gain knowledge about the world and ourselves in relation to it. When we build our store of knowledge, we are more likely to gain insight and even develop empathy, which leads us to think more deeply and critically. When kids learn to read in this way—thinking as they go—they frequently come to care about the subject matter, issue, or question and, ultimately, may even take action.

Reading with a Purpose

When we were kids, we obediently kept our noses in our school books without knowing why we were reading or what we were expected to get out of it. We were passive readers, because we learned that we had little to do with anything in the text and that our thoughts and opinions didn't matter. Our task seemed to be to answer some end-of-chapter questions, make an outline, and remember the author's ideas long enough for the end-of-chapter test. Thinking about what we were reading was beside the point.

The truth is we weren't very engaged and remember very little, since we viewed ourselves as ancillary to the whole reading process. In the field of education, the instructional pendulum swings widely from one extreme to the other. In the 1950s and '60s in our school experience, all that mattered were the author's words. As we began teaching, we were grateful for the emergence of a more reader-centered approach. Advocates such as Louise Rosenblatt, Donald Graves, and Nancie Atwell focused on the reader, not merely the reading.

Now, however, as we write this new edition, the text-centric paradigm has reemerged, particularly with standards that are primarily concerned with the text as the focus and the reader as an afterthought. But we know readers matter—more than anything. All writers know that their purpose is to get readers to read, question, and think. So we keep the perspective of Louise Rosenblatt foremost in our minds and in our instruction.

Efferent Reading and Aesthetic Reading

Louise Rosenblatt talks about two distinct reading stances, efferent and aesthetic (Rosenblatt 1996). Efferent reading is reading to learn, where we take away facts or information or synthesize big ideas. It is the stance we take when we are reading informational text. There is often too much information for a reader to take in without stopping and thinking. We read nonfiction in fits and starts, as if we are watching a slide show, one image at a time. If we see a hurricane swirling over the ocean, we simply have to stop and respond right then and there. In classrooms where we work, nonfiction texts burst with sticky notes and text codes. When readers read nonfiction, they need to read it with a pencil gripped tightly in hand. Efferent reading gives readers the best shot at learning, understanding, and remembering information.

The fiction and literature reading we do is what Rosenblatt refers to as aesthetic reading. Unlike efferent reading, aesthetic reading is more like watching a movie in your mind, where the projector runs unfettered: "In aesthetic reading, the reader's attention is centered directly on what he is living through during his relationship with that particular text" (Rosenblatt 1996). Aesthetic reading allows us to live through the stories of others and to visit a time and place we have never experienced. Aesthetic reading nurtures our soul, connects us to others, and may even transform our lives.

Michael Lynton (2000), CEO of Sony Entertainment, has said, "The book is the greatest interactive medium of all time. You can underline it, write in the margins, fold down a page, skip ahead. And you can take it anywhere." And this from a guy who has spent his career making movies. Sometimes we worry that kids don't see the interactive nature of a book. Given our increasingly plugged-in world of laptops, iPads, video games, and YouTube, reading is at risk. We're half expecting to see books appear on the endangered species list.

The truth is books are nothing without readers. When readers interact with text, a good read is as active as a fast-moving video game. Books and reading are every bit as enticing as roller coasters and sporting events. Teachers know this. They come up to us with dog-eared copies of books brimming with sticky notes, tabs, and margin scrawls, recounting stories of how neighborhood book clubs have transformed them as readers, how reading great books with their kids has spawned a community of learners, and how reading professionally has changed their teaching. When teachers flood their rooms with great text, teach kids to comprehend, and give kids plenty of time to read, their classrooms explode with thinking. Kids can't wait to share their excitement, talk about burning questions, express opinions, and even take action based on their reading and learning.

Chapter 2

Reading Is Strategic

Steph slid her chair up next to Alverro to confer with him. A second grader, he was reading Diana Short Yurkovic's *Meet Me at the Water Hole*, a non-fiction emergent-reading book filled with captivating photographs and interesting cutouts to stimulate thinking. He turned to a picture of a baby giraffe drinking at the water hole and began to read the one sentence of text that constituted the entire page: "When a baby giraffe is born, it is already six feet tall." Stunning information, to say the least!

Alverro read easily through the first clause and then stumbled on the word *already*. He tried a couple of decoding strategies to figure it out, including sounding it out and parsing the word. After several tries, he got it. He read *already*. His teacher beamed, deservedly so. She had dedicated considerable time to teaching Alverro those very decoding strategies. And now here he was, using them to crack the code independently without teacher intervention.

When Alverro reached the end of the sentence, however, he went right on to the next page without taking even a moment to ponder the remarkable fact about giraffe birth size.

"Whoa! Not so fast," Steph said. "What did you just read?"

He scrunched his nose and looked at her quizzically. "*Already?*" he asked.

"Besides that."

But he couldn't answer. He had no clue. He had committed himself single-mindedly to decoding the word *already* and had lost all track of meaning in the process. Worse, so pleased was he with his decoding triumph that he didn't real-ize that he had missed the meaning. Steph suggested he read the sentence again and think about what the words meant. As he did, his face lit up. He pointed to the life-size cutout of the class's favorite basketball star and made an authentic connection. "Wow, baby giraffes are almost as tall as LeBron James on the day they are born! That's incredible!" And he was right, of course; that is incredible.

Alverro had successfully activated strategies to decode text but had diffi-culty figuring out the words and gaining meaning simultaneously. When emergent readers are working hard to decode, meaning often takes a backseat.

Strategic Reading as a Thinking Disposition

Steph and Alverro then talked about what had happened in his first reading of the sentence. Together they decided that from now on when he reached the bottom of the page, he would stop and think about what he had just read. The end of a page became a sort of red light for Alverro to remind him to think about what he was reading. Alverro needed a strategy to monitor meaning, in this case to stop, think, and react to the information at the end of each page. Stopping to digest and synthesize information periodically helps readers con-struct meaning. Steph explicitly taught Alverro how to become more aware of his thinking, to realize when the text doesn't make sense, and to monitor understanding. Monitoring comprehension is a thinking disposition (Ritchhart 2002), which means that when kids read, they are inclined to use strategies to repair and focus on meaning.

Perkins and Swartz (Perkins 1992) define four aspects of metacognitive knowledge that are helpful for understanding how learners adapt strategies to their purposes. These aspects illustrate how learners move from less to more sophisticated ways of monitoring their own thinking. We have adapted their ideas to apply to readers and reading and identify four kinds of learners/readers here.

- *Tacit learners/readers.* These are readers who lack awareness of how they think when they read.
- *Aware learners/readers.* These are readers who realize when meaning has broken down or confu-sion has set in but who may not have sufficient strategies for fixing the problem.
- *Strategic learners/readers.* These are readers who use the thinking and comprehension strategies we describe as tools to enhance understanding and acquire knowledge. They are able to monitor and repair meaning when it is disrupted.
- *Reflective learners/readers.* These are the readers who are strategic about their thinking and are able to apply strategies flexibly, depending on their goals or purposes for reading. They monitor their thinking and understanding and according to Perkins and Swartz, they also "reflect on their think-ing and ponder and revise their use of strategies" (Perkins 1992).

Alverro, a second grader still learning to decode, is an example of a tacit learner/reader, one who is not yet aware of his thinking while reading. When Steph intervened to help Alverro think about the content, she nudged him toward becoming a more strategic and metacognitive reader, one who knows when meaning breaks down and has a plan of action to repair comprehension,

Amanda and Jonathan, the fourth graders who responded to the buffalo hunting piece in the previous chapter, were able to use visualizing and questioning to enhance their understanding of content. They are well on their way to becoming strategic if not reflective learners/readers. When readers have the disposition to stay on top of their thinking as they read, they are better able to access the strategies that best suit their purpose. According to Paris, Lipson and Wixon (1983), it isn't enough for students to simply understand a given strategy. They must know when, why, and how to use it. We teach readers to be active, flexible thinkers who are capable of responding to a variety of reading texts, tasks, contexts, and purposes with a repertoire of strategies.

Developing Metacognitive Knowledge: Monitoring Comprehension

Readers take a giant leap toward independence when they develop the ability to monitor their comprehension. When readers monitor their understanding, they have an inner conversation with the text. They listen to the voice in their head speaking to them as they read, which allows them to construct meaning. They engage in the text and learn from what they read. We need to teach readers to be disposed to think about their thinking throughout their reading process, moving toward becoming the strategic, reflective learners that Perkins and Swartz describe. Engagement matters. Once readers are made aware of and engage with their inner conversation, reading changes. The refrains of "What time is lunch?" and "When's recess?" become an anthem of "Can we please go read now?"

One good reason to teach kids to listen to their inner voice and monitor their understanding is that only when they do that will they notice when they stray from making meaning. Proficient readers—adults and children alike—proceed on automatic pilot most of the time, until something doesn't make sense or a problem arises and understanding screeches to a halt. Both of us read before turning in for the night. We mark the chapter and turn off the light. Or we wake up with lights blazing at 2:00 a.m., our glasses cocked, our books sprawled across our chests. But whichever the case, we've each had the same experience of picking up the book the next night, opening it to the marked page, and having no clue what the last page or so was about. We might scroll back a few paragraphs or might even flip back several pages to reconstruct meaning. The fact is that all readers space out when they read. Kids need to know this, or they risk feeling inadequate when it happens to them. We share these stories of our attention lapses with our students. When they learn that adult readers space out, too, they are less likely to brand themselves poor readers at such times and more likely to forge ahead with the text.

When meaning breaks down, experienced readers slow down and reread, clarify confusions before they continue, and apply appropriate strategies to cruise on down the road. They might ask a question when they need more information. Perhaps they infer a theme from a character's actions. Or they might activate their background knowledge when reading an editorial and disagree with the author's premise. Readers who monitor their understanding can access many different strategies—asking questions, visualizing, or inferring—to construct meaning in the face of problems. A reader's repertoire of strategies needs to be flexible enough to solve comprehension problems with words, sentences, or overall meaning.

Leaving Tracks of Thinking

The Wisconsin that Steph described in Chapter 1 is Wisconsin in the heart of the summer. Wisconsin in the dead of winter is a different animal. One of Steph's annual winter childhood games will give you an idea; it involved counting the string of subzero highs each January in hopes of breaking the established record. But what northern Wisconsin lacked in Fahrenheit each winter, it made up for in beauty. The rooftop icicles, the frosty pines, and the drifting snow lent winter a luster one never forgets. Each morning after a fresh snow, northern Wisconsin kids would scan their backyards for critter tracks. They knew whose paw prints were whose, and they leapt out of bed at the crack of dawn to see who had trespassed during the night.

We tell kids these stories about fresh tracks in the snow, or in the sand for those who live near water. We explain that fresh tracks let us know who's been there, even after they've gone. In the same way animals leave tracks of their presence, we want readers to "leave tracks of their thinking" as they monitor their comprehension. The reading comprehension instruction described in this book encourages students to annotate text, so they can remember later what they were thinking as they read. These thinking tracks provide a window into kids' thinking, and teachers use them to assess understanding.

Strategies That Work

The reading strategies we explore in this book have stood the test of time. For thirty years and counting, they have provided a foundation for comprehension instruction in classrooms around the globe. The good news is we don't have to teach and kids don't have to master hundreds of strategies. Ongoing research confirms that the most effective way to teach comprehension is to ground instruction in a small repertoire of strategies. Pearson et al. (1992) summarize the strategies that active, thoughtful, proficient readers use when constructing meaning from text as follows:

- Monitor comprehension
- Activate and connect to background knowledge
- Ask questions
- Infer and visualize meaning
- Determine importance
- Summarize and synthesize

Monitor Comprehension

We monitor our comprehension and keep track of thinking in a variety of ways. We notice when the text makes sense and when it doesn't. When our understanding breaks down, we stop, think, and take action to repair meaning. From our perspective, monitoring is more of a thinking disposition than a specific strategy. When we monitor our comprehension, we use a repertoire of strategies to maintain and further understanding. We ask questions, make connections, infer, and synthesize, all in an effort to promote understanding. We teach readers to

- become aware of their thinking as they read;
- listen to their inner voice and follow the inner conversation;
- leave tracks of their thinking by jotting down thoughts when reading;
- stop, think, and react to information;
- respond to reading by talking and writing;
- notice when they stray from thinking about the text;
- notice when meaning breaks down and detect obstacles and confusions that derail understanding;
- employ "fix-up strategies" when meaning breaks down—reread for clarification, read ahead to make sense, use context clues to break down unfamiliar words, skip difficult parts—and see if meaning becomes clear;
- examine evidence, check and recheck answers; and
- know when, why, and how to apply specific strategies to maintain and further understanding.

Activate and Connect to Background Knowledge

Nothing colors our learning and understanding more than what we bring to it. Whether we are questioning, inferring, or synthesizing, our background knowledge is the foundation of our thinking. We simply can't understand what we hear, read, or view without thinking about what we already know. We teach readers to

- refer to prior personal experience;
- make connections between texts and media;
- activate background knowledge of the content, style, structure, features, and genre;
- connect the new to the known—use what they know to understand new information;
- merge thinking with new learning to build a knowledge base; and
- activate their schema to read strategically.

Ask Questions

Questioning is the strategy that propels learners on. If we didn't wonder about the text, why would we bother to continue reading? Human beings are driven to understand the world. Questions open the doors to understanding. We teach readers to

- wonder about the content, concepts, outcomes, and genre;
- question the author;
- question the ideas and information;
- read to discover answers and gain information;
- read with a question in mind;
- wonder about the text to understand big ideas; and
- do further research and investigation to gain information and acquire knowledge.

Infer and Visualize Meaning

Inferential thinking allows learners to grasp the deeper essence of text and information by "reading between the lines." Readers infer and visualize meaning by taking their background knowledge and merging it with clues in the text or the images to draw a conclusion, surface a theme, or arrive at a big idea that is not explicitly stated in the text. We teach readers to

- use context clues to figure out the meaning of unfamiliar words;
- merge their background knowledge with text evidence to draw conclusions ;
- gain information from the visual and text features as well as the text;
- predict outcomes, events, and characters' actions;
- surface underlying themes;
- answer questions that are not explicitly answered in the text;
- create interpretations based on text evidence;
- create mental images drawn from their background knowledge; and
- visualize as well as hear, taste, smell, and feel the words and ideas.

Determine Importance

What we determine to be important in text depends on our purpose for reading it. When we read nonfiction, we are reading to learn, understand, and remember information. When we read fiction, we are often reading to nurture our soul, connect to embedded themes, or experience the world from a perspective other than our own. We teach readers to

- sift important ideas from interesting but less important details;
- target key information and annotate and code the text to hold thinking;

- distinguish between what the reader thinks is important and what the author most wants the reader to take away;
- construct main ideas from supporting details; and
- choose what to remember.

Summarize and Synthesize

Summarizing and synthesizing information nudges us to see the bigger picture as we read. It is not enough for readers to simply recall and restate facts. Thoughtful readers merge their thinking with the information to come to a more complete understanding of the text and the topic. Sometimes we add new information to our store of knowledge; other times we completely change our thinking based on our reading. But either way, we summarize and synthesize to gain a more thorough understanding and to acquire knowledge. We teach readers to

- take stock of meaning while reading;
- add to their knowledge base;
- paraphrase information;
- move from facts to ideas;
- read to get the gist;
- use the parts to see the whole;
- rethink misconceptions;
- tie opinions to the text;
- revise thinking during and after reading;
- merge what is known with new information to form a new idea, perspective, or insight; and
- generate new knowledge.

From Theory to Practice: Research That Supports Comprehension Instruction

A few years ago, an exciting email landed in Anne's mailbox. It announced that Pasi Sahlberg, the former Finnish education minister, Harvard visiting professor, and worldwide advocate for progressive education, was coming to Denver! But this wasn't an exclusive conference he was keynoting, it was a Saturday morning get-together of parents and educators interested in opting kids out of state tests. Wow!

Sign me up, state tests are sucking the soul out of education

Steph and Anne hung on Mr. Sahlberg's every word, especially his description of Finnish schools where teachers are respected, well trained, and treated as the knowledgeable and committed professionals they are. It was balm for souls tired of educational policies that advocated for testing kids 24/7, accountability masquerading as reform, and billionaires and hedge fund managers who commandeered the educational policies of a nation.

It's sad that "child-centered" is considered progressive

But what we most remember about Mr. Sahlberg's wonderful speech was his explanation of how Finland transformed what he described as a moribund system into a child-centered, progressive model that educators from around the world flock to visit. Then he asked the group a question: "You know, don't you, where many of these good ideas come from?" He went on to share that the practices that had led to major changes in Finnish education were grounded in educational research done right here in the United States. Perplexed, he continued, "Why is it that Americans come to Finland to see what we are doing when so many of the ideas originated right here in the US?"

This was surprising to read and sad. The solution is right here yet also so far away

Good question! Pasi Sahlberg reminded us of what we practitioners ought not forget: we have a long, robust, and well-respected tradition of educational research in our universities and teacher-education institutions. Educators throughout the world rely on this research as they develop their own educational practices, pedagogies, and policies. In recent years, policy makers and federal, state, and local governments have completely ignored this body of work in favor of policies that have little or no foundation in research.

In previous incarnations of this book, we've woven in research studies that support effective comprehension instruction. We've thought about the implications of work by mentors and guides P. David Pearson, Nell Duke, Dick Allington, Peter Johnston, and many others. In this research review, we share both long-standing studies and recent research.

Long-Standing Studies

For many years, educators studied struggling readers for clues about the best ways to teach reading. Reading research took a different tack in the 1980s, when researchers identified and systematically investigated the thinking strategies that proficient readers use to understand what they read. Why the shift? In 1979, Dolores Durkin jolted the reading world when she concluded, after many hours of observation in classrooms, that the questions in basal readers and on worksheets were really focused on assessing comprehension, not teaching it. We teachers thought we were providing instruction in comprehension through the use of story questions. Durkin argued that comprehension was much more than answering teacher-posed questions.

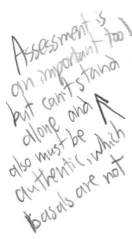

Assessment is an important tool but can't stand alone and also must be authentic, which basals are not

!!! Preach !!!

The reading world paid attention and got busy. P. David Pearson and Linda Fielding (1994) describe the shift in our thinking about comprehension: "Once thought of as the natural result of decoding plus oral language, comprehension is now viewed as a much more complex process involving knowledge, experience, thinking and teaching." The original studies of comprehension strategy instruction examined ways to teach a targeted strategy, such as questioning (Gavelek and Raphael 1985), drawing inferences (Hansen 1981), or creating text summaries (Brown and Day 1983). When researchers explicitly taught kids these comprehension-fostering strategies, kids learned to apply what they were taught, and these methods had positive effects on students' general comprehension as well. Along with these studies, Pearson and Gallagher's (1983) gradual release of responsibility framework provides pedagogical guidance for effective ways of teaching comprehension and thinking strategies explicitly.

According to Trabasso and Bouchard, "There is very strong empirical, scientific evidence that the instruction of more than one strategy in a natural con-

So important

text leads to the acquisition and use of reading comprehension strategies and transfers to standardized comprehension tests" (2002).

Recent Research

In a recent review of the research, Wilkinson and Son (2011) summarized how reading research has "evolved from laboratory and classroom-based strategies of single strategy instruction to studies of teaching small repertoires in more flexible ways in more collaborative contexts."

Research studies became grounded in more authentic classroom settings. Researchers such as Annemarie Palincsar investigated teaching students thinking and learning routines and "packages" of strategies that incorporate comprehension strategies as part of ongoing classroom instruction. Palincsar's original work in reciprocal teaching (Palincsar and Brown 1984) illustrates how comprehension strategy instruction improves students' learning from text. Teaching students to become more metacognitive with respect to their thinking about their reading has also proved effective. Block et al. (2002) focused on "process-based" comprehension instruction, teaching kids to articulate the processes they used to make meaning. She found that students' comprehension scores on both standardized and criterion-referenced measures improved.

Beginning in 1989, Michael Pressley and his colleagues built on ways to teach students multiple strategies. According to Wilkinson and Son, their approach, transactional strategy instruction (TSI), "emphasized transactions between readers and text, transactions between participants (students and teacher), and joint construction of understanding" (2011). Reutzel, Smith, and Fawson (2005) compared this approach with a single-strategy approach (teaching strategies one at a time) and found that second graders who were taught multiple strategies in a context that emphasized discussion about science content and student self-regulation of strategy use performed much better on tests of comprehension and science content knowledge than those who were taught one strategy at a time.

Discipline-based reading instruction that integrates thoughtful comprehension practices with content learning has been and continues to be a promising area of research and a source of effective, engaging instructional practices. For a number of years, Guthrie (2003) and others have investigated the effectiveness of what they call CORI—concept-oriented reading instruction—which focuses on teaching science concepts and ideas in an environment that combines experiential learning, engaging texts, and discussion to motivate students and to build scientific knowledge. P. David Pearson and others at the University of California, Berkeley, continue to demonstrate that combining scientific exploration and experimentation with comprehension instruction as students read science texts increases students' acquisition of science content knowledge (Cervetti et al. 2007). Their work focuses on the idea that "knowledge from this perspective does not refer to a litany of facts, but rather to the discipline based conceptual understandings . . . [that] engage students in becoming experts on the world around them" (Cervetti, Jaynes, and Hiebert 2009).

Duke et al. (2011) confirm that there are a small repertoire of strategies that, if effectively taught, improve reading comprehension as assessed by a variety

Exactly, students must be able to apply strategies to authentic reading or else what's the point?

of measures. This list of strategies varies from one research review to another but includes the strategies that form the heart of this book.

In Part II of this book, we have included an extensive collection of lessons in chapters organized by comprehension strategy. This organizational structure is not meant to suggest that we teach strategies one at a time or in a particular order. Rather we share a constellation of comprehension lessons that we teach our kids based on their needs and our curricular goals.

So what have we learned from over thirty years of research on comprehension instruction? One thing we know for sure is what we often call a strategy is really a whole package of strategic possibilities for reading to understand and remember. Kids need an arsenal of tools to think deeply about text. We don't simply teach a strategy one time and call it a day, nor do we focus on a single strategy unit for weeks on end. Instead we share multiple ways to provide kids with a repertoire of strategic tools that allow them to delve into the text, work out their thinking to construct meaning, and turn information into knowledge and actively use it.

This body of research gives practitioners many recommendations for effective comprehension instruction. As you read this book, we hope you keep the following in mind. We are not researchers. We are practitioners. We have spent the past thirty years learning from and thinking about ways to apply research in our classroom practice. But don't take our word for it. We suggest you take a look at our *Comprehension Toolkit* series (2016); Ellin Keene's *To Understand* (2008); Debbie Miller's *Reading with Meaning* (2012) and *Teaching with Intention* (2007); Peter Johnston's *Choice Words* (2004) and *Opening Minds* (2011); Dick Allington's *What Really Matters for Struggling Readers* (2011); Nell Duke's *Inside Information* (2014); and Franki Sibberson and Karen Szymusiak's *Beyond Leveled Books* (2008).

Secondary teachers will enjoy Cris Tovani's *I Read It, but I Don't Get It* (2000) and *So What Do They Really Know?* (2011). Harvey "Smokey" Daniels and Nancy Steineke have published two reading strategy books designed for middle and high school teachers: *Text and Lessons for Content Area Reading* (2011) and *Text and Lessons for Teaching Literature* (2013). For secondary content-area teachers, Smokey Daniels and Steve Zemelman's *Subjects Matter: Exceeding Standards Through Powerful Content Area Reading* (2014). In *Comprehension Going Forward: Where We Are and What's Next*, edited by Daniels (2011), leading practitioners and researchers give an idea of where the research suggests we should be heading in the future. For ways to merge comprehension instruction with inquiry and investigations, check out *Comprehension and Collaboration: Inquiry Circles for Curiosity, Engagement and Understanding* rev. ed. (Harvey and Daniels 2015).

A Common Language for Teaching and Learning

When you really think about it, teaching boils down to two things: what teachers say and what they do. This book is all about the teaching language and the teaching moves we educators use to teach comprehension and engage kids.

It can be helpful for readers only if teachers settle on a common language for teaching and talking about reading comprehension across grade levels in

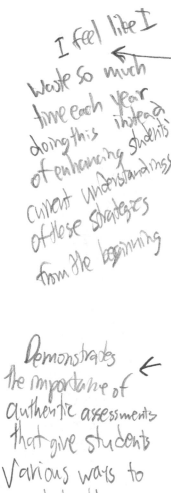

I feel like I waste so much time each year doing this instead of enhancing students' current understanding of these strategies from the beginning

Demonstrates the importance of authentic assessments that give students various ways to demonstrate their understanding

schools. It makes sense to develop clear explanations for each strategy that remain consistent from one grade level to another. When children come into the classroom knowing how to make connections, visualize, or determine important ideas, teachers don't have to reinvent the wheel each year, although they must remember that children's understanding of, say, inferential thinking changes over time, becoming more sophisticated and complex as kids encounter more challenging texts and tasks.

We encourage teachers to work together to become conversant with a variety of comprehension strategies and decide as a group on the language that makes the most sense for their kids. For example, the terms *background knowledge, prior knowledge,* and *schema* actually represent three different ways of referring to a similar concept—the knowledge and experience that readers bring to the text. You will notice that we tend to use the term *background knowledge* in this book when referring to this idea. We want our kids to be understood outside of school as well as inside. So we do our best to avoid "educationese." Choose whatever terms make the most sense to you, but remember to talk with your colleagues to develop a consistent language of comprehension across grade levels. This way we won't confound kids with our ever-changing jargon.

child centered. so important

One caution on the language front, however. P. David Pearson, reading researcher and professor emeritus at the University of California, Berkeley, reminds us that "just because readers say they are using a strategy to better understand what they read doesn't necessarily mean that they are. And conversely, just because students do not articulate the thinking behind the strategy doesn't mean they aren't using it to better understand what they read" (1995). In schools where we work, it is not unusual to hear one first grader turn to another and say, "I inferred that . . ." Our initial inclination is to pat ourselves on the back for all the wonderful teaching we have done. But we hold our exuberance and check with that child to see if she really did make an inference. Or is she just playing with the new language or trying to impress the teacher? We determine whether readers are using strategies to better comprehend by having conversations with them, reading their written responses, and observing them closely.   *"How do you know?"*

The cumulative effect of teaching comprehension strategies from kindergarten through high school is powerful. When kindergartners who have learned to visualize hit first grade, they are more likely to activate that strategy when they hear the word again, see their teacher doing it, and try it themselves. Each year teachers build on strategies the kids already understand, emphasizing a common language and how to use strategies flexibly with a variety of text. We can teach all of these strategies in developmentally appropriate ways to kids at all grade levels. *This framework is huge but takes a lot of communication*

We wouldn't consider spending the entire kindergarten year on teaching kids to make connections while ignoring their questions and inferences. It's not unusual to see a kindergartner look up at a dark, cloudy sky and infer that a thunderstorm is on its way. Fourth graders get hooked on compelling topics and synthesize the information to weigh in on the issues and even take action. As Vygotsky reminds us, "Children grow into the intellectual life around them" (quoted in Ritchhart 2015). It's up to us to create a culture that stimulates and challenges their thinking, and to introduce them to strategies that enrich their reading and learning about the world.

Ultimately, the language we use and the strategies we teach send a clear message to kids that their thinking matters. We can't read kids' minds, but one way to open a window into their understanding is to help them bring to the surface, talk about, and write about their thinking. Having knowledge of the strategies and the language to articulate their thinking goes a long way toward creating proficient, lifelong learning.

Comprehension at the Core: Building Knowledge Through Thinking-Intensive Reading

We've heard that E. B. White once said, "Always be on the lookout for the presence of wonder." In a room that is filled to bursting with great text, stirring images, engaging artifacts, and more, we can't help but ask questions and wonder. Content-rich classrooms make wondering irresistible. Stimulating environments fuel kids' natural curiosity. Teachers who create classrooms like this instill a disposition to explore, investigate, read on, and learn more (Ritchhart 2015). The real world is rich, fascinating, and compelling, and since kids are living in it, let's replicate it in our classrooms.

We don't save comprehension instruction merely for the literacy block. Comprehension is about building knowledge across the curriculum. For many years, we have advocated for teaching comprehension strategies as tools for building content knowledge (Harvey and Goudvis 2007, 2013, 2016). But we are convinced that conventional content instruction needs to be turned on its head. Content learning is not about slogging through textbooks, answering a bunch of questions about dates and events, or spending two periods of twenty minutes a week on science. Rather than simply skimming the surface, kids should be grappling with and constructing ideas for themselves across all content areas, 24/7. In content-rich classrooms, kids are asking questions, inferring, discussing, debating, inquiring, making things, and generating new ideas. David Pearson suggests a simple motto that says it all when it comes to content learning across the curriculum: READ IT, WRITE IT, TALK IT, DO IT! (2006b, emphasis added).

Comprehension strategies are at the foundation of our work in schools. Across the day, across the curriculum, and throughout the year, it is *comprehension at the core*. Collaboration among students, teachers, and others in the school environment relies on an understanding of how we think when we work together. Learning content requires that kids use thinking strategies in science, social studies, literature study, and so forth. And we want to emphasize that English language arts is a content area as well, which includes literature, grammar and mechanics, word study, genre investigation, and on and on. Whew . . . a lot of content to tackle in ELA.

We want all kids to understand that whenever they are reading, listening, or viewing in any content area, they need to be thinking. We teach the terms *thinking-intensive reading*, *thinking-intensive listening*, and *thinking-intensive viewing* even to our youngest kids, so they learn right from the start that reading, listening, and viewing are, above all, about thinking. And not just thinking per se, but doing so with a critical eye and a skeptical stance. As we scan the political landscape, we can't help but wish that civics and history were up front and center as opposed to relegated to the back burner and that kids were reading, writing, and thinking about these important issues and ideas every day. Democracy demands it.

Thinking-Intensive Learning

For kids to understand and remember what they learn, reading must be thinking and learning-intensive, so say no less than the President and Fellows of Harvard College (Harvard College Library 2007). Here's the good news: we have noticed that with most kids, it is the content that is seductive, so thinking seems to come naturally when content is mesmerizing. When kids are surrounded with compelling content, they are motivated to read, learn, and gain knowledge. To build intrigue, knowledge, and understanding, students read, learn about, and interact with the questions, mysteries, controversies, discoveries, events, issues, and drama that are the real stuff of content learning. This kind of deep dive often leads kids to acquire knowledge and to care about and even act on what they are learning.

Arthur Costa maintains that the acquisition of knowledge is only the beginning. "The deeper [the] knowledge one has, the more analytical, experimental and creative one's thought processes . . . Content literacy is all about what kids do with their new knowledge—how they make sense of it and use it in their daily lives" (2008). Thus, acquiring knowledge is a powerful jumping-off point, but kids get truly engaged only when they have a chance to spend some real time exploring significant issues and ideas. So going deeper into the essential questions and bigger ideas across disciplines gives kids a much better shot at "enduring understanding" (Wiggins and McTighe 2005).

The Comprehension Continuum

In this section we share a landscape of understanding that runs the gamut from answering literal questions to actively using knowledge. To explore the multiple ways that knowledge and experience interact, it is helpful to think about the many different purposes for comprehension. The continuum shown in Figure 3.1, which we have adapted from *Comprehension and Collaboration* (Harvey and Daniels 2015), includes five comprehension processes and the teaching language that matches each. This continuum is not necessarily sequential. It is rather a continuum of sophistication that begins with literal comprehension and moves through a spectrum that includes understanding content and acquiring, using, and acting on knowledge. The teacher language on the continuum moves from practices that emphasize literal understanding to more sophisticated questions that encourage analysis and synthesis. The prompts in the last three columns nudge kids toward more thinking-intensive responses. The teacher language suggested here is not a recipe for recitation, but rather a tool that teachers can use to guide students toward higher levels of thinking and deeper understanding.

Answering Literal Questions

Answering literal questions is the least sophisticated practice of comprehension. Students may demonstrate that they can recall information, but simply skimming and scanning to find the answers to questions at the end of a chapter does not guarantee understanding. It goes without saying that literal understanding is an important foundation of knowledge acquisition and use, but practices that begin and end with literal questions, be they from the textbook or the teacher, are unlikely to lead readers to a deep understanding and do little to engage the reader in learning.

Retelling

Retelling involves short-term recall and recounting a sequence of events. We recognize that retelling is a foundational skill for learners and that it is more sophisticated than answering literal questions, but retelling in and of itself does not demonstrate understanding.

Merging Thinking with Content

True comprehension begins when we merge thinking with content. Here's where kids use thinking strategies so that understanding takes root—engaging and connecting, questioning, inferring, visualizing, determining importance, and synthesizing information. These strategies facilitate kids' active engagement with their reading and provide them with an arsenal of tactics to construct meaning.

Comprehension Continuum

Answers Literal Questions	Retells	Merges Thinking with Content	Acquires Knowledge	Actively Uses Knowledge
Answering literal questions shows that learners can skim and scan for answers, pick one out that matches the question, and have short-term recall. *Only demonstrates surface understanding.*	Retelling shows that learners can organize thoughts sequentially and put them into their own words. Shows short-term recall of events in a narrative and bits of information in nonfiction. *Does not, in and of itself, demonstrate understanding.*	Real understanding takes root when learners merge their thinking with the content by connecting, inferring, questioning, determining importance, synthesizing, and reacting to information. *Understanding begins here.*	Once learners have merged their thinking with the content, they can begin to acquire knowledge and insight. They can learn, understand, and remember. *Shows more robust understanding.*	With new insights and understandings, learners can actively use knowledge and apply what they have learned to the experiences, situations, and circumstances at hand to expand understanding and even take action. *Understanding used for problem solving and acting.*
Teacher Language	**Teacher Language**	**Teacher Language**	**Teacher Language**	**Teacher Language**
What is...? Where did...? Who was...? How did...? How many...?	Tell me what happened. Tell me what this was about. Retell what you read. What comes first, second, third? When did...?	What do you think? What did you learn? What does this remind you of? What do you wonder? What do you visualize? What do you infer? What is this mostly about? What makes you say/think that? How did you come up with that?	What did you learn that you think is important to remember? Why does it matter? What do you think the author most wants you to get out of this? What evidence can you cite to make your claim? What do you think are some big ideas here? What difference does it make? What, if anything, confuses you?	What do you want to do about this? Why do you want to take action? Is there a way you can get involved? How do you think you can help? How would you convince others of your point of view? What is your plan? How might you engage the help of others?

Harvey & Goudvis © 2016, adapted from Harvey & Daniels © 2009

Figure 3.1 The Comprehension Continuum

Acquiring Knowledge

Once readers begin to consciously merge their thinking with the content, they are able to turn that information into knowledge. Integrating content and comprehension instruction means that "strategies . . . help students make sense of the content, and the content gives meaning and purpose to the strategies" (Wilkinson and Son 2011).

Actively Using Knowledge

Understanding strategies and having the disposition to use them encourages students to take an active rather than a passive stance toward learning. We can integrate our knowledge and actively apply it to experiences, situations, and circumstances in our daily lives. In this way, we come to realize the power of our own thinking. We may come to care about what we learn and apply that knowledge in practical, authentic ways. Knowledge undergirds informed decisions about how to behave, persuade, and act in the real world. You might ask yourself what the active use of knowledge looks like in your classroom. Sometimes the active use of knowledge means kids learn something new, integrate that information, and apply it in their daily lives. Other times it means kids are inspired to make a difference in the world, form a plan, and take action. For example, as kindergartners listen to *The Peace Book* by Todd Parr, they may make connections to their own lives and learn ways to get along with others and develop a sense of community at school. Fourth graders reflecting on Patricia Polacco's *The Art of Miss Chew* may come to understand how important it is to follow your passion. And middle school kids who read Michael Pollan's *The Omnivore's Dilemma*, Young Readers Edition (2009) may change their eating habits after learning about our processed food culture.

In *Proust and the Squid: The Story and Science of the Reading Brain*, Maryanne Wolfe suggests that as we read, "the dynamic interaction between text and life experience is bi-directional. We bring life experiences to the text and the text changes our experiences of life" (2007). We teachers have understood for a long time that reading changes thinking and that thinking changes reading. What better reason for us to ensure that readers understand that, above all, their thinking matters.

Current Trends

Times change. As we write our third edition of this book, we see a number of educational developments that were not trending back in 2007 when we wrote the second edition. The evolving role of content literacy is a development of such importance that we dedicate two chapters to it in Part III, where we share how we integrate comprehension instruction with content and inquiry. To our delight, content literacy is no longer a bit player; now it's the star of the show! Other trends we explore here include

- career and college readiness and 21st century skills;
- close reading, listening, and viewing;
- text complexity; and
- critical thinking.

Career and College Readiness and 21st Century Skills

Education is always rife with buzzwords: *outcome-based education* in the 1980s, *No Child Left Behind* in the first decade of the 21st century, and *career and college readiness* since 2008. Considering the alternative, not career and college ready, we're okay with this. We'd rather have kids 21st century ready than not! But we have a problem; we have no idea what those careers will look like, and it's tough to prepare kids for 21st century careers when they don't even exist today.

The year 2014 marked the twenty-fifth anniversary of the World Wide Web. Hard to believe that during our early years as teachers, online research was not even a concept—let alone an option. Facebook erupted onto the scene only in 2004. Google didn't exist in the early 1990s, and now it's a verb. Phones were stationary, for goodness' sake. The reality is that the careers of the future are as much a mystery to us now as Google, Facebook, and iPhones were a few dozen years ago! And although we may not know what our kids will be doing when they leave school in 2017 and beyond, we have a pretty good idea of what the real 21st century skills are. Curiosity, for example. Kids will always need to ask questions and investigate. Former Google CEO Eric Schmidt was once asked what he thought education should look like going forward in the 21st century. Schmidt answered succinctly: "Teaching will be learning how to ask the right questions. I was taught to memorize. Why remember it? Now you just need to learn how to search for it. Instantaneous access really changes your life. What never changes is the need for curiosity. What you really need to do is teach people to be curious" (2009).

We agree with one minor exception. You don't really need to teach people to be curious. Human beings pop out of the womb brimming with curiosity. But by fifth grade that curiosity wanes. Children are naturally curious. We need to make sure we don't snuff that wonder right out of them. Instead we need to fan the flame of curiosity throughout their school lives. Teaching kids to ask questions, read strategically, think critically, create, communicate, and collaborate rank at the top of our to-do list. That's what career and college readiness looks like to us. These are the real 21st century skills.

Close Reading, Listening, and Viewing

You can hardly swing open a car door without hearing the term *close reading* these days! And with the recent focus on close reading, teachers often ask us what close reading looks like with emergent readers, with English language learners, with kids who find reading challenging. Well, the truth is, it is about more than close reading. Much of the information this generation will encounter will be auditory and visual. Close viewing and close listening offer the reader more information than simply reading and also provide entry points for kids who need added support. We want kids to listen closely and view closely as well as read carefully. So let's take a closer look at these approaches.

"In literary criticism, close reading is the careful, sustained interpretation of a brief passage of a text. A close reading emphasizes the single and the particular over the general, effected by close attention to individual words, the syntax, and the order in which the sentences unfold ideas, as the reader scans the line of text" (Wikipedia 2016). Close reading as it was initially conceived focused primarily on the author's intent rather than the reader's interpretation.

Steph and Anne both went through high school when reading was highly text centric. It was the reader's job to ferret out what the author was saying, with little thinking, comment, or response on the part of the reader. Both Steph and Anne had a sense of déjà vu when close reading came roaring back, with its admonition to "stay within the four corners of the text." Too often the practice of close reading emphasized literal understanding of text at the expense of what readers bring to it. Some interpretations of close reading went so far as to say that readers were not supposed to access background knowledge as they read.

This makes no sense and is our biggest quibble with the idea of close reading in its current iteration. Research on schema theory explains how our previous experiences, knowledge, emotions, and understandings have a major impact on how we read and learn (Anderson, Spiro, and Anderson 1978). As P. David Pearson has quipped, "Asking readers to read without thinking about what they already know is like asking people to breathe without oxygen" (2015). Not possible! The upshot is that nothing colors our learning and understanding more than what we bring to it.

In practice, what we really want to do is make sure kids get in the habit of connecting the new to the known. How else could they possibly make sense of brand-new information? Over the past few years, however, we have occasionally noticed teachers spending too much time building background knowledge before students begin to read. There is no doubt that it's important to take a bit of time to have kids think and talk about what they already know about the topic, and perhaps view an image to stoke their thinking. So we take five or ten minutes to build some background and fire kids up so they get excited and want to read more. Then kids spend most of their time reading, because the best way to build background knowledge is through reading, listening, and viewing. After all, "Today's new knowledge is tomorrow's background knowledge" (Pearson 2014).

Our Take on Close Reading

We believe close reading is *strategic* reading! We want all kids to be able to read challenging text closely and carefully to better understand it. We want them to learn about interesting content, immerse themselves in great literature, engage in rich talk about text, and read extensively. The more complex the text and the tougher the vocabulary, the more thoughtful and strategic the reader must be. When kids encounter unfamiliar concepts, vocabulary, and text that is above their reading level, they are likely to meet words they can't read and ideas they don't understand. Using comprehension strategies allows them to hurdle the background-knowledge gap as they grapple with meaning. Inferring is frequently the life raft when close reading because it allows readers to construct meaning from text in the absence of explicit information. To read complex text for understanding, readers need strategies that allow them to make sense of unfamiliar words, concepts, issues, and ideas. Text that is challenging requires us to pay careful attention.

When Readers Read Closely, They Need To

- Slow down their rate and reread for clarification,
- Consider what they already know to better understand and be prepared to revise misconceptions,
- Annotate their new learning and confusions,
- Question the text,
- Think inferentially to figure out unfamiliar information,
- Determine importance by analyzing the information,
- Synthesize the information to get the gist, and
- Reread to expand understanding.

We teach kids when and why they need to read closely. We let them know that they probably will need to read closely and carefully when the information is extremely important and/or when the text is really hard. They need to think strategically and be able to apply thinking strategies flexibly and seamlessly to understand complicated text. The same applies when they debate complex issues, address problems, argue about solutions, and attempt to come to resolutions. They need to slow down and analyze the problem to construct meaning and solve it. So close, strategic reading can be helpful when readers are in text that demands it.

But unfortunately, too often close reading has become a default practice that kids are asked to use with text that doesn't require it. The fact is, most reading does not require this close, analytic routine. So we don't ask kids to do a litany of close readings every week, and we avoid published close-reading programs like the plague. If close reading happens constantly, we may commit what Kelly Gallagher refers to as "Readicide: noun, the systematic killing of the love of reading, often exacerbated by the inane, mind-numbing practices found in schools" (2009). To avoid this frightening fate, we fill the room with wildly interesting books and let kids *just plain read text they can and want to read* every single day.

Close Listening

In addition to the emphasis on close reading, we are teaching kids to listen carefully and actively. We know that all children can engage deeply and thoughtfully as they listen to stories and hear information. So we continue to read aloud every day and engage them in rich talk about text. We show them how we carefully consider and respond to the pictures, features, words, and ideas in the text. When children are taught to listen closely, ask questions, make connections, and infer big ideas, they will be far better able to think and delve into the deeper ideas.

Discussion Prompts for Close Listening

- What do the words make you think about?
- What do you wonder?
- What does it remind you of?
- What did you hear that makes you think that?
- What do you want to hear more about?
- What did you hear that is evidence for that idea?
- Do you agree or disagree? Why or why not?

Close Viewing

Visual literacy is an increasingly important genre in the 21st century. Regarding visual literacy, Ken Burns, the famous documentary filmmaker, says, "I treat the photograph as a work of great complexity in which you can find drama. Add to that a careful composition of landscapes, live photography, the right music and interviews with people and it becomes a style" (2017). We want kids to take time to ponder images in picture books, nonfiction trade books, and websites, noticing their beauty, their style, asking questions, inferring, and more. So we share photographs, diagrams, illustrations, infographics, charts, graphs, and so on, and model how we think about them so that kids will look more closely and learn from these features.

And now with devices, kids can make movies, music videos, reflection videos, and more. All kids can learn a lot from closely viewing these sources. Practices such as See Think Wonder, a thinking routine for exploring images, videos, objects, and more, can be very useful to help kids glean more from a visual text (Harvard Project Zero 2017). Teachers ask kids, "What do you see?" "What do you think about that?" "What do you wonder?" The routine fosters careful observation and thoughtful interpretation. Check out VisibleThinkingpz.org.

The *New York Times* offers a visible thinking lesson every week called "What's Going On in This Picture?" They publish a photo stripped of its caption every Monday. Teachers have kids talk and wonder about the image. The *Times* recommends three prompts to stimulate close viewing: *What is going on in this picture? What do you see that makes you say that? What more can you find?* On Thursdays, they add the caption and the back story. Kids can't wait until Thursdays! Close viewing gives us an entrée into our visual world that a cursory look simply can't reveal.

Discussion Prompts for Close Viewing

- What do you notice?
- What do you see?
- What does it look like?
- What does the image remind you of?
- What do you wonder?
- What are you thinking?
- What do the graphics make you think about?
- What in the visual feature makes you think that?
- What do you infer about the character(s) from the picture?
- Where is the evidence for that idea?
- What do you see that makes you want to learn more?
- What do you want to know more about?

Now, please don't get us wrong; no one loves books and textual literacy more than we do, but we ignore visual literacy at our kids' peril. We need to teach all kids to think beyond merely the words and use all sources available to them to construct meaning and build knowledge.

Text Complexity

Along with the resurgence of close reading comes the notion of text complexity and the idea that children of all ages should spend some time reading text that is challenging and perhaps above their level. Of course, we want our kids to have the wherewithal to attack challenging text, but we also know that to grow as readers they need to spend a great deal of time reading text they can and want to read (Allington and Gabriel 2012).

Hiebert and Martin (2015) have found that "the new standards . . . require fifth graders to read at a text complexity level previously expected of eighth graders." They go on to say that this is "an epic shift." We've noticed this ourselves as we spend time in schools, as has any sentient being who has spent any time with kids in classrooms in the past five years. Nothing concerns us more than kids sitting in front of text that is too difficult. How unfair. Three grade levels higher than previously expected? And where is the evidence that hard text makes kids better readers? It flies in the face of all the research that Stephen Krashen (2001) has gathered over the years. As he says, "Readers will [simply stop] reading texts if they are not comprehensible or if they are dull."

It's important to understand what leveling text even involves. To level texts, be it DRA levels, Lexile levels, and so forth, software leveling programs generally consider two aspects of a text: the number of words in a sentence and the number of syllables in a word. An unintended consequence of these software programs is that when the program doesn't recognize a word, it ups the level. This anomaly leads a text such as Rowling's *Harry Potter and the Chamber of Secrets* to garner the same level as Hemingway's *The Old Man and the Sea*. We know which one has more complex ideas. In American schools, students read *The Old Man and the Sea* in high school; they read the Harry Potter series in fourth or fifth grade. Scholars write their doctoral dissertations on the work of Hemingway. But Rowling's long sentences and numerous unfamiliar multisyllabic names stoke the Lexile engine enough so that both of these texts have the same Lexile level. *Henry and Mudge* (Rylant) Lexile levels out at 460 and *Sarah, Plain and Tall* (MacLachlan) at 430. Why? you ask. The repeated use of the unfamiliar word *Mudge* bumps the level of this kid-friendly book sky high (Hiebert 2012). And the highest Lexile level we have seen assigned to a simple text is a whopping 1090 to *Tikki Tikki Tembo* (Mosel)! Software leveling programs offer a ballpark idea of the text level, but that is about it.

There are some things that computers do better than people and some things that people do better than computers. One of those things thoughtful teachers are much better at is knowing their kids as readers. Leveling programs can't know that Jeremy is crazy for Ford pickups or that Suzanna wants to be an astronaut. Interest is at the heart of book selection. Interest is crucial when it comes to reading success. The role that interest plays in reading is at the core of a successful teacher's ability to increase their kids' reading, learning, and achievement. Use levels as a guide, but use your own common sense and judgment when helping your students select a text.

Text complexity is about much more than how dense the text is and how technical the vocabulary. Complexity resides in complicated ideas with multiple perspectives that can be presented in a myriad of ways. Complex text demands the reader's recognition and thoughtful consideration of the multifaceted nature of an issue or a problem. Readers need to consider a variety of aspects and implications of a problem or an issue, including economic implications, cultural implications, political implications, and so on. As we think about it, probably one of the most complex sentences in literature has one of the lowest Lexile levels: Shakespeare's "To be, or not to be: that is the question." Ultimately, complexity is about ideas, not merely words.

Teachers can help kids understand anything they read more completely by posing questions that encourage kids to work out the meaning. Some question prompts adapted from Peter Johnston's books *Choice Words* (2004) and *Opening Minds* (2011) follow. Keep in mind that these are not questions with a designed answer, but rather questions to encourage discussion and conversation.

Discussion Prompts to Support Understanding of Complex Text

- What in the text makes you say that?
- How do you know?
- What makes you think that?
- How did you come up with that?
- Where is the evidence for that?
- Where in the text did you get that idea?
- Who has another idea?
- What is the evidence for that idea?
- Who might disagree?
- How might you explain the different interpretations?
- How might you persuade someone to change his or her mind?
- What is the author trying to prove?
- What kind of proof does the author use?
- What is the author assuming the reader will agree with?
- Is there something the author leaves out that would strengthen the argument?
- Is there something the author included that hurts the argument?
- Does the author adequately defend the argument?

Critical Thinking

The trend toward teaching critical thinking is perhaps the most important trend in reading practice and theory since our previous edition. According to critical thinking specialist G. Randy Kasten, "The ability to think critically is one skill separating innovators from followers. Critical thinking reduces the power of advertisers, the unscrupulous and the pretentious, and can neutralize the sway of an unsupported argument" (2015). In this era of "alternative facts" and "fake news" this is the ultimate skill for the survival of our democracy. Kasten goes on to say that most students enjoy thinking critically "because they see immediately that it gives them more control." And Kasten points out that "every educator is in a position to teach students how to gather information, evaluate it, screen out distractions and think for themselves . . . When students are educated about information-gathering and critical thinking, they have the tools necessary to see through spin and make decisions based on fact, rather than myth or propaganda" (2015).

We couldn't say it any better. Our take on critical reading and thinking is pretty straightforward: it's not a program to be trotted out at 2:00 p.m. when it's "thinking skills time." For starters, kids need to be strategic and agentive, to read and think with a critical eye and a skeptical stance every time they open a book, listen to a podcast, or fire up their tablet. But what does this mean and how can we ensure kids are prepared? In a culture of nonstop information, images, and TMI on a daily basis, preparation and vigilance in the thinking department make a lot of sense.

If kids are to become thoughtful, versatile, independent readers and thinkers who can read between the lines, they need a classroom community that values and expects kids to interact, think, and question all day, every day. The critical thinker in chief, of course, is the teacher who works to enculturate an environment where critical thinking flourishes.

In these classrooms, teachers do the following:

- *Foster a strategic spirit.* Tishman, Perkins, and Jay suggest that "the truly versatile thinker is one who is able to construct, invent or modify a thinking strategy to meet the unique demands of the situation" (1994). This kind of original and flexible thinking energizes learning, so students are inclined to troubleshoot, solve problems, and take action through creative thinking.

- *Cultivate creative confidence.* David and Tom Kelley offer another take on immersing kids in a culture of thinking. They extoll the virtues of creative confidence. "Creative confidence is the natural human ability to come up with breakthrough ideas and the courage to act on them . . . When you have creative confidence, you can change things. You can do what you set out to do" (2013). As Kasten says, too often people do not "recognize the significance of their own perceptions" (2015). We need to work hard in our classrooms to change this. Confidence has the potential to move mountains.

- *Develop kids' sense of agency.* Agency represents the idea that "the environment is responsive to our actions" (Johnston 2004). Kids with a sense of agency believe that they are the kind of kid who can figure things out, find and solve problems, and make things happen. But kids are unlikely to develop a sense of agency if they lack strategies. When kids are reading independently and come to an idea, word, or issue they do not understand, they can move forward only if they have a repertoire of strategies to fall back on. According to Dyson, "A child must have some version of 'Yes, I imagine I can do this.' And a teacher must also view the present child as competent and on that basis imagine new possibilities" (1999, quoted in Johnston 2004).

To create an environment that builds a strategic spirit, a sense of creative confidence, and agency in every student, teachers must

- let kids know that their thinking matters and ensure that they can speak up without fear of being criticized;
- make sure kids feel comfortable expressing their opinions and taking a stand;
- give kids time to explore on their own and run with their passions;
- ensure that kids have daily opportunities to read, listen to, and view a variety of sources with many different perspectives;
- encourage kids to express their curiosity and inquisitiveness;
- value kids' ideas and honor their open-mindedness;
- refrain from stigmatizing mistakes and encourage kids to experiment;

- provide multiple opportunities for kids to try out new ideas and take risks;
- support kids in thoughtfully and respectfully challenging each other's ideas; and, above all,
- model and create these conditions in their classrooms—showing kids what this kind of learning environment looks like and how to live it every day.

Critical thinking is all about reading between the lines, being able to interpret underlying messages that may not be obvious on the surface, and discerning what the communicator is actually trying to say. Unfortunately, we live in a world where many people—politicians, marketers, celebrities, bloggers—put forth whatever they choose whether it's truthful or not, often intending to mislead people. If readers swallow everything they read or hear whole, we've got a problem. Critical thinking, therefore, becomes an increasingly important 21st century skill.

We must teach kids to sort and sift accurate information from hyperbole, ferret out fact from fiction, distinguish an off-the-top-of-the-head opinion from an informed opinion, and develop the habits of mind to trust their own interpretations and decisions. In Parts II and III of this book, we have tried to include lessons and practices that spark critical thinking.

Critical thinkers are encouraged to do the following:

- Reread, rethink, and reflect
- Adopt a skeptical stance
- Look beneath and beyond the information given to gain insight
- Ask authentic questions about information, ideas, evidence, expertise, and so forth
- Develop empathy and imagine the world from multiple perspectives
- Give credence to varied opinions, interpretations, and ideas
- Question varied opinions, interpretations, and ideas based on evidence to the contrary
- Analyze and synthesize to make connections across disciplines
- Create their own take on information and issues
- Imagine possibilities and formulate original interpretations, including how things could be different
- Integrate thinking to see all aspects and facets of a problem
- Go beyond problem solving: discover and surface potential problems before they occur
- Develop world awareness: be a global citizen, aware of our impact on the environment and society both close to home and beyond

Sounds like a tall order, but we don't have a choice! Eleanor Roosevelt punctuates this point: "Every effort must be made in childhood to teach the young to use their own minds. For one thing is certain: If they don't make up their own minds, someone will do it for them" (quoted in Beane 2005).

Chapter 4

Twenty-First Century Reading: Books and Beyond

Winston Churchill once said, "If you cannot read all of your books, at any rate handle, or as it were, fondle them—peer into them, let them fall open where they will, read from the first sentence that arrests the eye, set them back on the shelves with your own hands, arrange them on your own plan so that you at least know where they are. Let them be your friends; let them at any rate be your acquaintances" (quoted in Gilbar 1990). We know from whence Mr. Churchill spoke. At last count, between the two of us, we had nearly two dozen books on our nightstands of which we had not read a word. But we have held them, flipped through them, and introduced ourselves to them. The pile, however, just seems to grow. So we hold Churchill's words dear, and dream of when we might have time to read them all. This holds true for our children's-book reading as well.

Each year, huge numbers of children's books roll off the presses. We can't read them all; we can't even meet them all. So how do we get to know more books and get them into the hands of kids? Share those books you love with your colleagues. Spend some time each week talking about books. Your repertoire of picture books, trade books, chapter books, and collections will grow with each conversation. Get up close and personal with the library. School librarians and children's librarians in public libraries have the most in-depth knowledge of children's literature of anyone we know. They regularly read and review publications such as *Horn Book Magazine* and *Book Links*, both of which include extensive reviews of children's books on every conceivable theme and topic. Not to mention blogs from passionate book lovers such as Donalyn Miller and Teri Lesesne.

"Read widely and wildly," suggests literacy educator Shelley Harwayne (1992). The mini-lessons in this book incorporate a wide range of genres, including realistic fiction, historical fiction, nonfiction, and poetry. Kids love to read in every genre. It's the compelling text and images in Elizabeth Rusch's *Electrical Wizard: How Nikola Tesla Lit Up the World*, the realistic fiction about peer relationships in Jacqueline Woodson's *Each Kindness*, and the beautiful nature poetry in Joyce Sidman's *Swirl by Swirl* that hook our kids. We need to fill our classrooms to bursting with text of every genre and topic.

We wrote this book, in part, to ease the job of choosing from among so many books, not to mention websites, e-books, and other digital text forms. On the companion website for this book, we have included an extensive bibliography of picture books, trade books, and subject-area texts that has been updated from the previous edition of this book as well as an updated list of web reading. We hope they are both helpful. (See the table of contents for how to access these online resources.) But we know that you may find your favorite picture book or blog missing from these lists. We simply couldn't include them all, so by all means improve this list by adding those you dearly love.

But all of this book love doesn't amount to much if kids don't have access to scads and scads of books and time to read them. In *Readicide: How Schools Are Killing Reading and What You Can Do About It* (2009), Kelly Gallagher suggests several reasons why kids get turned off to reading, including a dearth of interesting reading material in their classrooms, limited opportunities for kids to choose their own text, and a limited amount of time for real reading and writing during the school day. Guthrie and Humenick found that when kids had access to a wide range of interesting text that they selected and were able to read, their motivation for reading increased, as did their reading comprehension (2004). When kids don't have access to books in their lives outside of school, they need even more opportunities to read in school every day. *Access plus choice plus time equals volume.* Each of these components is essential for kids to develop as readers. Throughout this book, we emphasize the need for extensive free voluntary reading across the day and across the year to grow their literate lives.

Text and Media Matter

Down with innocuous text, both print and digital! Alfred Tatum, author of *Teaching Reading to Black Adolescent Males* (2005), suggests that literacy holds power for young black men when it relates to their lives and concerns, when it is authentic, and when it raises issues that matter to them. We believe this holds true for *all* of us. Text in all forms matters—a lot. If children are not reading engaging, interesting, thought-provoking text, why bother? We surround kids with text that includes a variety of perspectives, opinions, ideas, issues, and concepts to read about, write about, and talk about. When students read and respond to text that provokes thinking, they are much more likely to become active, engaged readers. We flood our classrooms with text, images, videos, kidcasts, and infographics of all different types and on tons of topics, so we have a better shot at reaching all of our kids. How we choose text and how kids choose their own makes a difference in their literate lives.

Many of the lessons in the upcoming chapters use text that we've chosen because it furthers the purpose of the lesson. It is important, however, to keep in mind that these lessons can be done with many different texts of various lengths and genres, both online and in print. *Strategies That Work* is all about teaching the reader, not merely the reading. Choose those texts that serve your purpose or that you love, and teach with those.

This chapter shares our thoughts about the need for using a variety of short text forms for literacy teaching and learning, such as picture books, trade books, magazines, newspaper and web articles, and so on. It also describes ways to support teachers in choosing the best possible text for instruction. Last but not even close to least, it shares how teachers can teach their kids to select texts they can and want to read. When kids read text at their level and of interest to them, they are more likely to further their understanding and have a great read. Choice makes a difference for both teachers and kids.

The Possibilities of Short Text

We often ask teachers to write down the different types of reading they've done over the past few weeks. Usually, they mention blogs, newspapers, magazines, e-mail, manuals, social media, cookbooks, brochures, reports, newsletters, and so on. Many also have a novel, biography, or self-help book going. But about 80 percent of the reading they report is of the short-text nonfiction variety. This is what the "Twitterverse" most often refers to as "short reads." And since the advent of the Common Core State Standards and other new state standards, short nonfiction has also flooded the schools. Well-written short text gives kids an opportunity to read a piece quickly, dig into the themes, and respond to them.

The many forms of short text in magazines, newspapers, and websites—including essays, editorials, feature articles, sports stories—give kids the widest range of possibilities for finding and reading interesting text. And more and more frequently much of our reading and research comes from the web. Internet articles give us the most current and up-to-date information. We need to pack our classrooms with magazines, newspapers, and websites as well as with books. Short reads often rescue us from turning a mini-lesson into what we sheepishly call a maxi-lesson. When we use just a little bit of text for a demonstration, students can get the point, we can stick to the point, and everyone can get on with what's most important: students reading and practicing on their own. (See our list of magazines, newspapers, and websites online. Directions for accessing the list are in the table of contents of this book.)

Choosing Short Text for Instruction

Before she got her iPad, Steph used to haul a carry-on bag the size of a small Buick filled with reading material onto each and every flight. She remembers a time when she checked it by mistake and found herself facing four hours of flying without a single thing to read. While contemplating what she might do during the flight, she reached into the seat pocket in front of her and pulled out *Hemispheres Magazine,* the United Airlines in-flight magazine. Although she flew regularly, she had never opened one before, and her expectations were less than sky high. She turned to an article on cruising, which began as follows:

> *When I was young and slippery as a sea squirt, I spent a sun-splashed summer polishing brass for the glory of waterborne commerce. In those long glorious sea days, we glided into tropical ports—dead slow—in the early morning, the sea like melted glass, the ship causing barely a ripple. You could feel the faint beat of the engines and hear the steady wash of creaming water alongside. The anchor chain went out, the bridge telegraphed "finished with engines" and we looked wonder of wonders on a foreign land. My old cargo line called at dusty little coffee ports, but they were Paris, London and Rome to me. I thought then that traveling by ship was the best way to see the world. I still do.* (Keating 1998)

They say necessity is the mother of invention. If Steph hadn't mistakenly checked her reading material, she would have missed this stunning text. Compelling short text is everywhere. We just need to live in a way that lets us find it. Pore over newspapers, online essays, magazines, travel books, blogs, and picture books. The next time you read an article, a poem, or a short story that really grabs you, think about why. Don't just toss it away. Don't just press *delete.* Save it even if you don't know exactly how you will use it. In all likelihood, you will find a place for it in your teaching sooner or later. When we collect and save short text, we consider the following:

Purpose
When we design instruction around print or digital short text, we need to be clear about what we want children to learn from the particular experience. Do we want to model a specific strategy or build background knowledge on a particular topic? Sometimes a thoughtful picture book may be the best way to launch a discussion about a pressing issue like racism or an unfamiliar topic like the Great Depression. Other times a video or podcast may draw kids immediately into the topic. The clearer we are about our instructional focus, the easier it is to match texts with our teaching goals.

Audience and Relevance
The interests, ages, and learning needs of our students are paramount in choosing texts for teaching. Awareness of our students' backgrounds and experiences is essential if we are to select texts for our students that, as librarian Fran Jenner says, "touch their souls."

Genre
We choose a variety of genres in short-text form, including poetry, short stories, essays, letters, blogs, podcasts, feature articles, and columns to expose our stu-

dents to the different characteristics of each form. The wide variety of available nonfiction trade books has made it possible to teach almost any genre or topic with picture books and other nonfiction text.

Topics

We collect books in relation to a specific topic or curricular focus. In science and social studies, kids do not all have to read the same textbook, nor should they. We keep topic-related texts at a variety of levels in baskets and include trade books, picture books, magazines, and newspaper articles, as well as images, videos, and artifacts. These resources build kids' background knowledge and engage kids in delightful ways to explore, learn more about the topic, and share what they learned. The time we spend collecting these texts is worth it, because it allows us to differentiate instruction and gear our teaching to students' needs and interests. And kids love to join in on the collecting as well. We are often amazed at what they find at home, online, or in the library and bring in to share with all of us.

Writing Quality

We look for vivid writing like that in the cruising article from *Hemispheres Magazine*. A *Denver Post* article that has always appealed to us described a phantom snowstorm as follows: "The forecast for Friday promised much of Colorado a full-fledged affair with the snow, but all the storm could muster was a cheap kiss on the cheek. An overnight snowstorm that swirled its way into the state barely flirted with the metro area but dumped up to 10 inches in parts of southeast Colorado" (Esquibel 1999). What a charming metaphor!

Text and Visual Features

We hunt for and save different short-text forms that showcase a variety of graphics and features. We find articles that are framed around a specific text structure, such as compare and contrast, and look at them closely to better recognize and understand the structure the next time we meet it. We look for pieces containing features and visuals, such as headings, bold print, and charts and graphs, so that we can show authentic examples of these and discover their purpose. Infographics were not even on the radar screen during the previous edition of this book, and now they are ubiquitous. We share them to teach kids how to read them, and kids even create them in their writing.

When choosing short text we need to be thoughtful consumers of fiction and nonfiction. We might ask the following questions:

- Is the information accurate and up to date?
- Is the writing well crafted?
- Does a piece strike our imagination, allow for interpretation, and make us think?
- Is a nonfiction text logically organized and easy to understand?
- Do visuals and features augment the information?
- Is the infographic clear and well organized?
- Is the language clear and vivid?
- Does the author's choice of information and presentation pique our interest in a subject?

We choose short text for the purpose of comprehension instruction for the following reasons:

- It is easily read out loud, which gives everyone in the room a common literary experience and builds classroom community.
- It is readily available on the Internet and is easily projected on interactive whiteboards, document cameras, and visualizers for shared reading and lesson instruction.
- It is easily accessed on all manner of devices, and kids can respond quickly with virtual sticky notes and annotation apps.
- It is often well crafted, with vivid language and striking illustrations or photographs.
- It provides an intense focus on issues of critical importance to readers of all ages.
- It has a beginning, a middle, and an end in short order.
- It is authentic and prepares children for the reading they will encounter outside of school.
- It is self-contained and provides a complete set of thoughts, ideas, and information for the entire group to mull over.
- It is easily reread to clarify confusion and better construct meaning.
- It is accessible to readers of many different learning styles and ages.
- It allows even very young children to engage in critical and interpretive thinking of text they might not be able to read on their own. Ideas about the reading are easily shared and discussed.
- It provides ample opportunities for modeling and thinking aloud.
- It provides students with anchor experiences that they can call upon later to help comprehend longer or more difficult text.

Choosing Short Text to Launch Comprehension Instruction

We recognize that all text—in its many genres and forms—spawns a wide range of thinking, but we find that certain ones lend themselves to particular strategies for the purpose of instruction. When we launch comprehension instruction, we are likely to choose such a text to teach the strategy and support kids to utilize it effectively.

Choosing Text to Introduce a Specific Strategy

Activating and connecting to background knowledge. When kids read text on familiar topics, they are more likely to connect new information to that which they already know in order to construct meaning. So we choose text with topics that kids are likely to have some prior knowledge of, such as family, school, pets, and common childhood experiences. Realistic fiction and memoir often nudge readers to make connections such as these to their own lives.

Questioning. Texts and topics for which readers lack background knowledge often spur them to ask questions. We also choose text that sparks their imagination and initiates wonder.

Inferring. We choose text that is ambiguous and nudges readers to think about what they know. By merging their thinking with clues in the text, kids can make an inference or draw a conclusion. Mysteries often offer opportunities for readers to infer.

Visualizing. We choose vivid text in which the writer paints pictures with the words—shows not tells. Active verbs, specific nouns, and descriptive adjectives prompt mental images. Poetry is often used to launch the visualizing strategy.

Determining importance. We choose text that focuses on a big idea. Text that includes details that come together to support a big idea is ideal for launching the determining importance strategy.

Monitoring, summarizing, and synthesizing are strategies that we use with every text we read right from the start. By the end of each text, we've used a full repertoire of thinking strategies. Certain texts prompt readers to use a certain strategy to comprehend, but thinking strategies are most effective when employed simultaneously and flexibly in conjunction with one another.

Harnessing Technology to Enhance Comprehension Instruction

Technology is a natural vehicle for the active literacy practices and strategy instruction featured in this book. Likewise, comprehension instruction is essential for introducing meaningful ways to use technology in the classroom. It works both ways. We help students see the natural links between the strategies they use in print text and the strategies they use when navigating and reading online as well as some of the differences.

Digital Reading

In a digital world, strategies matter now more than ever. Ziming Liu, a professor at San Jose State whose research focuses on comparing print and digital reading, concludes that "skimming has become the new reading. The more we read online, the more likely we are to move quickly without stopping to ponder any one thought" (quoted in Konnikova 2014). This confirms what we have noticed. The more readers skim and scan, the less they seem to comprehend. So teaching online readers to slow down or stop to think and react to information is essential to their learning, remembering, and understanding.

Recent research on digital literacy suggests that reading and thinking strategies are critical to navigating, learning from, and understanding text online. Julie Coiro (2011) has long reiterated the importance of reading and thinking strategies, but she makes a distinction between offline and online reading comprehension. "Offline texts," she says, "reside in the familiar and bounded spaces that remain static over time, while online texts are part of a dynamic and unbounded information system that changes daily in structure, form and content" (Coiro and Moore 2012).

For those of us used to pictures and words between two covers, this is new territory for sure. But our kids are growing up and going to school in this constantly shifting, dynamic, "unbounded" environment. We need to expand our literacy toolkit to incorporate practices that help them deal with this ever-changing world. Coiro (2011) suggests that there are four crucial comprehension processes that are essential to online learning:

Approaching Online Reading Tasks with a Purpose in Mind
Active readers approach digital reading with a variety of purposes in mind. Sometimes readers google the answer to a question. Sometimes readers surf the web at their whim. Other times they are looking for specific information that helps them make a decision. They use a variety of strategies to gain understanding, depending on their purpose.

Navigating and Negotiating Online Texts
Just as in print reading, we show kids how to navigate the page, use search features and links, pay attention to bold text, view images, and so forth. Digital readers must determine important ideas and information, question information they encounter, connect information to their purposes for reading, and evaluate the accuracy of information. We explicitly teach kids specific ways to evaluate Internet information: noting hints that may signal less than reliable sources, attending to clues that cue inaccurate information, and/or comparing a variety of sources.

Monitoring Comprehension of and Pathways Through Online Texts
Readers need to constantly monitor their understanding of information and ideas and pay attention to and utilize the most effective ways to navigate their online reading. We teach them ways to avoid Internet distractions and follow their designated search. Even when we read print, we sometimes find ourselves drifting off and thinking about something else. This is compounded exponentially when visiting websites with their constant distractions, such as ads tailored to the individual reader pinging up every moment. Steph has been encouraged to buy her own *Nonfiction Matters* (1998) countless times while surfing the web. She once thought that everyone was getting these ads, until she learned of the modern marketing techniques!

Responding to Online Texts
Digital readers use a repertoire of strategies to respond to information in text and communicate their thoughts about it. Just as we share our learning in the sharing portion of the reading workshop, kids now have the ability to share their responses 24/7 with people from around the globe. Technological tools such as Padlet, digital annotation apps, Edmodo, Google docs, and TodaysMeet all stimulate collaborative conversations in small and large groups with a worldwide audience. As kids respond in all these different ways, we remember to teach them the habits of being solid digital citizens.

Recent research summarized in Wolf (forthcoming) and Konnikova (2014) explores the similarities and differences between book and online reading. This research suggests that the shift from print to digital reading "may come at a cost to understanding, analyzing and evaluating a text" (Konnikova 2014). Many teachers have pondered this as they observe kids flitting from one website to another or falling hook, line, and sinker for a compelling but less than accurate piece of information. As we write this book, many studies are in progress. In one study, fifth graders were taught to annotate their reading by interacting with online text (Chen and Chen 2014). Researchers found that explicitly teaching kids to leave tracks of their thinking on an interactive annotation app "improved their reading comprehension and strategy use." Konnikova (2014) notes that kids can "read deeply" on devices as long as they receive explicit instruction in how to do so.

It's not difficult to see how the comprehension strategies laid out in this book are woven throughout these approaches to digital reading and are necessary for kids' understanding when reading online. Leaving tracks of thinking, asking questions, synthesizing the big ideas—all of these comprehension strategies are essential to online reading and learning. But students may not automatically apply them. We have to explicitly teach them how to think strategically when they are online just as we teach them with print. At the time we wrote the previous edition of this book, online reading was a new experience for many kids, whereas now, it is ubiquitous for all of us. See Part II for a variety of lessons that share how to support kids to construct meaning and remember new learning when reading and researching online. For more information and lessons on enhancing comprehension instruction with technology, check out our book *Connecting Comprehension and Technology* (Havey et al. 2013)

Principles for Integrating Comprehension and Technology

Since the previous edition of this book, we have had the amazing opportunity to spend time in the fifth- and first-grade classrooms of Katie Muhtaris and Kristin Ziemke at Burley School in the Chicago Public Schools. They have an iPad for every student, which we used to call "one to one," but thanks to tech guru Alan November, we have all come to realize that classrooms where every child has a device are really "one to world," because of the global connectivity. In their book *Amplify* (2015), Katie and Kristin focus on teaching reading and thinking strategies for content learning, and part of that is teaching students ways to navigate, evaluate, collaborate, and communicate through digital resources.

As we enter Kristin's room, one child sketches a squid on the Drawing Pad app, noting its tentacles and sharp beak identified with labels. Another group creates a podcast about which pet they have chosen for their classroom decided by an online survey. Yet another pair creates a reflection video about the book they just finished as a book recommendation for their classmates. Fifth graders in Katie's room use their iPads to research the Berlin airlift as they surface questions while reading the picture book *Mercedes and the Chocolate Pilot* (Raven). Others create imaginative book trailers to share with classmates, their families, and a larger online audience. They work together online, holding real-time discussions, collaborating on documents, and responding thoughtfully to one another's ideas and questions.

Katie and Kristin are guided by six principles that effectively integrate comprehension and technology. To enrich comprehension instruction, we use technology to do the following:

Enable all students to participate and engage more deeply. When we think about collaboration in a digital world, we provide our students with pretty much immediate access to the thinking of others. For example, when kids engage in a back-channel discussion, they view and respond to the ideas of their peers during a read-aloud. Primary kids can share the ideas behind their images on Drawing Pad. These options engage students in multimodal responses and provide additional ways to share and build new knowledge.

Provide access to resources, specialists, and texts that would not otherwise be available. Technology totally changes the nature, depth, and variety of content kids can experience and learn from. These online explorations provide kids with real-time experiences that are immediate, not vicarious. For instance, second graders become ornithologists as they watch a webcam at Cornell University, observing eaglets hatch in real time. Eighth graders interview geologists at Palmer Station in Antarctica to discuss melting glaciers and climate change with those who are experiencing it firsthand.

Open up a real-world audience for thinking and learning in the classroom. Communicating to a wide audience gives learning an authentic purpose, exposes kids to a wide range of ideas and perspectives, and enables them to participate in a world that was previously reserved for adults only. As kids blog, they publish their ideas, read the work of others, and have their own work read and commented on. They communicate regularly with kids in other classrooms, their extended families, and the larger online community.

Monitor and assess digital products and projects. Technology allows for 24/7 assessment. As kids annotate with Edmodo on their devices, the teacher can see the class screen at a glance and note who is participating, interacting, and thinking. Kids create reflection videos to share their learning for themselves as well as their teachers and parents. Technology can help both kids and teachers organize work, follow up on and communicate progress, and reflect on goals.

Meet the needs of diverse learners. Adding a visual or auditory component to a learning experience provides natural differentiation and continued learning. Kids watch videos to build background knowledge about new and unfamiliar concepts. They can take lessons on just about anything on YouTube. They read infographics of all sorts to get information quickly. And teachers can design digital text themselves, creating e-books filled with visual and sensory images that are a valuable scaffold for all kids. Options abound!

Build a foundation for 21st century digital citizenship. Just as we teach our students to practice good citizenship in their face-to-face lives, we need to teach them the same kinds of skills for their online lives. Internet safety and responsibility go hand in hand. We teach kids about protecting their privacy, avoiding inappropriate sites, treating people with respect, steering clear of cyberbullying situations, and sharing any concerns that arise with adults they know. In turn, we teach them to respect and cite the work of others and contribute content appropriately and responsibly.

(Adapted from Harvey, Goudvis, Muhtaris, and Ziemke [2013]
and Harvey and Daniels [2015])

Access for All: Differentiate with Technology

Resources on the web for reading, learning, and understanding have infinite possibilities. Graphics, both videographic and image based, allow kids who might not be able to read the text or are learning a new language to effectively comprehend information they might not otherwise have access to. When kids are reading on a personal device, no one is the wiser about the level of the text they are reading. So kids don't have to worry about others knowing that they are reading a book below their grade level. This has powerful implications for reluctant readers since we know that one of the most important factors in reading achievement lies in what kids think of themselves as readers (Howard 1992).

Podcasts are an especially engaging way for kids to get information and bridge the gap between their reading level and their comprehension level. We believe in equity and don't want to deny kids access to information that might be beyond their reading level. Technology provides a way to give kids access to complex and more challenging information without having to decode it.

Digital tools such as smartpens allow kids to hear the passages as they read in order to understand the text. Speech-to-text programs transcribe spoken words into text. Technology doesn't even have to be fancy. We know teachers who use iPods or phones to record information that kids can listen to as they follow along in the text, which encourages both comprehension and fluency. And just to be clear, all of these tech approaches or devices require kids to use the same tried-and-true comprehension strategies that they use when reading print.

And let's not forget audiobooks. We love them! They captivate us. We don't even mind traffic jams any more as long as we have a good audiobook. According to recent research, kids are no different (Flynn et al. 2016). Mary Burkey (2016), in an article on the website the Booklist Reader, reviews the study of Flynn et al. on the importance of "just listening" to audiobooks. It turns out that just listening matters, a lot. She cites findings that compared second- and third-grade students who listened to audiobooks for a total of an hour a week at school and forty more minutes at home to those who didn't. The treatment group outperformed the control group on measures of reading comprehension, understanding vocabulary, and, most surprisingly, reading motivation. Burkey suggests that the implications are that kids should do more listening: in school, in the car, during summer, at home, just about anywhere. We wholeheartedly agree. For more information on audiobooks, check out her "Voices in My Head" column for *Booklist* and her book *Audiobooks for Youth: A Practical Guide to Sound Literature* (2013).

The Jury Is Still Out

There are a number of current research studies comparing print and digital reading. Most of these studies, however, are with college students or young adults, which implies that they focus on proficient readers, not young children learning to read and understand. Some of the findings suggest that readers are more adept at skimming, scanning, and getting details when reading digitally and more proficient at understanding complex ideas, inferring underlying themes, and getting the gist of a problem when reading in print.

Other research suggests that when students read in paper text, they are more engaged and attentive, which results in deeper understanding (Willingham 2016; Dartmouth and Kaufman 2016; Sparks 2016). In one of few studies done with younger children, Merga and Roni (2017) report data from nearly 1,000 intermediate-grade children in Australia. The study found that kids who had regular access to e-readers, tablets, and mobile phones did not use these devices primarily for reading, even though the kids were daily book readers. A more stunning finding was that the more devices a child had access to, the less he or she read in general. One interpretation is that print books are still preferred by kids this age when it comes to reading.

From our standpoint it is not a competition. Books still matter, especially if understanding and deep reading are the goals. We have both noticed that when we really need to dig in to understand newer, more complex ideas, we want the book in hand, or a printout of the article. It's still much easier to reread and annotate our thinking right on the page to synthesize the information. But you can't beat devices for instant access. So ultimately, we offer a range of possibilities, both print and digital, to connect kids with the big, wide world through reading.

The Possibilities of Picture Books

Picture books offer certain unique advantages when we deliver instruction. Of all literature that lends itself to reading comprehension strategy instruction, picture books top the list. Why? We believe that interest is essential to comprehension. If we read material that doesn't engage us, we probably won't remember much. Engagement leads to remembering what is read, enhancing understanding, and acquiring knowledge. Picture books, both fiction and nonfiction, are more likely to hold our attention and engage us than dry, formulaic text. There's nothing like a striking photograph of the flukes of a killer whale jutting out from a sky-blue sea to capture a reader's interest. Readers are more likely to comprehend material that interests them and that is written in a compelling way.

Picture books have been a prominent feature of elementary classrooms for decades. Elementary teachers the world over share compelling picture books with kids. But elementary kids can't have all the fun! There is a picture book for every reader and a reader for every picture book. The wide range of themes, issues, language, and ideas reach out into classrooms like tentacles drawing in each member, regardless of the different learning styles, ages, reading levels, or prior experiences. We need to think about *all* the students who can benefit from picture books. The teachers portrayed in this book use picture books with the broadest spectrum of students for many different reasons.

Building Background Knowledge and Teaching Content

Teaching students to read text strategically sharpens and enhances their understanding of the content. At the same time, we can bring up issues, problems, and concerns without deluging students with facts and information. Unlike longer nonfiction or reference materials, picture books and other short texts focus our attention on one issue or topic at a time. Curricular stalwarts such as history and geography benefit from an ever-growing collection of picture books covering every conceivable time period and culture. Science trade books provide ample opportunity for children to ask and answer many of the questions they have about the natural world.

Challenging Kids to Think

Just as we read difficult texts ourselves, it's important to share books that are a stretch for children. We've noticed that stories and narratives set in foreign cultures or unfamiliar historical periods often result in more rather than less interest. We know many students who would rather read nonfiction than a riveting mystery or adventure story. Students are fascinated by books on unfamiliar but compelling topics, such as *On a Beam of Light* (Berne), a story about Einstein's curiosity; *Enormous Smallness* (Burgess) the story of e. e. cummings's life in poetry; and *Will's Words: How Shakespeare Changed the Way You Talk* (Sutcliffe), all books about remarkable people. We have found over and over again that we should never underestimate what kids can understand when motivated to do so.

Differentiating Instruction

Picture Books with Young Children
We have found that we can begin teaching comprehension in preschool and kindergarten. When we read out loud to kids, we expose them to more sophisticated text that requires them to think. We eliminate the barriers that face young readers who can't decode text yet.

Picture Books with Older Children
Traditionally viewed as a genre reserved solely for younger children, picture books lend themselves to comprehension strategy instruction and guided discussion at every grade level. Older kids may balk when you first share picture books with them. Comments such as "Why are you reading those baby books?" will dissipate, however, when you share powerful picture books that are filled with sophisticated content best suited to older students.

Picture Books with Striving Readers
Equity matters. All kids deserve books that contain inspiring, sophisticated content and prompt stimulating discussion. Kids should not be left out because they have difficulty decoding the text. There are no better print materials to use with developing readers than picture books. The pictures complement the text to help less proficient readers access meaning. Readers can choose from many

different levels and genres on a single topic. The shorter form is less intimidating than longer chapter books and other forms of dense text.

Picture Books with Linguistically Diverse Learners

For kids who are learning English, any text with pictures can be a lifeline. When illustrations, photographs, and other features make content and vocabulary concrete and visible, kids have a better shot at making sense of the sophisticated ideas, compelling story lines, and complex information in the text. Picture books on science and social studies build background and make the content comprehensible for English language learners. Adding interesting picture books into our daily lessons makes a huge difference in kids' interest, engagement, and understanding. See our video *Reading the World: Content Comprehension with Linguistically Diverse Learners* (2005b) for additional ideas for teaching English language learners.

Choosing Picture Books Just Because We Love Them

We remember the words of the writer C. S. Lewis when we choose books for reading and instruction: "No book is really worth reading at the age of ten which is not equally (and often far more) worth reading at the age of fifty" (quoted in Cullinan 1981). When we find a book that inspires our teaching, we can hardly wait to see how children will respond to it. We are hopeful that it will engage them. The best reason of all to read a picture book to a group of students is simply that you love it. Anne and her colleague Nancy Burton made frequent trips to a local bookstore to purchase books for their classroom library. One day they became so engrossed in choosing books that they never noticed when an overly efficient bookstore employee unloaded the mountain of books they had stacked in their cart. Thinking no one in their right mind would buy that many books, she had quietly reshelved each one of them. So, unless you live next door to the public library, beware. Children's books can be habit-forming.

Enthusiasm for books is contagious. Sometimes we become so focused on a theme or curricular topic that we put off sharing our favorites. Big mistake! Steph still often reads Margaret Wise Brown's *The Sailor Dog* to kids regardless of their age. It was the first book she ever really read, and she can't not share it with kids because it means so much to her. Kids pick up on this. Invariably, the moment she closes the book, they leap up and grab for it en masse, even eighth graders. We also choose books we have always wanted to read but have never gotten around to. Anne has a list of several dozen. Once in a while, she picks one up and reads it to the kids. In this way, they learn about the book together, which gives everyone a fresh, authentic experience.

Sharing our thoughts about why we love a book allows students to get to know us better and shows them how discerning we are about what we read. Children in classrooms where everyone talks about books, teachers included, aren't afraid to venture their own thoughts. There's no better way to encourage readers than to ask them to contribute their favorites to a classroom text set. And students can't resist when we consistently ask them to voice their honest opinions.

Beyond Picture Books: Choosing Longer Text

Many of the texts that launch the lessons in this book are short—picture books, magazine and web articles, poems, and so on. Don't get us wrong. We love long text too, and our kids all read novels and other longer forms as well as short pieces. As we work with book clubs and literature circles or when everyone in the class has a different novel going, we remind our kids of the many lessons we have done with short text so they will apply what they learned to their ongoing independent reading in longer text.

Our kids read long novels and love them. And they also read lengthy nonfiction—anthologies and trade books. They may not read these nonfiction books cover to cover, but they get important information from them. Books like Phillip Hoose's *We Were There, Too!* a compelling compendium of vignettes of children in American history, engage students who are surprised at the roles kids played in history, and Joy Hakim's series on history (A History of US) and on science (The Story of Science) are among our favorites for getting essential content information written in an interesting way. So as you work with the strategies in Part II of this book, think of ways to apply them in longer text.

Choosing Books: Interest, Readability, and Purpose

When teaching kids to choose text, Cris Tovani (2003) focuses on the following three criteria:

Interest
Readability
Purpose

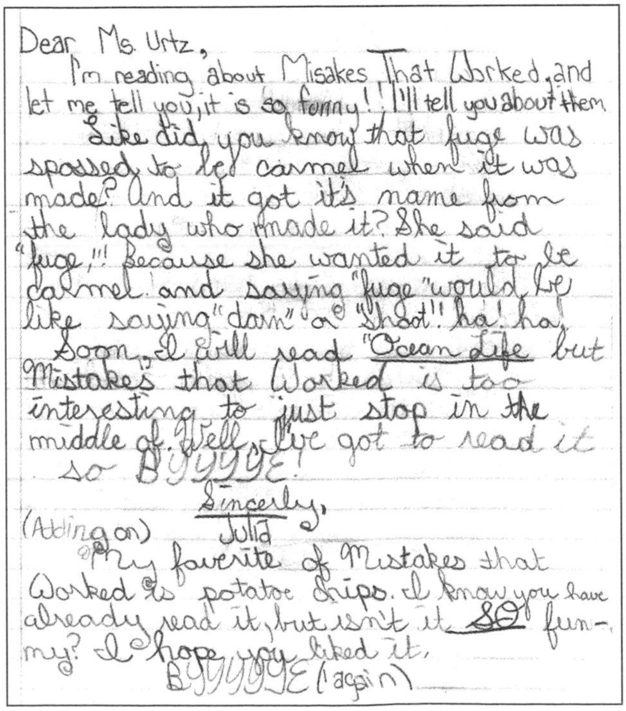

Interest

Of course, we read out of interest. Nothing compels readers more than their personal interest in a piece of text. We have noticed that readers can read more difficult books if they are interested in the material. Text that addresses a reader's interest promotes engaged reading. Fifth grader Julia was so engaged in reading *Mistakes That Worked*, Charlotte Foltz Jones's book about inventions like Post-it notes that came about serendipitously, that she simply couldn't put it down. Her enthusiasm burst forth in a letter to Mary Urtz, her fourth-grade teacher, in which she mentioned that she would soon get back to a science book titled *Ocean Life* but not until she finished *Mistakes That Worked* (see Figure 4.1). For personal reading, adults primarily choose books based on their interests. Why expect kids to be any different?

Figure 4.1 Julia's Letter About *Mistakes That Worked*

Readability

In recent years, leveled books and leveled libraries have proliferated in schools, and they are a useful guide for teachers to support kids to find books they can read. But we mustn't become slaves to reading levels. We know we're in trouble when we ask a young reader what she's reading, and she answers, "I'm an M." Reading is about so much more than a level. And choosing what to read is about more than kids reading "at their level." But they need to be able to read what they choose. So we share three different categories of books:

- *Easy books.* An easy book is a book in which you can read every word and understand all the ideas.
- *Challenging books.* A challenging book is a book where there are many words you can't read and many ideas you can't understand.
- *Just-right books.* A just-right book is a book where you can read most of the words, but not all, and you can understand most of the ideas, but not all.

To demonstrate how we choose books by readability, we bring in examples of our own books that fall into each category. We model how we choose easy, just-right, and challenging books for ourselves. We share one of each type—easy, challenging, and just right—and create an anchor chart of these categories. We do this authentically so kids can see that even though we are grown, proficient readers, we still encounter books we want to read that are a challenge. And they also see that we still read beach books. As our demonstration nears an end, we reiterate that if we choose only easy or challenging books, we won't get better at reading so we try to choose just-right books most of the time.

Another thing we share with our students is an exciting outcome of classifying books into these three categories: as we grow as readers, books that were once challenging suddenly seem just right and eventually even become easy. These easy, just-right, and challenge designations can help readers recognize reading progress.

Purpose

Readers read for many different purposes. We want kids to think through why they are reading. Cris Tovani (2011) demonstrates this by asking her readers to list some different purposes they have for reading, and she records their responses on a chart. The following are some of their purposes:

- To compete school assignments
- To find out information
- To be entertained
- To read instructions
- To cook something
- Just for fun

Cris emphasizes that these are but a few of the many purposes for reading and that purpose affects our book selection. She encourages the students to add more purposes to the chart whenever they arise.

Joaquin, a seventh grader at Horace Mann Middle School in Denver, noted that one of his purposes for reading was to put his little sister to sleep at night. Cris asked him if he chose easy or hard books to do that. He said easy books, so his five-year-old sister could understand them. And as for interest, he said he might choose Cinderella because princesses were a big deal to his sister. In other words, his primary purpose in this instance was reading to his little sister. Help your students think of the many purposes for reading. Ideally, they won't forget enjoyment. If they neglect to mention it, add it, or any other purpose you deem worthy, to the list.

Helping Kids Select Books to Read

To scaffold book selection, we ask kids how they choose a book. What exactly do they do when they reach for a book on the shelf? We record their responses on a chart in hopes that some of these suggestions will be contagious. The kids in Leslie Blaumann's fourth-grade class compiled the following list for how they choose books:

- Reading the back
- Reading the flap
- Reading the first page—an interesting lead can reel us in
- Reading the first few pages
- Reading the table of contents
- The title
- The length
- The level
- Flipping through the pages
- Reading the last page
- The pictures
- The cover
- The author
- The subject
- The series
- The genre
- Recommendation

All of these are helpful suggestions, but Leslie understands that if she merely copied this list each year and posted it, the kids in her class would likely ignore it. This list makes sense to them because they create it based on their own needs and practices.

Don't be afraid to weigh in here, however. You, too, are a member of the reading community in your classroom. Leslie recognized that she generally chose a book based on the recommendation of someone close to her. "Recommendation" never made the original list. So Leslie added it. Books recommended by friends and family who know her tend to be books that capture her interest.

Teachers need to pay close attention to students' interests in order to fill the room with books they want to read. Post a chart where kids can record their interests and, more specifically, some topics they would like to read about. That way, when you order books or head off to libraries, garage sales, and bookstores, you can look for those special books that kids in your classrooms yearn for. Debbie Miller, author of *Reading with Meaning* (2012) and *Teaching with Intention* (2007), suggests three questions kids can ask themselves when it comes to text selection:

- Can I read most of the words?
- Is it interesting?
- Does it give me something to talk and think about? (Miller 2017)

A Word About Reading Aloud

Jim Trelease, author of *The Read-Aloud Handbook* (2013), says that the purpose of literature is to provide meaning in our lives. He believes that literature is the most important medium, more important than television, film, and even art, because it "brings us closest to the human heart." He says that reading aloud serves to "reassure, entertain, inform, explain, arouse curiosity and inspire our kids."

We wholeheartedly agree. Some of our best moments have come from reading aloud or being read to. Steph first encountered Dr. Seuss in kindergarten when Miss Buehler read *The 500 Hats of Bartholomew Cubbins*. Anne remembers reading E. B. White's *Charlotte's Web* to her five-year-old daughter, Allison, and finding herself unable to continue through the tears when Charlotte died. The recent proliferation of audiobooks illustrates our love affair with listening to great read-alouds.

Thoughtful teachers everywhere dedicate time each day to read out loud to their students in all genres and content areas. When teaching reading comprehension, we do a good deal of instruction via reading aloud. But we need to remember that if we read aloud only for the purpose of instruction, we will ruin reading aloud. We need to read aloud every day for the sheer joy of it!

Chapter 5

Effective Comprehension Instruction: Teaching, Tone, and Assessment

Anne closed Allan Baillie's *Rebel* after reading the last page out loud to a group of eighth graders. This clever picture book, about the courageous response of a group of rural Burmese peasants to a dictatorial military strongman, was one of her favorites. She glanced up at the clock and noticed the time slipping away. She really wanted to confer with the kids, and she couldn't wait to read their responses to this compelling story. Feeling pressed for time, she asked the kids to divide a sheet in half and mark one column What the Text Is About and the next column What the Text Makes Me Think About. She had found this form useful in the past to get at children's deeper thinking. Although she had never introduced the form to this group, it appeared to be self-explanatory.

As the students returned to their tables to respond on this form, Anne sat down at one table and began to confer with Jasmine. Others at the table soon joined in, and a lively book discussion ensued. The kids brimmed with questions and comments. With Anne present, they talked about what really went on in the story, where it took place, who these people were, and why they were fighting.

As she began to construct meaning from the discussion, Jasmine wrote the following in the first column: "This was about some people in Burma who used to be free and now were under the control of a bad government and an even worse general. The people rebelled in a surprising way." "Great thinking," Anne commented to Jasmine. In the second column, Jasmine wrote that the book reminded her of stories her grandfather had told about Vietnam. Anne felt pleased with Jasmine's summary and viable connection. She left the table with Jasmine writing about her grandfather's Vietnam experience and her table group writing about all kinds of things.

The bell rang and Anne collected the forms as kids filed out the door. Her heart sank as she paged through them. With the exception of the kids at Jasmine's table and a few very prolific writers who always filled entire pages regardless of the instruction, most of the forms stared blankly at her, hardly a word written in either column. She knew the form couldn't be at fault; it had worked effectively in the past. As Anne pondered the disappointing results of her instruction, she realized that she had once again made a familiar mistake.

Almost every time she reflected on why a certain lesson had been ineffective, she concluded that it was because of a lack of explicit instruction. She either hadn't modeled explicitly enough what she was trying to do or she hadn't given her students enough time to practice what she had shown them. If she had modeled how to use this form on the document camera rather than giving a series of directions, she suspected, things would have gone quite differently.

The next time Anne saw Steph, she described the debacle. Steph could only smile knowingly. She herself had repeatedly told her own kids that it was okay to make a mistake as long as they didn't make the same mistake over and over. But when it came to delivering instruction, she, too, continued to make the same mistake over and over. Like Anne, whenever Steph cut corners on modeling, her instruction suffered.

Don't surrender to the clock. It takes time to show kids how, but it is time well spent. When it comes to instruction, it is nearly impossible to be too explicit.

Effective Comprehension Instruction

Teaching kids to comprehend means we show them how to construct meaning when they read. Strategy instruction is all about teaching the reader, not merely the reading. Comprehension instruction is most effective when teachers do the following:

- Teach with the end in mind
- Plan instruction that is responsive to the individual needs of students
- Model their own use of comprehension strategies over time
- Remind students that the purpose for using a strategy is to construct meaning and engage in the text
- Articulate how thinking helps readers better understand what they read

- View strategies as a means to an end with the goal of building a repertoire of thinking strategies
- Model their oral, written, and artistic responses to the text
- Gradually release responsibility for using strategies to the students, always moving them toward independent reading and thinking
- Provide opportunities for guided and independent practice
- Show students how comprehension strategies apply in a variety of texts, genres, and contexts
- Help students notice how strategies intersect and work in conjunction with one another
- Build in large amounts of time for actual text reading by the students
- Make sure students have many opportunities to talk to each other about their reading
- Provide opportunities for students to respond by writing and drawing
- Take time to observe and confer directly with students and keep records of those observations and conferences to assess progress and inform instruction
- Use student work and talk to assess past instruction, guide future instruction, and assess and evaluate student performance

Explicit Instruction: The Gradual Release of Responsibility

When teaching, our job is to make what is implicit, explicit. Explicit instruction means that we show learners how we think when we read, as Steph did in Chapter 1 when reading *Up North at the Cabin* (Chall). We explicitly teach reading comprehension strategies so that readers can use them to construct meaning. We are likely to teach a strategy by modeling it; guiding students in its practice in large groups, small groups, and pairs; and providing large blocks of time for students to read independently and practice using and applying it. This is what Pearson and Gallagher (1983) call the gradual release of responsibility framework for instruction.

In our work, we make a distinction between what might be called "mentioning" and explicit teaching. Published reading programs often simply mention comprehension strategies rather than teach them. For example, basal teacher's guides might direct teachers to ask readers to infer a character's motivation without teaching kids how to infer. This entire book is about explicitly teaching the thinking that is at the foundation of comprehension instruction. Effective instruction always involves modeling, guiding, and giving kids time to practice.

We've adapted Pearson and Gallagher's gradual release framework as follows:

Gradual Release of Responsibility

Connect and Engage

- The teacher builds intrigue and interest in the topic.
- The teacher activates and ascertains students' background knowledge.
- Students interact to connect the new to the known.

Teacher Modeling

- The teacher explains the strategy.
- The teacher models how to effectively use the strategy to understand text.
- The teacher thinks aloud when reading to show thinking and strategy use.
- Students turn and talk to express their thinking.

Guided Practice

- The teacher purposefully guides a large-group conversation that engages students in a focused discussion that follows a line of thinking.
- The teacher and students practice the strategy together in a shared-reading context, reasoning through the text and co-constructing meaning through discussion.
- The teacher scaffolds the students' attempts and supports student thinking, giving specific feedback and making sure students understand the task.

Collaborative Practice

- Students share their thinking processes with each other during paired reading and small-group conversations.
- The teacher moves from group to group, assessing and responding to students' needs.

Independent Practice

- After working with the teacher and with other students, the students try practicing the strategy on their own.
- Teachers confer during independent reading to meet the needs of each reader.
- The students receive regular feedback from the teacher and other students.

Sharing

- Students come together to share thinking, learning, and understanding.
- Students reflect on their reading process and the reading content.

Application of the Strategy

- Students use the strategy in authentic reading situations.
- Students use the strategy in a variety of different genres, settings, contexts, and disciplines

(Fielding and Pearson 1994; adapted by Harvey and Goudvis in 2016)

In the past few years, we have come to understand that modeling should be short and sweet. Kids' waving hands and whispered comments have sent us this message loud and clear. If all we ever did was think out loud about a piece of text, kids wouldn't listen for long. So we model for a few minutes, just long enough to get our point across, and then quickly engage kids in guided practice. Most of our instructional time is spent in guided practice, because that is where we can best support students as they move toward independence. We ask them to talk to each other frequently throughout the lesson, process the information, and share their thoughts and opinions. As soon as we sense they are ready, we send them off to practice either collaboratively or independently. At the conclusion of the work time, we bring kids back together to share their thinking. For more on modeling that keeps kids engaged, check out Debbie Miller's chapter "Not So Gradual Release" in *Comprehension Going Forward* (2013).

Teaching Comprehension in the Reading Workshop

Strategic reading takes hold in classrooms that value student thinking. In our work in classrooms, we've noticed that the classroom context makes all the difference for effective strategy instruction. The comprehension instruction described in this book is a natural complement to the workshop model. Our notion of workshop has expanded in recent years so that we now include researching workshop, where we teach science and social studies, as well as reading and writing workshops. Kids read a variety of genres, texts, and topics in these workshops. They read poetry and literature to enhance their understanding and love of reading. They read a wide range of nonfiction and they do a great deal of focused content reading in science and social studies.

In the workshop, the teacher models a whole-group strategy lesson and then gives students large blocks of time to read and to practice the strategy in small groups, pairs, or independently. During this time, the teacher moves about the room, slides her chair up next to readers, and confers with them about their reading. Sometimes the teacher meets with small, flexible groups to provide additional needs-based instruction. At the end of the workshop, the whole group comes together to share their learning.

The workshop model emphasizes choice in book selection. Reading researcher Richard Allington recommends that readers choose much of what they read. We know that readers get better at reading when they choose books they can and want to read. Kids can choose from any book under the sun or they can choose from a number of options the teacher offers. Allington refers to the latter as "managed choice" (1994). For instance, a language arts teacher may offer several books from which kids choose and form literature circles. A social studies teacher may offer a dozen picture books on the Civil War to build background knowledge of the topic. We need to fill our rooms with terrific books at every level, on every conceivable topic, to ensure that kids get their hands on books they want to read. In Chapter 4, we describe how we choose books and how we help students choose their own books to read independently when practicing various comprehension strategies.

But it is important to keep in mind that comprehension strategy instruction can and should be taught in any classroom context and with many different materials. Some teachers use a four-block instructional model; others organize their teaching around guided reading and balanced literacy. Some use published anthologies, basal readers, or scripted programs. But whatever resources or structures you choose, kids need comprehension instruction to read, write, and talk about their thinking. And they need to learn reading strategies that support them to understand what they read.

Strategy Instruction: A Means to an End

Comprehension instruction is not about teaching strategies for strategies' sake. It *is* about teaching kids to use strategies purposefully to read any text for any reason, and to walk away from their reading experiences with new understanding that may generate still more learning. Comprehension strategies are interrelated, and we don't keep this a secret from kids. We show them how strategies overlap and intersect. We demonstrate how readers weave them together for a more engaged, rewarding read.

We frequently walk into classrooms and hear kids bursting with connections and questions. As the conversation continues, we sometimes find ourselves feeling a little queasy if it appears kids are using strategy language without understanding the thinking behind it. This suggests that they may not realize that the purpose of a strategy is to help their understanding. Comprehension strategies are not an end in themselves, but rather a means to understanding. Our classroom instruction must reflect this.

Launching Strategy Instruction

There's a big difference between introducing and teaching kids strategies for the first time and how they will eventually use a repertoire of strategies to construct meaning. For practical purposes, when we first teach a strategy, we model the strategy on its own so we don't confuse kids. If we introduce all the strategies at once, kids simply can't handle all the information. When we launch a strategy, we clearly explain and demonstrate how we use it to better understand what we read. For instance, we show kids how we think when we ask a question and how that question helps us to make meaning. Then we give kids time to practice with their peers and on their own.

Our launch lessons don't resemble classic mini-lessons, in that they take longer than five or ten minutes. When we launch a strategy, we keep kids up close for about half of the workshop time. Armed with clipboards, sticky notes, and pencils, they interact with the text and one another throughout the lesson. After we have modeled for a few minutes, we quickly engage the kids in doing the work right in front of us. Our purpose is twofold: first, we can see what they are doing and notice who is on target and who needs more support. Second, and most importantly, we are scaffolding the lesson, so that they can get a full, rich, complete experience with using a strategy to understand an entire text.

One at a Time? For How Long?

We are often asked, "Should I really teach the strategies one at a time?" Or, "I've been teaching inferring for seven weeks. When should I move on?" The real questions are whether or not we teach strategies in isolation and how long we focus on a particular strategy. The short answer is that we introduce the strategies one at a time but quickly move on to introduce additional strategies so that kids build a repertoire of strategies and use them flexibly to understand what they read. Otherwise, instruction may become all about the strategy rather than using the strategy as a tool for understanding. If kids think about strategies only in isolation, they tend to think about how many connections they can come up with rather than how their connections foster understanding. The last thing we want is for strategy use to become rigid and rote.

And we don't wait very long to let kids know that readers don't use strategies in isolation. Why would we teach them only to ask questions throughout an entire book or make connections just as they read a poem? Readers weave a variety of strategies together to make sense of text. Comprehension strategies work in concert. Once kids ask a question, an inference is never far behind. So when we hear kids making inferences before we've introduced inferring, we celebrate their great thinking. "Oh, oh! No inferring today. Remember, we are working on questioning right now!" is not a refrain we hope to hear. The last thing we want to do is limit kids' thinking, directing them away from one strategy because we happen to be teaching another.

In *The Comprehension Toolkit* (2016), a resource we created for comprehension instruction with informational text, we share lessons that demonstrate how the strategies build on each other over time as well as a range of options for teaching comprehension strategies. Time frames vary, but in our opinion it makes sense to introduce all of the comprehension strategies described in this book within a reasonably short time period. For instance, we might introduce and explore all the strategies within a couple of months. Kids need to learn how to infer the meaning of unfamiliar words long before February comes around. Even as we introduce a new strategy, kids keep using the ones already in their repertoire. That is the point. We don't introduce a strategy and never mention it again. We continue to model, introduce, and use various comprehension strategies throughout the year and across the curriculum. We teach and reinforce the strategies in all curricular areas, including science, social studies, and mathematics. Comprehension instruction is cumulative and recursive.

Is There a Sequence?

One question that crops up more than any other is, "In what order should I teach the strategies?" Although we believe there is no one sequence for strategy instruction, teaching kids to monitor their comprehension comes first. We begin by explicitly teaching students to monitor their comprehension, listen to their inner voice, and leave tracks of their thinking. Once they understand how to monitor their thinking, they are able to use a repertoire of strategies and apply them when reading.

For clarity's sake, we introduce specific strategies in each chapter. But we do not believe there is any one sequence for teaching comprehension strategies.

What matters is that children use them flexibly according to the demands of the text and the task they encounter. For instance, we view activating background knowledge as a foundational strategy, because it is something kids need to do from the get-go. They will need to be taught to notice new information and learning before they can determine important information. On the other hand, we may want to teach kids to infer the meaning of unfamiliar words on the first day of school because they're reading complex text with a ton of unfamiliar concepts and vocabulary. So rather than following a prescribed sequence, we consider what our kids need to learn, what they are reading, and which strategies will best facilitate their learning.

Above all, we take our cue from the kids. So as you read this book, let your kids lead the way. Maybe you go through the strategy chapters in order, or maybe not. Perhaps your fourth graders learned as much as they ever needed to know about making connections in the primary grades, so skip some of the connection lessons. After all, if we find ourselves teaching connections year after year after year, Houston, we've got a problem! So as you use the lessons in the second part of this book, we suggest dipping in and out of the strategy chapters on an as-needed basis. Our goal is to teach a repertoire of strategies to further engagement and understanding and to build knowledge.

Setting the Tone: Building a Literate Community

In a thinking-intensive classroom, literacy is an active process. Teachers set a tone that values student curiosity and thinking and respects all voices and visions. We work hard to build a community of thinkers, expressers, listeners, and learners, a community where kids and teachers care and wonder about one another's interests and ideas and take time to talk about them, think about them, and explore them. Some of the principles that guide our practice follow.

Foster Passion and Curiosity
Einstein said, "I have no special talent. I am only passionately curious." An interesting assessment, considering the source. It was his passion and curiosity that led to his discoveries. Passion is contagious. So we share our own. Students enter our classrooms brimming with curiosity, and we want school to encourage rather than squelch it.

An Environment That Values Collaborative Learning and Thinking
In classrooms that promote thinking, students and teachers co-construct meaning in large groups, small groups, and conferences; through discussions, book groups, and partner work. Everyone gets a chance to weigh in with meaning.

Large Blocks of Time for Extended Reading and Writing
The importance of independent reading cannot be stressed too much. Reading volume is a strong indicator of reading achievement (Cunningham and Stanovich 2003). The more we read, the better we read. If we want students to get better at reading, they need to read a lot and think about what they are reading. If we only went to a piano lesson on Monday and never sat down to practice the rest of the week, we wouldn't get any better.

We need to build in time for readers to read on their own and practice using strategies in self-selected text that they can and want to read. Richard Allington (1994) notes that high-achieving students spend much more time reading than their lower-achieving counterparts, providing evidence that time spent in independent reading makes a difference. Reading actually makes you smarter (Stanovich 2000), and our kids need to know this.

Language Matters

The language we use determines what happens in our classroom far more than the lamps, desks, and bookshelves. In his books *Choice Words: How Our Language Affects Children's Learning* (2004) and *Opening Minds* (2011), Peter Johnston suggests that teaching and learning are all about language. What we say and how we say it make a difference for our kids. Using respectful language that values their thinking sets a tone that encourages their participation and their trust. When we begin to hear kids using and understanding language that we have shared through instruction, we know that they are learning in ways that matter. We hope our kids adopt and adapt our teaching language as their learning language. Language shapes and expands thinking.

Authentic Response

In active literacy classrooms, students have opportunities to respond to reading in a variety of ways—talking, writing, drawing, blogging, creating, and so on—giving them an opportunity to make their thinking visible and bring it to life.

Responsive Teaching and Differentiation

One size does not fit all. Responsive teaching is intentional, flexible, and adaptive. Good instruction is good instruction for all kids. We want all of our students to experience the kind of lessons we have designed in this book. Participating in shared reading allows all kids to be part of a community of thinkers and learners. We understand that children differ, so we differentiate by offering a range of response options and a variety of text at different levels. For more information on ways to differentiate instruction for kids with special needs, pick up a favorite of ours, Patrick Schwarz's *From Disability to Possibility* (2006).

Text Matters

Surround your students with text of every conceivable genre, style, form, and topic. Richard Allington reminds us that when teachers use a "multi-source, multi-genre curriculum" (1994), instruction tends to be more thoughtful and effective. When rooms are filled to bursting with a vast array of print, kids pick it up. For more on this, see Chapter 4, "Twenty-First Century Reading: Books and Beyond."

Room Arrangement Matters

Long gone are classrooms characterized by desks in rows and no talking. It's nearly impossible to participate in the discussion if all you see is the back of someone else's head. In classrooms that value thinking, kids sit at tables or desks in clusters so that they can easily talk to one another and collaborate. We provide instruction in a comfortable meeting place where kids, no matter their age, sit up close in front of the teacher so they easily focus on the instruction and listen to and interact with one another. We also create quiet spaces and nooks and crannies for them to read independently or work in small groups. When we create our classroom spaces, we keep bookstores or libraries in mind. Kids thrive in intimate, comfortable surroundings.

Accessible Resources

In classrooms that value thinking, resources that support literacy are easily accessible. Clipboards act as portable desks so kids can sit up close to the teacher and respond. Pads of sticky notes top the supply list. Notebooks and journals fill student cubbies and desks. Books, although we love them, aren't the only resources. Sharing short articles, images, infographics, and videos that we can project for all to see makes text accessible to everyone. And good news! Many online resources are free.

Assessing Comprehension: Teaching with the End in Mind

Reading assessments, like rodents, run rampant. DIBELS, DRAs, IRIs, SATs, ACTs. You name it, kids have taken it, and sometimes for hours and hours on end. Unfortunately, too often test preparation has become the default curriculum. Assessment is not only about what our kids do, but also about how effective our instruction has been. When we reflect on evidence of their learning and understanding, we revise and shape our subsequent instruction. Authentic assessment provides us with three very important pieces of information that guide our instruction:

1. *Our students' learning and progress.* By looking carefully at our kids' work and listening to their words and thoughts, we derive an authentic understanding of how they are doing and what they have learned or not learned.

2. *Past instruction.* What kids learn depends on how well we have taught it. If kids don't get it, we need to rethink our instruction and change it accordingly. If most of the class doesn't get it, it is our responsibility. If 25 percent of the class doesn't get it, it is still our responsibility. And frankly, if one child doesn't get it, it remains our responsibility. It's not about teaching the same lesson over and over again, because that doesn't work. We need to redesign our lessons, keeping in mind what we have learned from our kids and letting that information guide our instruction.

3. *Future instruction.* Responsive teaching and assessment go hand in hand. Based on what we see in students' work, the evidence of their understanding, we design subsequent instruction that is tailored to what they need. We plan our next steps based on what we notice in their work that needs attention and elaboration. Kids all have different needs. Some are quickly ready for independent practice. Others need more time, support, and guided practice. We may convene a small group or we may confer individually, depending on need.

Finding Out What Students Are Thinking

When we lead a discussion, we notice and evaluate children's responses. When we look over their written responses after class, as Anne did after reading *Rebel* (Baillie) out loud, we learn what we have to teach or reteach the next day. The only way we can confidently assess our students' comprehension is when they share their thinking with us. Readers reveal their comprehension by responding to text, not by answering a litany of literal questions. Personal responses to reading give us a window into students' minds. We connect with their thinking when we know what's going on for them as they read.

All the lessons, discussions, and responses described in this book have one purpose: to move kids toward independence as readers. What ultimately matters is that students internalize comprehension strategies that promote understanding.

We find out if readers are understanding what they read in the following ways:

We Listen to Kids
We can't stress enough how much we learn about kids' reading and thinking by simply listening closely to what they say. If we listen, they will talk. Sometimes kids might say, "I made a connection" or "I'm inferring." Using the language isn't enough, however. We check to see that there is substance underlying their statements.

We Read Kids' Work
We read their responses closely, looking for evidence that they are constructing meaning. And we use these responses to design future instruction.

We Confer with Kids
The reading conference provides an ideal opportunity to talk one on one with students and help them sort out their thinking and come to a deeper understanding of how reading strategies support comprehension. Sometimes, discovering what readers are thinking only takes asking them. Those natural talkers are only too happy to fill you in on their thinking. Those more reticent kids may surprise you and open up, too, if you only ask.

We Listen In on Conversations
Even though we were both taught that eavesdropping is rude, we know that it's invaluable when trying to find out what kids are thinking about their reading. Listening in on conversations kids have with one another is a surefire way to get at their honest thinking.

We Observe Behavior and Expressions
A scrunched-up nose, a raised eyebrow, or a quizzical look lets us know what a reader is thinking. We watch kids carefully and notice their expressions while they read to give us a glimpse into their thinking.

We Chart Responses
We record what kids say in class discussions on charts. This holds their thinking and makes it visible, public, and permanent. Students can refer to the

charts during discussions or use them as guides when crafting their own responses.

We Keep Anecdotal Records of Conferences and Conversations

In classrooms where we work, teachers keep track of student thinking by taking notes of interactions they have with students and reviewing them regularly. Teachers have a wide variety of resources in which to record student learning and progress, including notebooks, binders, and so on. Current technology apps makes documenting and sharing kids' learning a breeze.

The chapters in Part II of this book include a variety of comprehension lessons. At the end of each chapter, we share some student work accompanied by our running commentary. We show and explain how we look at the work and think about it to get an idea of how our kids are doing and where they need to go next.

What About Grades? Moving from Assessment to Evaluation

There is no need to grade students on what they know when they walk in the door. We need to grade them on what they learn from what we have taught. When we give students grades to evaluate them, we make sure the grades are based on evidence gleaned from ongoing and authentic assessment. This is how assessment informs evaluation. When we assess our kids' progress, we look for a demonstration of understanding. Work samples, student talk, and artifacts are the evidence we use to assess their learning. Grades are all about evaluating what kids have learned through practice. We evaluate and give grades only after students have had a lot of time to internalize the strategies and skills we have taught. We base our grades on a substantial body of evidence that stands as proof of kids' learning.

Grading a stack of worksheets and packets doesn't provide us with information about authentic learning. So we look at constructed and more open-ended responses that require kids to show us their thinking and learning. This evidence comes in the form of responses on sticky notes, two- and three-column think sheets, short and longer summary responses, notes from discussions, thoughtful illustrations, and journal and notebook entries.

We constantly check what kids are doing against what we have taught them and the outcomes we hope to achieve. We review and save work that demonstrates understanding as well as work that doesn't, and we design instruction accordingly.

After students have had plenty of practice and we have collected a good deal of their work, we grade them, holding them accountable for what they have learned. Much of our grading is done using rubrics that directly correspond with and measure what we have taught. So in the end, we evaluate students to measure their learning, to "grade" their understanding, and to satisfy the norms of school and society.

Out of the Pens of Kids

We are often asked what comprehension strategies do for kids. How they help kids understand what they read. How they help kids engage in their reading. So we go straight to the kids and ask them. After all, who knows better than the kids if and how comprehension strategies help them understand and engage in what they read? Students love to share their ideas and talk about their thinking.

Fifth-grade teacher Eleanor Wright sees merit in having her students write about how strategies help them comprehend text. In her response, Amy writes about how visualizing helps her "get it" when she reads: "I had lots of trouble with reading. I mean I can read but I didn't get the book. Now, I have a film through my head like I am actually there in the book." Skilynn shows how she stops and thinks about her reading for a minute or two before going on—synthesizing, if you will:

> *This year I have been going home and reading for at least 30 minutes and I love it! Ever since we started the sticky notes, it has really been making me think a minute or two to understand what the book is about. When I go home, I always go back and look at my questions to see if I can answer them yet. I usually can.*

And Cassie, finally, has an outlet for those pent-up thoughts and feelings (see Figure 5.1). Eleanor was amazed by these responses. She was delighted that her students were so engaged in reading. The strategies helped them move between their lives and books in meaningful ways, and Eleanor had a thorough understanding of what they were thinking and learning.

Figure 5.1
Cassie's Thoughts on How Reading
Comprehension Helped Her

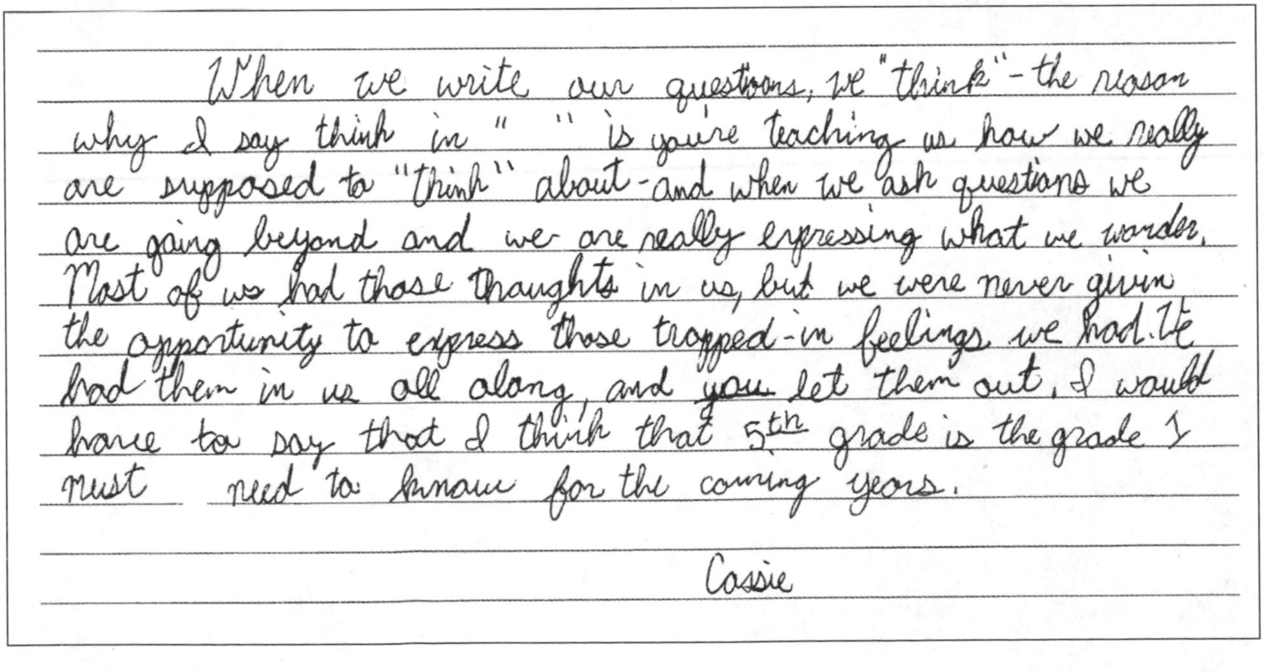

When we write our questions, we "think"—the reason why I say think in " " is you're teaching us how we really are supposed to "think" about—and when we ask questions we are going beyond and we are really expressing what we wonder. Most of us had those thoughts in us, but we were never given the opportunity to express those trapped-in feelings we had. We had them in us all along, and you let them out. I would have to say that I think that 5th grade is the grade I most need to know for the coming years.

Cassie

Part II

Strategy Lessons

Chapter 6

Instructional Practices for Teaching Comprehension

When we take the time to show kids how, we reap big rewards. The lessons in Part II of this book include a variety of instructional practices and response options that show kids how proficient readers read for understanding. We use these practices in different contexts, with different strategies, with different texts, with different content, and for different purposes. These practices and response options provide kids with a repertoire of strategic tools. Kids need an arsenal of tools to think deeply about what they read, listen to, and view. To demystify the comprehension process, we share our thoughts, surfacing our own inner conversation so kids can learn to do so independently.

We mix and match a variety of instructional techniques and response options to reach all kids, teach them, and keep them engaged. Sometimes we lead an interactive read-aloud. Sometimes we annotate the text. Other times we guide a group discussion. Children differ; so do their responses.

We model our thinking in whole-group instruction, small-group instruction, and individual conferences. Variety is the spice of life!

Before delving into the lessons in Part II and the content unit examples in Part III, we share these generic instructional practices and a list of response options that you will see throughout the lesson chapters. Each of the strategy lessons in Part II incorporate one or more of these explicit instructional approaches and response options to teach comprehension.

Instructional Practices

Thinking Aloud

The reading literature refers to the detailed process of making our thinking public as a "think aloud" (Davey 1983). Our definition of thinking aloud means that we peel back the layers of our thinking, show kids how we approach text, and make visible how understanding happens in a variety of reading contexts. Sometimes our think-alouds are strategy specific. Other times we share a variety of reactions and responses.

Rereading

The more kids hear or read a story or text, the more they love it, the more they learn from it, and the more they comprehend it. The teacher models how she rereads for clarification, for deeper understanding, and to build knowledge.

Interactive Reading Aloud

The teacher reads the text, models her own thinking, and highlights strategy use. Students listen, turn and talk to each other, and jot or draw their thinking, reactions, questions, and comments.

Annotating Text

Annotation is one of the most powerful thinking tools for learning, understanding, and remembering. We annotate through drawing as well as writing and use annotation on text, images, and other features. The teacher models and leaves tracks of his own thinking. Then the teacher and the kids reason through the text and images together as kids assume greater responsibility for annotation.

Co-constructing Anchor Charts

Anchor charts connect past teaching and learning to future teaching and learning. We cocreate anchor charts as a record of instruction, often including the language we use to talk about our thinking. Anchor charts hold kids' and our thinking about a text, lesson, or strategy so that we can return to it to review what we have learned.

Guiding Discussion and Student Conversation

The teacher facilitates a discussion about the ideas, issues, and concepts in a text. In this discussion, the teacher strives to weave the kids' thoughts and questions into a coherent conversation about the big ideas and helps shape the kids' responses into a line of thinking that moves the discussion forward.

Sharing Our Own Literate Lives

The ultimate way to show kids how we read and think is by sharing our own literate lives with them—what we read and write and our experience as readers. This way, kids will get to know us as people who read books, write for many purposes, and research to find answers to our questions. This is more than a practice; this is a daily demonstration of what it means to live a literate life.

Plan Ahead to Highlight Specific Teaching Points

We plan ahead and note places in the text where we want to model specific strategies and show how we analyze and interpret the text. We think about questions that zero in on important concepts or ideas that we stop and discuss with kids to further their understanding.

Share Aspects of the Inner Conversation

We share how we monitor and keep track of our thinking when reading. We note our reactions, connections, confusions, questions, and so forth. "In this book, *Gleam and Glow*, I think it would be really scary to have your dad off fighting in a war somewhere like the father in this story is doing." We also share how our attention can flag and our thoughts can stray from the text and how we repair this, so that kids will see how we get ourselves back on track. We jot and sketch our thoughts on sticky notes or in the margins to leave tracks of our thinking and stay on top of meaning.

Share How We Activate and Connect to Background Knowledge

We show kids how we merge what we already know with new information we encounter as we read. "I knew that sharks have big teeth, but they are even bigger than I thought they were. Wow!" We also show how our thinking changes as we read. "I always thought that sharks like to eat people, but now I know that they are very picky eaters."

Share Our Questions

We demonstrate the questions we have while reading. We note that some questions are answered and others are not. We show how we read with a question in mind and how one question often leads to another. "Why are the sea otters disappearing? Is there not enough food? Is a predator killing them? Is the water polluted?" In this way, we demonstrate how our questions can lead to a line of thinking.

Share Our Inferences

We model how we use the context to infer the meaning of unfamiliar words and concepts. We show how we infer themes in fiction. We show how we use illustrations, photos, and features to draw conclusions in nonfiction. "It says the radio guys on the *Titanic* were weary. I'm inferring it means they were tired, because the next sentence says they had been up all night."

Verbalize Confusing Points and Demonstrate Fix-Up Strategies

We monitor ongoing comprehension and show our reaction when meaning breaks down. "Huh? I don't get this part. This doesn't make sense." And we also show how we use fix-up strategies like rereading or reading on to clarify confusion, saying something like, "Oh, now I get it. I missed that the first time I read."

Share How We Sort and Sift Information to Determine Important Ideas

We demonstrate how we can't remember all of the details when we read. So we model how we pick out the information we want to remember. "Boy, there are a lot of details here about photosynthesis. But what's really important is how plants use sunlight to make their food. I can tell that because the writer talks a lot about the sunlight and its relationship to plants."

Rereading

Rereading is an effective way to clarify confusion, respond to questions, and understand a text more completely. We model how we reread for all of those purposes and others as they arise.

We share how we reread to do the following:

- Clarify confusions and misconceptions
- Revisit and address questions
- Find and confirm evidence
- Focus in on what we learned in the first read and expand our thinking and deepen understanding on subsequent reads
- Synthesize and infer the bigger ideas in complex text
- Stop and notice the author's style, use of words and images, and beautiful writing
- Further enjoy a text we loved the first time

Interactive Reading Aloud

As with thinking aloud, during an interactive read-aloud, we model our own thinking to show kids how we interact with the text and then quickly give them opportunities to talk with one another and respond on their own.

We build and activate background knowledge about the text by asking kids to turn and talk about what they think they already know about the topic at hand. Then we allow a minute or two for them to share some of this information. This engages our kids and prepares them to participate.

We read through a bit of the text and model our thinking as we read. We share our inner conversation, our use of a strategy, our confusions, our background knowledge, some content information, whatever the focus of the lesson was. We stop and record our thinking on sticky notes, a chart, think sheets, the margins, or in notebooks. After kids have observed us modeling, we often stop and ask them to share what they noticed us doing as a reader, so they can do it themselves when they are reading independently. We might record their thinking on an anchor chart, both what they noticed us modeling and their own thoughts.

During guided practice, we read a bit more and encourage kids to further discuss the ideas and issues. As we read, we stop and give them time to draw or write their responses and talk to one another.

Annotating Text

Annotation is the most powerful tool for holding thinking when reading, listening, and viewing. We need our students to be up close and personal, clipboards in hand, during our lesson as we read through the text, stop to demonstrate how we use a strategy, and invite them to annotate and draw their responses.

We explain that annotating means stopping briefly to write or draw our ideas in the margins, on sticky notes, or on think sheets as we read. Leaving tracks like this gives readers a place to hold and remember their thinking.

To highlight the power of kids' thinking, we often say, "Nothing matters more than your thinking when you read, and annotation is a great way to share it, hold it, and remember it."

We model our own annotations and share a variety of text codes, and kids contribute their own. Here are some possibilities:

- * for important information
- ? for a question
- L for learn
- R for "It reminds me of . . ."
- ! for amazing or surprising information
- I for inference
- V for visualize
- Huh? for confusion

Ⓡ This character is just like me, a little shy at first.

Ⓛ I never knew that dinosaurs lived on land & plesiosaurs lived in the water.

⊘ What is parkour?
Ⓐ A sport of running, jumping, climbing through obstacles.

Co-Constructing Anchor Charts

Anchor charts make thinking big, concrete, and visible. We co-construct them so that kids have ownership and continue to use them. They evolve over time as kids learn more and add to them. Everybody weighs in.

Anchor charts provide a record of our launch lessons. We co-construct anchor charts to record kids' thinking about a text, a lesson, a strategy, or the content so that we can return to it to remember what we have learned. Halls and walls teach in our classrooms.

We create a wide range of anchor charts to hold the learning and thinking from the lessons. A variety of anchor-chart types include the following:

- **Strategy charts.** During a strategy lesson, we co-construct charts incorporating the lesson content as well as students' comments and insights. We define the strategy, capture the language that demonstrates strategic thinking, and show examples of the kids' use of the strategy.

- **Content charts.** Content matters. Content anchor charts record the interesting and important information that readers discover when reading and researching. Sometimes we record new learning, how our thinking has evolved and changed, or new information we have acquired.

- **Genre charts.** We discuss and define the genre and share examples. As kids read in a particular genre and discuss what they know about it, we capture their thoughts in writing. So we might co-construct a chart about the features of nonfiction or the elements of fiction, which we post for all to see and remember.

- **Response charts.** We honor kids' thinking by collecting their thoughts, drawings, and all manner of responses on anchor charts. Many of these charts relate to strategy lessons we have taught as well as content they have learned.

MONITORING COMPREHENSION

When we monitor our comprehension we listen to the voice in our head speaking to us. We read Robin Cruise's <u>Little Mama Forgets</u>, the story of Lucy, a little girl who lives with her mom, dad, baby brother and her beloved grandmother. As her grandmother gets older, she forgets more and more things every day. But she never forgets how much she loves her little Lucy and the rest of the family.

After we read it, we wrote down what the story made us think about.

What the story makes us think about...

It reminds me of my favorite uncle who is really old but still loves to have fun.

It makes me think of my grandpa who forgets lots of stuff.

It makes me hungry when they eat all those tortillas for breakfast.

I don't like to take a nap either.

Why did she forget the stop light? That's dangerous.

I wonder why some people forget so much when they get old.

Guiding Discussion and Fostering Conversation

In planning guided discussions, our intent is to teach the art of conversation so that kids learn to hold these discussions themselves.

When planning for a guided discussion, we think about important parts of the text where we need to stop and discuss the big ideas.

We think about focus questions that nudge kids to weigh in with their ideas about important concepts.

We intentionally weave kids' comments into the conversation, using their thoughts to advance the discussion.

We teach them language for building on one another's thinking such as

> *That's an interesting idea that makes me think . . .*
> *Piggybacking off of . . .*
> *Just like _____ was saying, I am thinking . . .*
> *I respectfully disagree. What I was thinking was . . .*
> *I beg to differ . . .*

We ask open-ended questions to encourage deeper thinking such as

> *What makes you say that?*
> *Can you tell us more about what you were thinking?*
> *Anyone have another idea?*
> *How did you come up with that?*
> *Can you say more about that?*

Tips for Sharing Our Own Literate Lives

We let kids know every day that we are readers. We share learning from the newspaper, online, our book club, the book we are reading, and so on.

We bring in a huge variety of texts of interest and share our enthusiasm for the ideas.

We use our own text and our own writing to model lessons when it makes sense to do so.

We are always on the lookout for articles, images, essays, and other materials that relate to the content we are studying in the classroom and bring them in to share.

We remember to share readings that are difficult as well as those we love, so our kids get the idea that the going can get tough even for proficient readers, and as proficient readers we sometimes have to work hard to make meaning.

We share our visits to libraries, museums, concerts, plays, and lectures and let kids know how we continue to learn more about topics of interest outside of school.

Beyond Dioramas: Responding to Reading

Lucy Calkins, professor and director of the Teachers College Reading and Writing Project, notes that when she finishes a book late at night in bed, she doesn't grab her husband by the arm and say, "Oh, I just can't wait to get downstairs and make a diorama." We understand. For too many years, kids in classrooms all over the United States have been asked to do a laundry list of activities when they finish reading books. You know the ones—dioramas, shadow boxes, word jumbles, word searches, and so on. Reading response is more than these. Authentic responses don't have to be so contrived or complicated. As our colleague Harvey Daniels suggests, "Why can't kids do what real lifelong readers do when they finish a great book? Talk about it and then get another book."

In one way or another, every lesson described in this book incorporates student response. Be they oral or artistic or written, simple or sophisticated, responses tell us what children are thinking and learning. They let us know if our kids are engaged with their learning or tuning out from boredom. Student responses provide evidence of learning. They give us an inkling about whether students' understanding is in the ballpark or off the mark. And usually we know a whole lot more. Kids who have experienced comprehension instruction are only too happy to share their thoughts and opinions about their reading and thinking, and we can all learn a great deal from them.

Diverse, open-ended responses tell us the most about what children understand or don't understand when they read. The two most common forms of in-school responses have been oral and written. Many of the responses in this book fall into these categories. With the advent of technology, however, the response landscape has expanded exponentially. Kids can record videos, lay down music tracks, and become full-fledged second-grade filmmakers. They can interview their favorite authors or experts on a topic of study and record the entire interview to share with their class and online. They can create infographics that summarize new learning. They can take action by learning about local recycling practices and create flyers to inform neighbors. So response options have come a long way since the previous edition of this book. But regardless of whether they merely involve paper and pencil or represent the latest in tech wizardry, kids still use them to construct, demonstrate, and share their thinking, learning, and understanding. And we use them to thoughtfully and authentically assess that learning.

Oral Response Options

Literacy floats on a sea of talk (Britton 1970). Oral response options that you will see in the lessons in Part II include the following:

Turn and Talk
Turning and talking gives all kids, not only the most vocal ones, a chance to participate in the conversation and construct meaning. With young children, we model how to do this so kids can see what it looks like to interact with a partner in relation to the lesson.

Paired Reading

Kids may be paired around a common interest, question, or topic of study. We remind them that the listening is the most important job when working together. We often have the listener jot his or her questions and thoughts on sticky notes so that when the reader finishes, they can have a conversation about the reading.

Think Pair Shares

After the teacher models a strategy, pairs are encouraged to go back and work through text, talk about it, and respond together. We model this as well, so kids have a good understanding of how to do it most effectively.

Small Informal Discussion Groups

Three to five kids discuss and reason through a piece of text together. Sometimes they sit in the position of a compass, which allows the teacher to help move the conversation along by mentioning when North should finish up sharing and East can begin.

Jigsaw Discussions

When we ask kids to jigsaw articles on a theme or topic, we try to ensure that each article brings a different perspective and/or includes different information. Younger kids can jigsaw images or short segments of text.

Book Clubs and Literature Circles

Students read the same text and meet together to discuss and respond to it much the same way that adults meet in monthly book clubs. The authentic conversations that occur encourage participants to express their opinions, raise questions and issues, and connect the text to their own lives.

Informational Study Groups

In these groups, students work together to build knowledge about a common topic of interest. These topics may emerge from a facet of the curriculum or simply from student interest.

Inquiry Circles

In these small collaborative groups, kids investigate questions they are curious about and search to find information. (For more on this, see *Comprehension and Collaboration: Inquiry Circles for Curiosity, Engagement, and Understanding* [Harvey and Daniels 2015].)

Written, Artistic, and Digital Response Options

Whereas talk is likely the most immediate way to respond to reading, writing and drawing in many forms allow readers to work out their thinking in relation to the text. Response options that you will see in the lessons in Part II include the following:

Annotations

We use a variety of annotations both written and digital, including margin notes, text codes, sticky notes, electronic notes, think sheets, Google Docs, Edmodo, Padlet—all represent ways to capture thinking while reading

Short Constructed Responses

There are as many possibilities for short response as one can imagine, including one-pagers, quick-writes, blogs, surveys, listicles, infographics, and written conversations.

Response Journals

Lit logs, notebooks, Wonder Books, blogs, and more. Kids write, draw, sketch, paste in artifacts, and so on as they explore their thinking in relation to reading. These entries can often spur longer, more extensive writing such as poems, stories, and essays.

Creating and Making

A response option new since the last edition of this book comes out of the maker movement. The maker movement has taken advantage of the availability of low-cost computers and programming to provide a real-world, hands-on, constructivist experience for student learning. Students can build what they are learning and thinking about. We can also take the low-tech pathway, including assembling with Legos, creating models with paper and cardboard, and building with wooden blocks. If kids can envision it, they can create it.

Artistic, Dramatic, Musical Responses

Giant posters, murals, reflection videos, book trailers, songs, poems, plays, and more are included here. We work with kids to develop the broadest spectrum of meaningful responses. But *meaningful* is the key word here. We want to remember to keep these authentic and engaging. We are thrilled that the world has opened up in terms of response. Until recently, if kids were not the most accomplished writers or speakers in the class, times were tough. Now, however, kids are the ones leading the way, with creative response options that feature their talents and interests. If we stick to only oral and written responses, that future Georgia O'Keeffe, Sheryl Sandberg, or Leonardo DiCaprio may never emerge. But now the sky is the limit!

Chapter 7

Monitoring Comprehension: The Inner Conversation

"So tell me something. How many of you have ever found yourself reading something but thinking about something else?" Steph asked a group of seventh graders gathered in front of her during the last period of the day. The entire class shot their hands into the air. "Wow, all of you. Okay, take a minute and think about a time this has happened to you. Then turn and talk to a partner about what you were reading and what you were thinking about." The room exploded with chatter as kids shared their thinking. Apparently, this was routine stuff for them. After several minutes, Steph asked if anyone wanted to share his or her experience.

"It happened to me last period in science," Taunia ventured. "We were reading about atoms, but I was thinking about something else."

"So what were you thinking about?" Steph asked. Taunia explained that Friday would bring the first middle school dance of the year and she and her mom had made a deal that if she did all of her chores that week, her mom would buy her a top that she had picked out at T. J. Maxx the previous weekend. Today was the day, so she was focused on that top. Her main concern was whether it would still be there, since she knew that many of the items at T. J. Maxx were one of a kind. However, she had taken action to increase her chances of securing that top. She had moved it from the girls' junior department to men's coats, hiding it deep in the middle of the size 46 rack. Now, that's strategic!

If only all of our kids were as strategic about their reading as Taunia was about her outfit for the dance. Sometimes reading goes smoothly, and sometimes it doesn't. Sometimes readers can't get enough of a topic. Other times they couldn't care less about it. Sometimes a lack of background knowledge interferes with reading and understanding. Other times a compelling topic engages readers throughout the text. Sometimes readers proceed seamlessly; other times they stumble because the text is too hard. And sometimes they lose focus as Taunia did and don't even notice that they are no longer thinking about the words and ideas in the text.

Surprisingly, Taunia reported that she was able to answer the questions at the end of the atoms chapter, not because she understood what she read, but because all of the answers were in bold print. So she just skimmed the bold print answers and matched them to the questions they fit, another strategic act on Taunia's part. We want our kids to do more than skim bold print to discover answers. We want them to merge their thinking with the text information, building knowledge as they go. And we want them to stay engaged in their reading and be stimulated by their thinking.

In the lessons described in this chapter, we use explicit language that relates directly to monitoring comprehension. As you do these lessons, we suspect you'll hear your kids tell you that they need to stop, think, and react to the information, that they are listening to their inner voice, or that they have strayed from their inner conversation. We teach the language and lessons of monitoring so that our kids can monitor meaning and articulate their thinking, and in that way become strategic readers who develop new insights.

Strategy Lessons: Monitoring Comprehension

Following the Inner Conversation

Purpose: **Listening to the inner voice and leaving tracks of thinking**
Resource: ***Gleam and Glow* by Eve Bunting**
Responses: **Sticky notes on a piece of paper on clipboards**
Audience: **Intermediate and middle**

Reading comprehension is an ongoing process of evolving thinking. When readers read and construct meaning, they carry on an inner conversation with the text. They hear a voice in their head speaking to them as they read—a voice that questions, connects, laughs, cries. This inner conversation helps readers monitor their comprehension and keeps them engaged in the story, concept, information, and ideas, allowing them to build their understanding as they go. Once we have modeled the inner conversation, readers will more seamlessly activate a particular strategy, such as questioning, connecting, or determining importance, when they read because they are more likely to notice and consider their thinking.

Interactive Reading Aloud

Steph launched this lesson on the inner conversation with a group of eighth graders. Most of the kids in the class were immigrants from a variety of countries around the world, including Somalia, Sudan, Cambodia, and Mexico. Steph chose to use Eve Bunting's picture book *Gleam and Glow*, a gripping fictionalized account of a true story from the war in Bosnia. In this story, a family is separated by the ravages of war and eventually reunited in a refugee camp. Steph knew that many of the kids in this class could readily relate to this story, having been immigrants themselves, some even having lived in refugee camps at one time or another. She purposely chose this book since the kids would likely connect to it. You can view this lesson on our video series titled *Strategic Thinking* (2004).

Throughout the story the two young protagonists never forget the two pet fish, Gleam and Glow, they were forced to leave behind, but who, amid the great destruction of war, survive and flourish in a pond behind the family's former home. Despite the loss of material possessions and the disintegration of their former way of life, the family survives and emerges stronger than ever, which in many ways parallels the story of the two fish, Gleam and Glow. In the end, the story remains one of determination, hope, and survival.

With the kids gathered in front of her, Steph began by saying, "Nothing is more important during reading than the reader's thinking. I have chosen this book because it makes me think about so many things. When readers pay attention and think about the words and ideas in the text, they carry on an inner conversation with the text. It is a quiet conversation that happens in the reader's head."

She then gave some examples of the kinds of things readers hear in their heads as they read. "When I read and pay attention, I hear a voice in my head that says different things to me. For instance, when I am confused, I might hear something like *Huh, I don't get this part.* And when I read on, I might hear something like *Oh, now I get it.* Or when I meet new information, I might hear something like *Wow, I never knew that before.* This is the inner conversation that I have with the writer as I read. While I am reading to you, I want you to think about and notice what you hear in your inner conversation."

Steph then modeled her thinking with the first page of *Gleam and Glow*. As she did, she pointed out her connections, questions, and reactions and jotted her thoughts on sticky notes, showing how she left tracks of her thinking.

Next Steph continued to read the story, engaging the kids in guided practice. Sometimes she simply asked them to turn and talk about their thinking. This is an open-ended thinking prompt that we encourage teachers to ask frequently. Other times, she asked a more specific thinking prompt, such as, "Turn and talk about the mom in this story. What are you thinking about her role in this story?" This is a more specific thinking prompt to get kids to talk about a certain aspect of the story that may help them focus on a specific theme. What is important here is that she varied the thinking prompts from open ended to specific and gave kids a lot of time to interact with the text.

At the end of the story, kids got into groups of four and used their sticky-note responses to fuel a discussion of the story as Steph moved around between the groups and listened in on them. Upon the conclusion of the lesson, Steph asked them to share some of what they learned about monitoring comprehension and the inner conversation as well as their thoughts on the story. See Figure 7.1. (See additional examples of their inner conversations on sticky notes in the assessment section at the end of this chapter.)

Figure 7.1
Sticky Notes on *Gleam and Glow*

> The man is fair to animals and he understands that the fish need to live too. What is so important that the book would be named after them?

> Finally, something good happens !!! ...
>
> Family strength ...

> Poor Gleam and Glow! They cant get left behind. Oh Well at least I hope they find their father ...

> So good they found their father. But what about the bombs will their house be Okay? What about g+g?

> their mother is very courageous. She doesn't give up. Where does the stuff come from? Who's taking care of them? Do they have food?

> Where are g+g? They cant die because its the name of the book. If they died, they would float to the top Maybe they're hiding ...

Follow Your Inner Conversation When Reading Digital Text

Purpose: **Applying strategies used with print text to digital text in order to keep track of thinking.**

Resource: **A short poem or other short piece presented digitally through a website, a pdf file, or a shared document like Google Docs. We used "Street Painting" by Ann Turner (2011).**

Responses: **A paper graphic organizer or sticky notes for note taking while reading text digitally**

Audience: **Intermediate and middle**

We've noticed that as students read more and more text through a digital medium, they often forget to apply tried-and-true strategies that have helped them become proficient print readers. Students flexibly use these essential skills by drawing comparisons between print reading and digital reading. When students learn to follow their inner voice, they make the jump into becoming thoughtful and careful readers. Digital reading is even more demanding in this regard, as it often adds additional challenges.

Katie Muhtaris, a fifth-grade teacher, teaches students this strategy using a gradual release of responsibility model. Katie first asks them to sit and observe as she reads a model poem aloud. To get started she chooses a poem that requires a great deal of jotting and interaction to fully understand. Text matters, and a somewhat challenging and thought-provoking text will hit home the importance of keeping track of thinking.

> *Today we're going to work on making sure that we use our thinking brain to read a digital text. We've worked really hard on reading with a wide-awake mind this year. But do you ever notice that sometimes when you read on a screen, your brain sort of checks out? It's as if your mind says the words on the screen aren't as important as the ones on paper. We have to remind our brain that we need to think just as hard, if not harder, when we read a text on a computer.*

During the modeling part of the lesson, Katie uses a document camera so that students can see how she places the tablet computer with the poem and the graphic organizer side by side. She asks students to have their own organizer on a clipboard and to identify a turn-and-talk partner so that they can engage, observe, and debrief. As she works, she thinks out loud with phrases such as these:

> *What do you notice about what I'm doing right now? Am I rereading a lot? Yes! I feel like I need to work harder to focus when I read on a screen.*
>
> *Here I'm going to make sure to write my thinking as well as the text that the thinking is connected to.*
>
> *I notice that I'm not quite sure what this means. I'm going to add that to my organizer so that I can think on this more.*
>
> *This line seems especially important. I wonder what this means. Maybe it means . . .*

Katie then asks students to turn and talk about what they noticed. How did she apply the strategies they'd seen her use time and time again to the digital text? How did the digital text challenge her in new ways? She continues on a few more lines, asking students to jot their own thinking and share out with the class. Then students move off to work in partners to practice, taking note of their own challenges and successes as they work. See Figure 7.2.

Katie ends the lesson by asking the class to come together to discuss how they applied strategies, what they noticed about themselves as digital readers, and how leaving tracks of their thinking helped them make meaning.

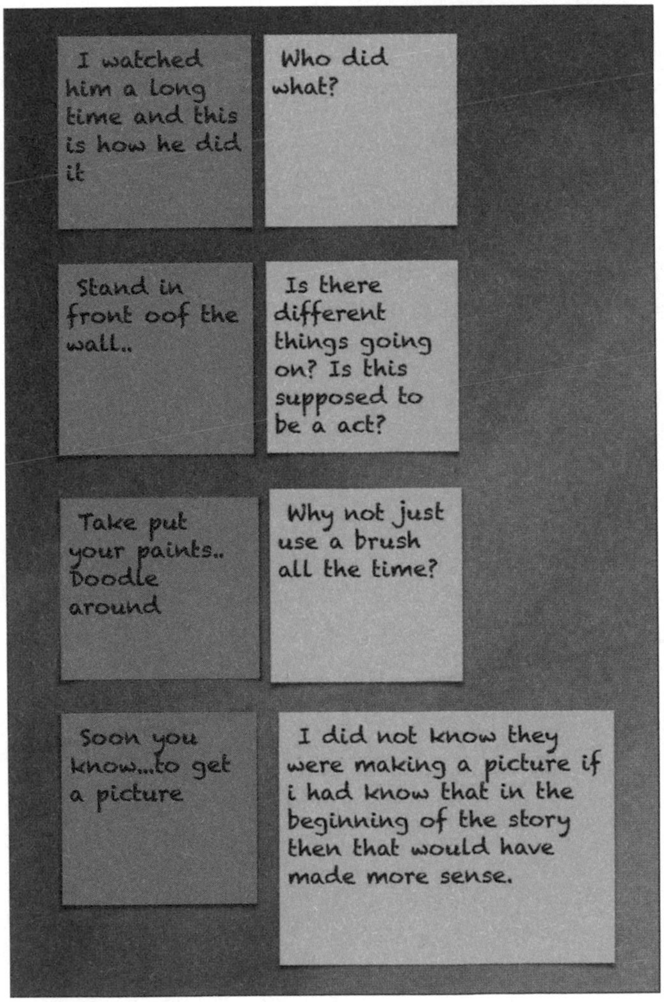

Figure 7.2
Students' Notes—Words and Ideas from Text (left) and Thinking (right)

Noticing When We Stray from the Inner Conversation

Purpose: **Monitoring the inner voice to focus thinking and "fix up" comprehension**
Resource: **A piece of adult text**
Responses: **Two-column chart titled Why Meaning Breaks Down/What to Do About It**
Audience: **Intermediate and middle**

Only when readers listen to their inner voice will they notice when they stray from an active inner conversation with the text. In truth, it is natural for our minds to wander when we read. Whether reading in print or digitally, an idea in the text may trigger a personal connection and suddenly we have no idea what we are reading about, but we can remember our first prom with clarity! Or we come to a part where we lack the background knowledge needed to process and understand; meaning breaks down and we find ourselves thinking of something else. Perhaps we are thinking about our to-do list and we simply can't concentrate on our reading no matter how hard we try. Or maybe we come to a hard part and abandon the text because we lack the strategies to fix up meaning. When we teach our kids to listen to the inner conversation and notice when they stray, they are more likely to catch their wandering minds sooner, stop, and refocus before they become completely befuddled.

There's nothing more powerful than sharing our own reading process with our kids, explaining and showing how we make meaning as well as how we fix it when it breaks down. Above all, our kids need to know that we are readers, so bringing in text we are reading at home is a great way for them to get that message. We take time frequently to share our own literate lives with our kids. But in so doing, we need to remember that although we teachers (most of us anyway) are prolific readers who love little more than curling up with a great book, we need to share when reading gets tough as well as when it is pleasurable. We can share stories with our kids of times we found our mind wandering during reading or of times when the text was simply too hard to comprehend.

Bring in a text of your own where you have noticed meaning break down and you have struggled to pay attention and understand. Model for the kids how you notice yourself straying from an engaged read when you come to a hard or boring part, and what you do to get back on top of meaning. Co-construct an anchor chart with the kids. Share a couple of reasons that meaning breaks down for you and write them on the chart. Then ask kids to turn and talk about what causes them to lose focus when they read and discuss what to do about it in partners, having them share their responses. You'll see some amazing ideas that we really need to take to heart when teaching reading! A co-constructed chart with a group of fifth graders follows.

Monitoring Comprehension

Why Meaning Breaks Down	What to Do About It
Fatigue	Reread to construct meaning.
	Put the text down when too tired.
Not enough background knowledge	Focus and read words more carefully than usual.
Thirst	Get up and get a drink of water.
Stress	Talk to a teacher or friend about what's on your mind.

Don't like the text	*Choose something else to read.*
Too hard	*Think about what you know and try to connect it to new information.*
Boring	*Choose another text if possible or talk to someone who finds the topic interesting.*

Noticing and Exploring Thinking

Purpose: **Distinguishing between retelling the story and merging thinking with it**
Resource: ***Little Mama Forgets*** **by Robin Cruise**
Responses: **Large sticky notes and an anchor chart titled What *Little Mama Forgets* Makes Me Think About**
Audience: **Primary**

Monitoring comprehension happens when readers pay attention to their own thinking and explore it. All of the lessons in this book promote active literacy. In some lessons, we have kids write as we read. In others, they write as they read. In many, they turn and talk while we read out loud. Sometimes they just read, read, read! In this lesson, we simply read a book without saying a word—that's right, no thinking aloud! Then we ask kids to jot or draw their thinking *after* we read, share their responses with a partner, and have a conversation. In primary classrooms, retelling is paramount, and we agree it is an important skill. But retelling is not all we do with primary kids when it comes to comprehension. We want our kids to merge their thinking with the ideas in the story, connecting to it, questioning it, inferring the meaning, and so on. We want them to understand that their thinking matters when they read, listen, or view.

Liz, a second-grade teacher, chose Robin Cruise's *Little Mama Forgets*, the poignant story of a little girl and her beloved grandmother, who is suffering age-related memory loss. In this book, the author explores the tender relationship between these two characters changing places as it were, the girl growing up and the grandmother forgetting more each day. Liz suspected that this text might remind kids of their own grandparents, other elderly people in their lives, or various family stories they had heard. She introduced the book by telling the story of her own adored grandfather, who became more forgetful as he grew old. She mentioned that this story reminded her of that relationship. Liz read the book aloud straight through. When she finished, she gave them each a large sticky note and explained that she didn't want them to retell the story, but rather to write down what the story made them think about, their thoughts and reactions, their inner conversation.

After kids jotted down their thinking, Liz asked them to turn to a partner and read what they wrote as well as talk about it. When kids finished their conversations, some shared their thinking with the whole group. To conclude, Liz collected the sticky notes and, with the kids' permission, put them all up on the chart titled What *Little Mama Forgets* Makes Me Think About. This became a wonderful anchor lesson and anchor chart to remind the kids to focus on their thinking when they read, not merely on the details, the plot, or the sequence of events of the story.

Read, Write, and Talk

Purpose: **Stopping to think and react to informational text**
Resource: ***Time for Kids*** **(2002) article, "Could You Survive a Week Without TV?"**
Responses: **Jotting thinking in the margins**
Audience: **Intermediate and middle**

Reading is a social act. We all love to talk about what we read: sharing the latest novel with a friend, reacting to an outrageous editorial with a colleague, or exploring a picture book with a child. Read, Write, and Talk is a practice that gives readers an opportunity to think, record their thoughts by annotating, and then talk about their reading. We model our own inner conversation with the text and jot down our thoughts in the margins of a piece of text and then give kids a chance to try it on their own. We explain that when readers read informational text, it is a good idea to stop and jot down their thinking while they read so that they can add to their store of knowledge, remember the information, and better learn and understand it. We teach kids to merge their thinking with the text by stopping, thinking, and reacting to the information—STR for short. When they finish reading, they can find someone who read the same piece and use their margin notes to talk further about their reading. When kids notice their thinking while they read, and engage in purposeful talk afterward, they comprehend more completely and think beyond the text.

Steph launched Read, Write, and Talk with a group of fourth graders, using an article from *Time for Kids* titled "Could You Survive a Week Without TV?" She modeled her own thinking, remembering to stop, think, and react to information as she read. In this way, she hoped that the kids would get an explicit idea of her thinking process—how she merged her thinking with the information by jotting down her connections, questions, and reactions.

After modeling her thinking by interacting with the text for a few paragraphs, Steph invited the kids to jot down their thinking on their own copies of the article during guided practice. She continued to read but stopped every few moments and asked them to jot their reactions in the margins and turn and talk to each other about their thinking. When she finished reading, Steph asked the kids to flip over their papers and write down three things:

1.   Something they learned that they think is important to remember
2.   How talking to a partner helped them understand what they read
3.   Any lingering questions that they still had

The kids shared their responses with the whole group and talked about how stopping, thinking, and reacting helped them understand what they read and if and how talking to a partner added to the experience.

After we do this together as a class, we suggest kids try it on their own. We usually offer a choice of three pieces at different levels and on different topics and ask kids to read a piece, jot down their thinking, and then find someone who read the same article and have a conversation with them. Some of their responses to different articles are shown in Figure 7.3. (See additional examples of kids' thinking tracks in the assessment section at the end of this chapter.) Read, Write, and Talk is not a lesson, but rather a practice that we implement with science, social studies, mathematics, and even textbooks. It sets up a way to interact with text and with each other. Kids of all ages can annotate. See the following lessons for annotating with kindergarten and second-grade students. For further information about how to launch this practice, see our video *Read, Write, and Talk* (2005a).

Figure 7.3
Student Responses to an Article and Their Talk with a Partner

People are actually supporting tests & I'm thinking if they were ever kids once!

My Conversation with Emma was very useful because we talked about How UNFAIR it is to test. she made me think about stuff I never realized when I read the article

I thought it was worth while Because it was interesting to see what othe People had to say, and what they thought was Cool.

I couldn't belive that 93,000 tigers died in 94 years! Also it's very cool that ever tige has different stripes.

TV Too much violence
TV makes children agressive

I learned some background knowledge.

We don't save Read, Write, and Talk merely for the literacy block. It is not a lesson that we teach once before quickly moving on to the next but a practice we do frequently across the curriculum. When we launch Read, Write, and Talk, we choose the most compelling text we can find on content that kids find irresistible, such as TV watching. If they are fascinated by the content, they are more likely to learn and understand the process quickly. Once kids have had more experience with this process, it becomes a practice to be done repeatedly both collaboratively and independently in ELA, science, history, and even math.

Leave Tracks of Thinking: Annotating in the Primary Grades

Purpose: **Viewing closely to learn and wonder about photos and captions**

Resources: ***Red-Eyed Tree Frog* by Joy Cowley and/or other nonfiction books with great photos and minimal text**

Response: **Writing around a photo and caption**

Audience: **Primary**

It's the third week of school and Jessica Noe's class of twenty-six kindergartners know just what to do with a clipboard, a sticky note, and a marker. As our colleague Joanne Durham notes, "A sticky note and a nonfiction book with provocative pictures are powerful things in the hands of a five- or six-year-old." Each day as they gather to listen to Jessica read fiction or nonfiction, her students eagerly respond to both. Charts filled with sticky notes of the kids' thinking about *Corduroy* (Freeman), *Sheila Rae the Brave* (Henkes), and nonfiction Big Books cover the walls.

Children express their thinking and learning by drawing, and if they can, writing in response to a photograph of a hairy tarantula, or a snowy avalanche. As kids become more practiced at responding to their reading, why not teach them to leave tracks of their thinking by annotating?

Listening to Joy Cowley's *Red-Eyed Tree Frog* provided an opportunity for the kids to think about and learn from the photographs and text. As Jessica read the book out loud, she modeled how to respond to the text and photos on sticky notes. She placed these on pages of the book. By the end of the read-aloud, kids could hardly wait to have at it. Each child had a photograph and caption waiting at their desk, and they went to work drawing and writing their new learning. Josiah, with a photo of the wings of a moth in the mouth of a tree frog, exclaimed, "Wow! I just learned the tree frog eats insects!" Using invented spelling, he wrote his question (Figure 7.4). At the end of the lesson, kids proudly shared their annotations—demonstrating the power of learning, from one enticing photograph.

Figure 7.4
Children's Written and Illustrated
Annotations Include Questions

Read, Talk, and Jot: Annotating Nonfiction Text and Images

Purpose: **Annotating text by writing and drawing to leave tracks of thinking**
Resources: **Magazine or newspaper articles, or other short forms of text**
Responses: **Ask questions, record reactions, write and draw new learning**
Audience: **Primary and intermediate**

Kids are eager to learn about the real world, and they often spontaneously connect what's happening in the classroom to the big wide world out there. During a class study of endangered animals, Lorena burst into the classroom waving an article from the local newspaper about disappearing polar bears. These second graders, concerned that such a magnificent creature might be endangered, gathered round to find out more.

Teacher Brad Buhrow knew this was the perfect opportunity for kids to leave tracks of their thinking in the margins of the text, asking questions, connecting to background knowledge, and jotting down new learning. Knowing the text would be a challenging read for most of the kids, he placed the article with its large photograph on a class chart, with a wide margin on either side. Together they annotated the text to leave tracks of their thinking.

In this shared read, Brad and the kids discussed their background knowledge about big concepts related to endangered polar bears and their changing habitats.

As Brad viewed the photograph, read the caption, and began to read the first part of the article, he reminded kids to pay attention to their inner voice—the voice in their head that they hear when they read, listen, or view. He shared what he was thinking about and showed the kids how he put the information in his own words and jotted it in the left-hand margin, under the heading Information. He paraphrased the information, leaving tracks of his thinking by writing "The sea ice is shrinking." Then Brad asked kids to turn and talk about this, telling them that they would put their thoughts in the right-hand margin, under Thinking. Hunei wondered aloud that if polar bears can swim, perhaps it wouldn't matter if they had less sea ice to live on. As Brad listened in, he pointed out that Hunei was bringing his background knowledge into the conversation. "It's really important what you are doing—you are making sense of the information in this article by connecting to what you already know about polar bears." The conversation that followed—about whether or not polar bears could survive in a habitat with less ice—highlighted the bigger issues about polar bear adaptations.

When the kids read the last part of the article, which explained that scientists studying and tracking the polar bear population learned that many had died, they were very concerned and eager to know what was being done about this problem. They were able to extrapolate the specific information about polar bears to consider bigger ideas about the consequences of habitat change and global warming. Although these are not easy concepts for second graders to grapple with, acquiring knowledge about issues like these engages kids in learning about the world beyond their classroom.

(See additional examples of kids' work in the assessment section at the end of the chapter.)

Figure 7.5
Anchor Chart of a Newspaper Article
with Annotations from the Kids and the
Teacher

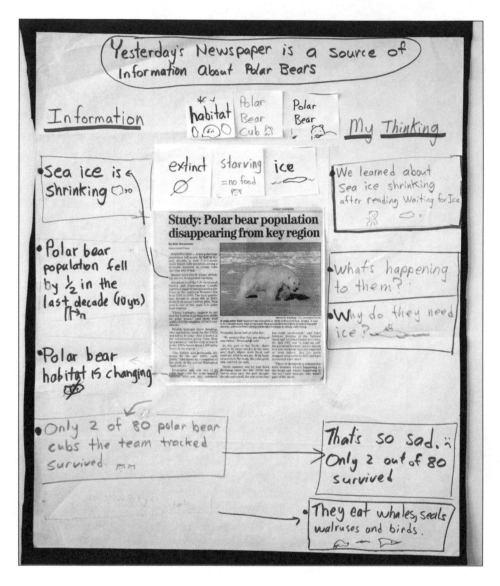

New

Monitoring Comprehension While Reading on the Web

Purpose: **Monitoring understanding while doing web reading by being aware of distractions and roadblocks**

Resources: **Current-events articles from a website like TweenTribune.**

Responses: **Students track distractions they encounter while reading on the web and create an anchor chart to help guide their online reading.**

Audience: **Intermediate**

Reading on websites can add an additional layer of confusion for students to deal with. Distracting ads, small text, and links further complicate reading that might already be challenging. This is why we intentionally teach kids about these distractions and what to do when they encounter them. As students become thoughtful digital readers, they also learn to apply strategies such as zooming in on text, refocusing their mind to the task, and looking for just-right websites.

We navigate these experiences as a class, sharing when we get distracted and what we do to get our minds back into the text. These whole-class read-alouds show students the skills and strategies needed to be successful. As students become more accomplished, we allow them to practice, take the reins, and give their feedback on what has worked for them.

Katie Muhtaris launches this lesson with her fifth graders by projecting an article from the Smithsonian's TweenTribune website. She models getting herself ready to read by previewing the text and by talking through a few of the distracting elements that she notices on the website. Katie then asks students to refer to the chart on monitoring for comprehension that they keep up in their classroom. This is a chart that she created with the students earlier in the year, and it holds a list of ways that meaning can break down when reading and fix-up strategies that students use.

As students review the chart, she poses a question: "When we're reading online, which distractions are specific to the technology and which ones are the same kinds of distractions we might encounter in our print reading? I'm wondering if reading online is so different from reading an article in a magazine." She asks students to keep this focus question in mind as she models actively reading an article from the site and working through distractions. Students jot notes in their notebook about strategies they see her use and share frequently through turn and talks.

Next, students practice on their own, selecting an article that they think might present a challenge. Katie feels it is important that students have choice in this area so that they can find an article that challenges them yet keeps them engaged. They keep track in their notebooks, as they read, of moments when they lose meaning, and pay careful attention to whether the distraction also occurs when reading print text or only with digital text.

Katie gathers students mid-workshop and asks them to share some of the work they've been doing with the class and make some recommendations based on what they're seeing. Students share that while they needed to engage some additional strategies to avoid distractions, this particular website didn't have too many, and it was easy for them to use technology tools like zooming in to avoid most of them. They also share that they noticed they needed to use many of their print strategies to understand the text, a fact that a few found surprising. Katie begins to collect their ideas on a chart.

Monitoring Comprehension While Reading Digitally

- Always go back to your fix-up strategies; reading is reading no matter what you're reading on.
- See if you can use your tech knowledge to get rid of distractions.

As Katie writes, one student points out that he was not able to annotate the text as he read digitally and that was a strategy he often used to gather information. Katie asks the students to brainstorm how they might continue to interact with the digital texts so that they can still hold their thinking. They add to their chart.

Ways to Stop and Think

- Jot in a notebook or on sticky notes while you read.
- Take a screenshot and use an app to annotate thinking.

Next Katie sends students off to work independently. She has provided links to a few other sites for kids to explore.

At the end of the lesson, Katie asked students to record a quick reflection video to share: how the day's reading went, how and when they applied the strategies, and whether they were successful. These reflection videos gave students an opportunity to reflect on the day's lesson and provided Katie with important assessment information.

(For an example of student work, see the assessment section at the end of the chapter.)

Monitoring comprehension is above all about engagement. When readers interact with the text, they are more apt to stay on top of meaning as they read. When readers are passive, not much happens and meaning eludes them. Passive may mean that readers are not interested in the text, find the text to be too difficult, or have insufficient background knowledge to understand. Whatever the reason, the result is that passive readers stray from an engaged read and lose track of meaning. Active reading is a dynamic process that puts the reader at the helm.

Teaching with the End in Mind: Assessing What We've Taught

Monitoring Comprehension

Based on the lessons in this chapter, we look for evidence that

1. *Students follow their inner conversation and annotate the text to leave tracks of their thinking.* We look for evidence of readers' thinking, including their reactions, questions, connections, and inferences. Students use sticky notes, graphic organizers, and a variety of apps to record their thinking.
2. *Students notice when they stray from the inner conversation and repair comprehension—use fix-up strategies.* We look for evidence that readers understand why meaning breaks down and how to go about repairing understanding.
3. *Students stop, think, and react to information as they read.* We look for evidence that nonfiction readers are stopping frequently, thinking about the information, and jotting down their thoughts and reactions.

Suggestions for Differentiation

Monitoring at this point is very open-ended. Readers may ask questions or draw inferences, but what is most important is that they have the disposition to think about and react to what they hear and read.

When modeling an interactive read-aloud, the teacher is doing much of the reading and the kids are listening. All kids are free to think about the ideas, because coding doesn't interfere. In this way, all kids can access the text. We ask them to leave tracks of their thinking. Those who are less developed writers are encouraged to draw a picture or use a short code to represent their thinking. We also encourage kids to turn and talk to each other before writing to hone their ideas and rehearse what they are going to write down or share. Those who are unable to write at all can still construct and share meaning by talking to someone about their thinking. When we confer with kids, we realize that English language learners may be able to say more about their thinking and reactions than they are able to write. So we make sure that we talk with them a great deal to give them an ongoing opportunity to sort out and share their thinking.

For younger kids or English language learners, we might make a large copy of the text and together we monitor our thinking and chart our response right on the text. The poster-size text becomes an anchor chart that guides kids as they do their own reading and practice monitoring their own comprehension. If they seem to be monitoring, and using a number of strategies, such as questioning, connecting, and inferring, we review these and quickly move on to teaching a more sophisticated strategy.

Monitoring Comprehension Assessment Commentary

Sticky notes from an interactive read-aloud with *Gleam and Glow* from the lesson "Following the Inner Conversation"

> What's Amonia? It must be hard. to carry all your stuff to move? I have two fish and they lived for one year. The family's brave to leave. I wonder if they would get dehydroted? Why would not people help them?

◄ When this child asks, "What is ammonia?" he is aware that he doesn't understand something, and we can tell he is monitoring his comprehension. In truth, we see a likely misconception; the girl in the story had *pneumonia*. We would stop and help the reader sort out the difference between the two words, but we would also let him know that by stopping and asking a question, he is doing exactly what we want him to. Additionally, we can see him inserting himself into the story with an inference, "It must be hard . . ." and a connection to his own fish as well as more questions.

▸ Here we see a drawing of a father leaving. We did not explicitly model drawing, but this student chose to illustrate his reaction, which is a terrific example of an authentic response to literature.

> I'm so glad they found their father, and he can stay too so they are together. They can go home now. But will their house be there? What about G & G? Oh no How will they live now? At least they are alive and together. G & G are ok. It's home even without the material things.

◄ On this note, we get a running commentary. Some kids are ready to write as we read; others need us to stop more frequently so they can collect their thoughts and jot them down. This child is really listening to her inner conversation when she says, "Oh no, how will they live now?" after seeing that their house has burned down. And she comes up with her own synthesis in the last line: "It's home even without the material things."

▸ This reader asks questions, expresses reactions, and shows her personality, especially when she says, "I am a woman. Hear me roar!" But the most important words come at the end when she writes, "We found Papa!" Notice the use of pronouns. She did not say, "They found their dad." Instead, she saw herself in the story at that point, which is one of those moments we live for as teachers.

-Why are the fish so special?
-Why did Victor do that w/ the fish?
- I feel bad for Marina!
-Will Al papa and them reunite?
-Which war is this?
-I roar fim a woman.Hear me
- Mini freedom fighters!
- WE FOUND PAPA!!!!!!!!!

why ⓠ did they bren ⓠ the houses? How could people do such a thing?

ⓢ there a live! ⓢ there gest like humens.

▲ ▸ This child is diagnosed with a processing deficit. He goes to the learning lab several days a week, and on two other days the special ed teacher comes into the classroom. He couldn't have read the book on his own, but he can think at the highest levels, as is evidenced from his notes. On the first sticky note, he reacts to the fact that the family's house was burned to the ground with the question "Why did they burn the houses?" and follows that up with perhaps the most important question of anyone in the class, "How could people do such a thing?" He also nails a parallel theme on the second sticky note, where he notices that Gleam and Glow survived just like the humans in the story. Many kids in the class did not recognize this, but interactive reading aloud levels the playing field and gives everyone a chance to weigh in with their thinking.

Think sheet used to monitor comprehension from the lesson "Monitoring Comprehension While Reading on the Web"

Jilleah

Why Meaning Broke Down	Print or Digital Distraction?	How I Fixed It
Distractions	Digital	Zoomed into the text.
Text is too small	Print	Zoomed even more into the text.
Links in articles	Digital	Ingnored the links.
Disinterest	Print	Read the rest of the article then went to another.
Unknown word		Infer what word means.
Distracting Connection	Print	
Distracting ads	Digital	Forget it and keep reading.
	Digital	Ignore it

◀ This think sheet supports kids to monitor and repair their comprehension as they read both in print and digitally. Jilleah has used a few fix-up strategies, including zooming in on the text, inferring the meaning of a word, and ignoring digital distractions.

A child's annotation of the polar bear article from the lesson "Read, Talk, and Jot"

▶ This second grader annotated her own copy of the newspaper article about polar bears. She asked questions, surfaced the big ideas, and expressed empathy (so sad!) for the plight of the polar bears. She accurately summarized what was happening in their habitat and the implications for their survival.

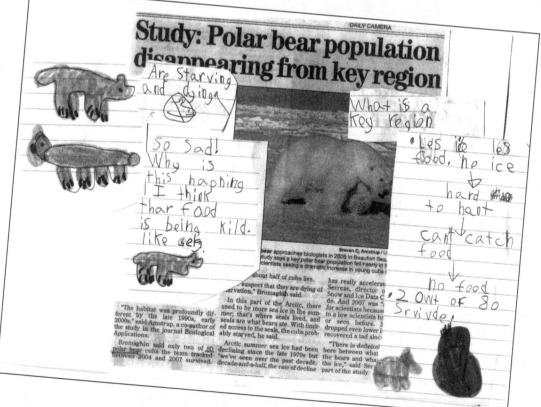

Chapter 8

Activating, Connecting, and Building: Why Background Knowledge Matters

A group of second graders swarmed around Anne as she read William Steig's delightful picture book *Amos and Boris*, the story of a friendship between a whale and a mouse, and the predicament they face when the whale becomes stranded on the beach. Amos, a tiny mouse, figures out how to get his gigantic friend Boris back into the ocean where he belongs. As they listened to a number of picture books by William Steig, the kids added more information to their store of background knowledge about his books, and they began to see a variety of connections. Rashid noticed that most of the characters were animals that could talk. Julianna observed that all the characters seemed to encounter difficult problems over the course of the story. The more these second graders read William Steig's books, the more they came to expect certain themes, humor, and ideas to emerge. This was not surprising. We can think of few authors whom we love quite as much and who evoke such enthusiasm from kids.

As serendipity would have it, the night after Anne read *Amos and Boris* to this group, she heard a remarkable story on National Public Radio of a whale marooned on a Texas beach. The local citizens of the town had turned out in shifts over a twenty-four-hour period to spray the whale with water in an attempt to keep it wet and alive till a helicopter could rescue it. Having once gone on a whale-watching expedition off the coast of California, Anne was drawn to the NPR story. When she woke up the next morning, all she could think about was that unfortunate whale, and she wondered if it had survived the night. She checked her phone to search the Internet for a news update. Much to her delight, the whale was still alive, so she took copies of the news bulletin to the classroom.

As the children listened to the unfolding story, the discussion turned to the similarities between the stranded whale in Texas and Boris's quandary in the story. Several students coded the news transcripts with connections they noticed between Boris and the stranded Texas whale, and later that day a small group found the sad news online that the whale had died. Two children wrote the following brief news account, noting the difference in the two endings: "Boris lived, but the Texas whale died. Sometimes stories have a happy ending. Sometimes real stories don't." Some students were so interested in this event that they continued to seek and find information about the plight of stranded whales and why whales beach themselves in the first place.

The background knowledge we bring to our reading colors every aspect of our learning and understanding. If readers have nothing to hook new information to, it's pretty hard to construct meaning. When we have a lot of background knowledge in a topic, we are much more likely to understand the text. When we have background knowledge of a certain writing style or structure, we more easily make sense of it. But when we know little about a topic or are unfamiliar with the format, we often find ourselves mired in confusion.

Making connections to personal experience facilitates understanding. The kids connected Boris to the Texas whale to better understand its plight. They knew that William Steig's animal characters would figure their way out of predicaments. They looked forward to Steig's humorous writing style, coming to expect laughter when they pulled his books off the shelf. Our prior experience and background knowledge fuel the connections we make. Books, discussions, experiences, newscasts, magazines, the Internet, and even nightly dinner-table conversations all forge connections that lead to new insight. We teach kids to activate their background knowledge and think about their connections so that they read in ways that let them discover these threads.

Connecting the New to the Known and Building Knowledge

When we begin strategy instruction with children, stories close to their own lives and experiences are helpful for introducing new ways of thinking about reading. Readers naturally make connections between books and their own lives. Once they have heard a wealth of stories and narratives, they begin to connect themes, characters, and issues from one book to another. When children understand how to connect the texts they read to their lives, they begin to make connections between what they read and the larger world. This nudges them into thinking about bigger, more expansive issues beyond their universe of home, school, and neighborhood.

Our suggestions for strategy lessons move from close to home to more global issues or cultures and places further removed from most children's lives. Although some lessons emphasize understanding literature, others focus on building knowledge of a particular topic. They have a common purpose, however: to use our personal and collective experience to enhance understanding and acquire and use knowledge. After twenty years of doing this work, one thing stands out above all others—using comprehension strategies promotes knowledge acquisition. Over the years, we have noticed that some of our work has been misunderstood. We will say it here, as we have in the past and even in the front of this book. *We don't teach strategies for strategies' sake.* Comprehension strategies are, above all, tools for building knowledge and understanding about ourselves, the text, and the world.

Toward the end of this chapter, we address some issues that sometimes crop up when teaching readers to activate their schema, build knowledge, and make connections. The purpose of making connections is to enhance understanding, not derail it. There are a number of pitfalls that cause kids to stumble when they focus too much on making connections. So we attempt to sort out some of the obstacles to understanding that can occur when kids make perfunctory connections.

Strategy Lessons: Activating, Connecting to, and Building Background Knowledge

Surfacing Big Ideas with Personal Connections

Purpose: **Connecting personal experience with ideas in the text to build empathy**

Resource: ***Each Kindness* by Jacqueline Woodson**

Response: **Interactive read-aloud with kids responding on sticky notes and grouping them to surface the big ideas in the text**

Audience: **Intermediate and middle**

In the hands of a skilled and thoughtful teacher, powerful picture books are both "windows and mirrors" for kids' own lives and experiences. *Each Kindness* by Jacqueline Woodson is one such book—it stretches and pushes kids to think beyond their own experiences and empathize with others. At the same time, it reflects and brings into sharper focus kids' understanding of themselves and their relationships.

In *Each Kindness*, Maya, a "new girl," comes to the classroom one day. Kids are distinctly unfriendly and remain that way. Despite Maya's best efforts, the class as a whole and one group of girls, led by Chloe, shuns her. When Maya disappears one day and doesn't return to the classroom, the kids who were so mean begin to have second thoughts. But it's too late—Maya is gone, and the kids in the story (as well as the reader) are left with a jumble of feelings, especially regret and sorrow. Here are two examples of teachers who shared this book with their kids to build community, each with a slightly different twist but a similar result.

At the beginning of the year, Hilary Barthel immersed her fourth graders in picture books about empathy and compassion to help build a caring community in the classroom. As kids delved into the characters in these books, Hilary guided them toward important conversations about their own relationships. She began with a discussion of empathy, sharing that people who are empathetic are able to put themselves in others' shoes. It's seeing the world from another perspective. Characters in books allow us to do this.

These fourth graders had lots of experience connecting books to their own lives. As they jotted their thinking on sticky notes during the read-aloud, they stopped occasionally to share some of their thinking and place their notes on a big chart. Right off the bat, they noticed that one of the important ideas was how the kids in the story were treating Maya. As Vera pointed out, "They are looking at the outside of Maya, not the inside." Silence fell as kids began writing about these ideas. One child wrote, "When Maya tried to share her new set of jacks, no one wants to play with her. That makes me feel angry and sad. It reminds me of the time there was a girl I was trying to impress. She rejected me and I felt just like Maya did. Finally, she started to be my friend and her friends became my friends, too. I am not sure that will happen to Maya."

As the class continued through the story, the kids noticed how the characters, especially Chloe, began to change. In addition to demonstrating themes of guilt, sorrow, and regret, the characters learned important lessons about kindness and empathy.

Jennifer Kennison, a third-grade teacher, tried something a little different with *Each Kindness*. Jennifer spends a lot of time at the beginning of the school year having conversations with her third graders about what it means to be a good citizen, a caring community member, and a trusted friend. As she introduced the book, she emphasized that the choices each of us makes every day have consequences. Then she brought in a bowl of stones and a glass bowl filled with water, just as the teacher in the book does. Jennifer asked students to think about a time when they had done something kind—a small act that demonstrated empathy toward someone else—and then invited them up to choose a stone to drop into the bowl. She asked them to think about what happens with the ripples in the water. In the story, the teacher explains that the stones represent kindness and the ripples represent the power that comes from acts of kindness.

Jennifer notes that during the reading of the book, "when the teacher in the story brings out the bowl and the rocks, just as we did before reading, the students felt an intimate connection to the characters, which showed on their faces and in their eyes when they realized they had done the same things only moments before. They were able to connect their experiences and acts of kindness to the characters in the story."

The kids in both Hilary's and Jennifer's rooms had similar reactions of shock and sadness when Maya never comes back. Kids this age are used to happy endings. But life isn't always like that. Don't we as adults feel that way about a powerful story? All of us, young and old, want to follow the characters with whom we feel a connection and hope for a positive resolution. When a book touches readers this deeply, however, one important outcome is that our empathy grows just like the ripples from the stones in the water. Stories such as these provide substantial and meaningful connections and serve as both "windows and mirrors," allowing us to reflect on our own feelings and behaviors as well as how we view, reach out to, and treat other people in our world. (See kids' work example in the assessment section at the end of the chapter.)

Connecting Text to Our Own Experiences: Relating the Characters to Ourselves

Purpose: **Understanding the text by thinking about our own experiences**

Resources: **Picture books by Kevin Henkes, including *Owen*; *Chrysanthemum*; *Julius, the Baby of the World*; and *Sheila Ray the Brave***

Responses: **Writing and drawing about how we connect to the text**

Audience: **Primary**

When Kristin Elder-Rubino and Melissa Oviatt introduced a Kevin Henkes author study at the beginning of the year, their kindergarten students found it easy to connect the text to their own lives. Kristin and Melissa use Kevin Henkes books year after year when teaching the idea of making personal connections. Henkes's characters are about the same age as their students and have similar problems and experiences. The kids were drawn to characters like Owen, who wouldn't give up his ragged old blanket, or Chrysanthemum, whose mouthful of a name was problematic for a kindergartner. Melissa and Kristin chose these narratives because they knew their kids would relate to them.

Just as Steph did in her *Up North at the Cabin* (Chall) think-aloud described in Chapter 1, Kristin and Melissa modeled their own connections for the kids as they read the stories aloud, putting a sticky note in the text with an *R* for "reminds me of" and perhaps drawing or jotting a few words about their own connections. As they modeled this, Kristin used the word *text* and Gerald waved his hand wildly in the air and asked, "What is text?" Kristin thanked him for his right-on question and explained that text is any print that is written down—a book, a newspaper, a poem, a magazine article, a post, an e-mail, and so on. These kindergartners had to understand the meaning of the word *text* before they could move ahead.

As they read *Sheila Rae the Brave*, Luis piped up and said, "Sheila Rae reminds me of my older brother. He is always bragging about how strong he is." As the children listened to a variety of stories by Henkes, they began to make connections between texts as well. They noted similarities between characters and their predicaments in his books. One kindergartner noted that Lily in *Julius, the Baby of the World* was every bit as stubborn about accepting the new baby in the family as Owen was about giving up his blanket. Melissa jotted down that across-text connection and pointed out that we make connections between the characters and ideas in different stories.

Having made strong connections between the characters in the stories and their own lives, these kindergartners had a greater understanding of Henkes's narratives. When kids make meaningful connections to the characters, problems, and events, they gain greater insight into the story and into themselves.

Distracting Connections

Purpose: **Teaching readers to identify distracting connections and fix up meaning**

Resource: **Any text or part of a text that triggers a connection that leads the reader astray**

Response: **Conversation**

Audience: **Intermediate and middle**

If we are going to teach our kids to make connections as they read, we must teach them about a type of connection that we have come to call the distracting connection. Distracting connections actually cause our minds to wander from the text and disrupt meaning rather than enhance understanding. This happens when a point in the text triggers a thought and the next thing we know we are thinking about that thought rather than constructing meaning from the text. There is nothing wrong with indulging a particular connection for a moment or two. The problem is continuing to read while doing it!

We teach the notion of distracting connections by modeling how it happens to us so kids will come to recognize when it happens to them. For Steph, it happens when she meets the term *Fourth of July*. She grew up in a town in central Wisconsin where nothing happened for 364 days a year, but the Fourth of July was unbelievable—the bike parade, the fireworks, the carnival that came to town. To this day, whenever she comes to the words *Fourth of July* as she reads, no matter what the context, she is back there in the Wisconsin of her youth, celebrating that memorable day.

To teach distracting connections, Steph models with a bit of text that mentions the Fourth of July. When she comes to those words, she stops and shares those vivid Fourth of July images. After a paragraph or two, she stops reading again and explains that she can't understand anything she just read, because she is still thinking about the Fourth of July. She explains distracting connections and then models how to go back to the point in the text where she got off track, in this case to the words *Fourth of July*. She consciously refocuses her thinking and begins reading from that point. After reading a few paragraphs, she stops and shares what she just read, showing that she understands the text now, because she successfully pushed the Fourth of July out of her mind and focused on the ideas in the text.

Find a topic or an idea in a piece of text that triggers another thought and causes you to stray from meaning as you read. The sky is the limit. Steph knows a teacher who comes across the word *fishing* and he is out of there. Another sees the word *golf* and she is on the fifteenth hole at Pebble Beach! Then do as Steph did and model the idea of the distracting connection for your kids so that they can recognize and repair meaning themselves when it happens to them.

New

Reading to Build Content Knowledge About Important Concepts

Purpose: **Connecting the known and the new to build content knowledge**

Resources: ***Bat Loves the Night* by Nicola Davies or any animal books that highlight big concepts, such as animal adaptations and survival**

Response: **Record new learning and questions on sticky notes and organize them according to bigger concepts.**

Audience: **Primary**

Mention almost any animal and kids spout off amazing details and surprising facts. We build on kids' curiosity and engagement by teaching them to connect new information about animals to what they already know. In this lesson, kids continue to build their knowledge store, but also begin to apply this knowledge to bigger concepts such as how animals are adapted to their habitats. They learn how an animal's physical features and behavior ensure its survival in the wild.

In this second-grade lesson, the interactive read-aloud is about bats and how they have adapted to various habitats in order to survive. Picture books such as *Bat Loves the Night* by Nicola Davies are engaging nonfiction narratives interspersed with factual information. Davies's narrative, with its rich description and highlighted facts, allows kids to connect the information about bats' behavior and physical features to the big idea that these adaptations ensure their survival. With this kind of knowledge under their belts, kids begin to see the big picture and grasp these important concepts.

Returning from the school library, a small group of kids waved a magazine article about bats using echolocation to navigate and find food at night. These young researchers wondered what other animals use echolocation and whether it is the same as bat echolocation. The kids scoured the animal books in the classroom, and the search continued online. They presented their findings, which included dolphins, some whales, and a small number of birds, in a teaching poster presented to the whole class. Building knowledge about the big ideas in science gives kids ways to organize all the information they take in each day. As they continue to learn new information and think about it in relation to these bigger concepts, they turn information into knowledge in important ways.

Making Connections Between Small Poems and Our Lives

Purpose:　**Illustrating and writing about connections to our lives**

Resource:　***Sol a Sol* by Lori Marie Carlson, poems in English and Spanish**

Responses:　**Kids read, make connections, and write short pieces about their lives and experiences.**

Audience:　**Primary**

Lori Marie Carlson's *Sol a Sol* is an engaging book of short poems about everyday events and happenings that all kids can relate to. Written in both English and Spanish and with vibrant illustrations, these poems are great models for kids' writing: they are short, full of action, and accessible. Centered on family life and everyday activities, the poems are on topics such as riding bikes, rolling back the rug and dancing after dinner, making tortillas, cats, grandmothers, and gazing at the sky and counting the stars. After we read some of these poems aloud, we create a "snippet," a short free-verse poem, together. The kids then turn and talk about their own snippets and then they are off—responding, connecting, drawing, and writing about their own lives. We often introduce making connections by eliciting kids' own personal snippets, showing them how we can draw and write down "just a piece of our experience." We often read, talk about, and write these snippets at the beginning of the year. It's a great way for new classmates to get to know one another and to share a small part of their lives with others. See Figure 8.1 for two examples of these snippets.

Figure 8.1
Students Get to Know Each Other by Sharing Snippets Such as These

Using Background Knowledge About Reading to Enhance Your Viewing Experience

Purpose: **Explicitly viewing media clips by applying what we know about being effective readers of print materials**

Resource: **Media clip "Toothpaste—Ingredients with George Zaidan" from the website The Kid Should See This, or any short media clip**

Responses: **Annotations on an anchor chart of reading strategies**

Audience: **Intermediate and middle**

We know most of our students spend hours staring at a screen. But when it comes to learning from video clips, passively watching won't get them far. They need to be active viewers just as they are active readers. In this lesson, we teach students to be active viewers by asking them to apply their background knowledge of reading strategies such as asking questions, monitoring comprehension, and making inferences.

Denton Harve, a fourth-grade teacher, opens this lesson by having students review an anchor chart that summarizes many of the reading skills they have been working hard at this year. He asks students to turn and talk about how each of the strategies listed helps them to be more thoughtful readers. (See the example in the assessment section at the end of the chapter.)

Thoughtful-Readers Anchor Chart

- Thoughtful readers ask questions before, during, and after reading. We read to learn more and know more! We keep reading until we find answers.

- Thoughtful readers connect parts of texts together to understand the big picture.

- Thoughtful readers take time to separate big ideas and details; they understand what the most important parts of the text are and use that to help them.

- Thoughtful readers make inferences about things not said in the text. They use the text to support their inferences.

- Thoughtful readers always stop and ask themselves, Does this make sense? Am I understanding this right?

As students turn and talk, Denton confers with pairs and gathers thinking to share with the whole group. He then asks a few pairs to share before moving on to the video portion of the lesson. Students share thoughts like the following:

> *We've learned a lot about how reading with a question in mind keeps us with the book. That strategy has helped me a lot because it kind of helps me think about what I need to read for.*

> *I used to get into the details a lot and now I know that I really have to think about the big picture. What is the thing I'm reading trying to tell or show me?*

As Denton continues the lesson, he explains the important work of learning for the day. "Readers, you've come so far using these strategies to help you be more thoughtful. Now it's time to apply your background knowledge about reading to a new medium. Videos! Today we're going to watch a video, and I want you to think about how you are needing to use your reading strategies to be a thoughtful viewer."

Denton provides students with copies of the chart and plenty of space to hold their thinking. The video he has selected is the first in a series by National Geographic called "Toothpaste—Ingredients with George Zaidan." He located this video on a favorite resource: The Kid Should See This, a website that offers a variety of videos for use in the classroom. The topic is toothpaste, and he knows that the content will both inspire and challenge his students, engaging all of their viewing strategies.

Next, Denton plays a short part of the video, models stopping and thinking about the strategies he's using as a viewer, jots a few thoughts down, and then moves on. He then hands the task over to the kids, asking them to turn and talk, stop and jot, and reflect on how their background knowledge of reading strategies is helping them to make sense of this new information. They jot their thoughts on the reading strategies chart.

At the end of the video he asks students to share their chart with a new partner, someone they weren't sitting with, and think about the strategies that were most helpful to them. Students share their annotated charts with the class at the end of the lesson (see Figure 8.2).

Figure 8.2
One Student's Annotations on an Anchor Chart of Reading Strategies

There were parts in the video—like in our books so we used that to see what we should know but we needed to see it twice.

Thoughtful Readers...
→ ask questions before, during, and after reading.
→ Connect parts of the text together to get the big picture.
→ take time to separate big ideas and details, understand the important parts.
→ make inferences about things not said, use the text to support their inferences.
→ Stop and ask—does this make sense?

I asked a lot of questions to help me understand.

Too many details—but if you waited he explained. rewatch like reread.

Noticing and Thinking About New Learning

Purpose: **Merging thinking with new information**
Resource: ***Avalanche* by Stephen Kramer, or other nonfiction trade books on various topics**
Response: **Sticky notes**
Audience: **Intermediate**

When readers read nonfiction, they are reading to learn new information. What they learn depends on their background knowledge. Noticing and thinking about new learning is one of the first lessons we teach to support nonfiction readers in gaining information and acquiring knowledge. When we encounter new information, we are likely to hear a voice in our head that says something like, *Wow, I never knew that before* or *Hmmm, interesting* . . . A compelling book such as Stephen Kramer's *Avalanche* engages kids easily and encourages them to listen to their inner voices and merge their thinking with the text. In addition, the book is so jam packed with information that every student will likely learn something new.

Most avalanches Ⓛ are snow slides. There are mud, rock and ice avalanches too.

Avalanches Ⓛ happen on snowy hills and mountains.

Wow! 100,000 Ⓛ avalanches each year in the US. A million around the world. So many.

Unstable snow Ⓛ causes avalanches. What is unstable snow?

I never knew that you could build snow fences to keep snow from sliding down a hill. Ⓛ

People can Ⓛ get caught in avalanches. Really dangerous! How many people die each year?

Figure 8.3
On Sticky Notes Like These, Students Record New Learning and Their Reactions to What They Learn

Steph launched this lesson with fifth graders by modeling the voice she hears in her head when she meets new information. She explained to the kids that it is not enough to simply regurgitate facts when we read but that we have to listen to the inner conversation we have with the writer, listen to our own "inner voice," and merge our thinking with the text in order to learn, understand, and remember the information.

As she read the text, she thought aloud, sharing her inner voice, particularly the voice she heard in her head when she met new information. For instance, on page ten of the text, she read that anything that slides down a mountain or a hillside—rocks, ice, mud—can be called an avalanche. She stopped and said to the class, "I never knew that anything that slid down the side of a mountain could be called an avalanche. I thought avalanches had to be made of snow. I'm going to jot this new learning on a sticky note because that is surprising, new information to me. Then I'm going to mark this sticky note with an *L* for *Learn* and write *Wow! I never knew there were different types of avalanches—rocks, mud, ice, and snow.* I'll place this note on the page near where I read the information so I can find it easily if I need it."

Steph continued reading and sharing new information she met as she read, marking sticky notes with an *L*, merging her thinking with the information, and jotting down the new learning to better remember it. After she read a page or two, she engaged the kids in the process. They were bunched up in front of her on the floor with clipboards with a blank page covered with six 3-by-3-inch sticky notes on both sides of the paper. When they heard new information about avalanches, they jotted down a word or two from their inner conversation along with the new information. When Steph stopped reading the text, she sent the kids off to practice independently in text at their level and on a topic of their choice. At the end of the workshop time, the kids formed a circle and shared some of the new learning they encountered in their own texts. Figure 8.3 shows some of the new learning students recorded.

Above all, we must be teaching readers to merge their thinking with text information—to stop, think, and react to the information throughout the read. When readers interact with text in this way, they are likely to remember the information way beyond Friday's quiz. To see a similar lesson in action, check out our DVD *Think Nonfiction! Modeling Reading and Research* (2002).

(Additional work examples are provided in the assessment section at the end of the chapter.)

Revising Misconceptions When Learning Something New

Purpose: **Celebrating the learning, not merely the knowing**
Resource: ***Surprising Sharks*** **by Nicola Davies**
Response: **Chart titled What We Think We Know/New Learning and sticky notes**
Audience: **Primary and intermediate**

Misconceptions get a choke hold on us. Steph was fully grown before she learned that the proper spelling of 40 was forty, not fourty. Somewhere along the way, someone must have corrected her, but she had learned this misconception and didn't relinquish it. We know it can be difficult to "replace" limited or incorrect knowledge with more accurate information. We also know that we need to explicitly teach kids how to leave their misconceptions behind and be open to and proud of learning new information.

For quite a few years, in an effort to both engage kids and activate their background knowledge, Steph and Anne would launch lessons by asking kids to share what they already knew about the topic at hand and then record it on an anchor chart. But it soon became apparent that some of what they knew was inaccurate, which is no surprise—they're young learners after all!

We both found it a tad uncomfortable, however, to write a glaring misconception from one of the kids on a two-column anchor chart titled What We Know/What We Learned. About that time, Tony Stead came to the rescue with a very slight change in language that made all the difference. In his book *Reality Checks: Teaching Reading Comprehension with Nonfiction K–5* (2005), he suggested titling the anchor charts and think sheets What We **Think** We Know rather than What We Know. That tiny language tweak has made a great difference.

Some kids are still uncomfortable when they share something inaccurate, so when doing a lesson such as this, we model a misconception of our own that we can revise. Then as we read, we revise it in front of the whole class as Steph does here. It is very powerful for kids to see the teacher revise a misconception when she learns something new. They get the message that we celebrate the learning rather than the knowing.

Steph modeled this lesson with Nicola Davies's *Surprising Sharks*, a wonderful book chock-full of shark information. She began by asking kids to turn and talk about what they thought they already knew about sharks, and then she jotted several of her own ideas on the anchor chart, including a misconception about shark skin.

What We Think We Know	New Learning
Sharks are predators.	
Sharks have smooth skin.	Sharks have tough, scratchy skin.

Building on the previous lesson where kids were taught to mark new learning with an *L* for *Learn*, Steph engaged the kids in an interactive read-aloud of *Surprising Sharks*. As she read, she and the kids jotted their new learning and marked their sticky notes with an *L* when they learned new information. When Steph came to a diagram that showed that sharks have very rough skin, she stopped and shared how she never knew that. She shared the term *misconception* and explained that it is an inaccurate fact. But more importantly, rather than acting embarrassed, she jumped up and crossed out her *misconception* and then wrote that sharks have tough, scratchy skin under New Learning, She expressed delight at learning this new information: "I am always amazed at how much I learn every day!"

Once kids see that we adults have inaccurate information and are always learning, they are far more likely to revise their own misconceptions without embarrassment. It's no surprise some kids have more trouble with this than others, so we don't just share our own misconceptions one time and call it good. We frequently say things like *I used to think _____, but I read something last night, and now I think _____.* The more we celebrate our new learning, the more kids are willing to jump on board.

When Steph began to confer with students, she stopped by Jessica's area and noticed a misconception. The book was clear that people are more dangerous to sharks than sharks are to people, but Jessica missed that, as her sticky note indicates. Once Steph conferred with her and asked her to go back and reread, Jessica cleared up her misconception, as you can see from the series of notes (see Figure 8.4).

Figure 8.4
Jessica's Sticky Notes About Sharks

> Ⓛ Sharks can Kill 100 million people.
>
> Ⓛ Sharks can be surprising and bite people.
>
> Ⓛ Many sharks are endangered ☆

"Research Lab" in Kindergarten

Purpose: Doing research in kindergarten to build knowledge
Resources: Photographs or accessible texts with photographs
Responses: Observing images and recording new learning and questions
Audience: Primary

A curious thing happened in kindergarten one day. A penciled sign in kids' invented spelling was posted at the entrance to the classroom's home-living center. It read as follows:

Research Lab
Cooper Tony
marsupials
No home living

> rezCH Ldb
> cooper tony
> md Rzqɛɛɛɫz
> NO home livg

Future Homemakers of America might have a problem with this, but unless someone wanted to do the dishes, this seems like a perfectly good use of the space. Books about various marsupials were piled high on the dining table, along with markers and sticky notes. Cooper and Tony were hard at work on their research about marsupials. Looking for a quiet work space, they simply posted their sign, temporarily closing the home-living center and declaring it the "Research Lab."

As the kids delved into their research, Cooper observed several images about kangaroos. He noticed two kangaroos engaged in what looked like a boxing match, and described them as "two wrestling kangaroos." He also wondered, "What do they eat?" "Where do they sleep?" "When does the baby leave the mom's pouch?" and his teacher scribed his thoughts around the photographs.

This research didn't happen by accident. The teacher's lessons before this set Cooper and Tony up to commandeer the home-living center. The class had been reading and responding to nonfiction from the first day of kindergarten, so kids were quite skilled at learning new information and asking questions. This prepared them to take matters into their own hands.

Tangential Connections: Pitfalls to Understanding

Once children understand the concept of making connections, there seems to be no stopping them. They link books, experiences, and ideas in delightful ways. In classrooms where teachers teach kids to think about their background knowledge and make connections and then build in time to practice strategy application, kids fill their pages with sticky notes coded with their connections. The truth is, however, we've encountered a number of pitfalls on the connections path. Sometimes, kids make tangential connections rather than meaningful ones. We need to keep a watchful eye out for tangential connections that do not enhance understanding. The lesson on distracting connections in this chapter addresses one of the obstacles we have to overcome when teaching kids to make connections. Some others follow here.

Connections in Common

Sometimes when we ask kids to share a connection they have, they burst forth with comments such as "The book mentioned San Diego and I've been to San Diego"; or, "The character is a boy and I'm a boy"; or, even better, "The coolest character's name is Jasmine and my name is Jasmine!" The primary reason for a reader to make connections is to enhance understanding, and it is highly unlikely that sharing a name with the main character or noting that you have been to the same city as mentioned in the book will do that. To be honest, these situations make us uncomfortable and present a bit of a dilemma. As teachers who believe that nothing matters more than the reader's thinking, it's tough to tell a reader these connections are unimportant since they are a part of the reader's thinking. And yet these connections are unlikely to add to understanding.

We've come to call these connections "connections in common"; for instance, if you share a name, birthplace, or relative with a character, you have that in common. And although these connections in common do not lead to understanding, they very well may lead to engagement, because kids like to read about characters with the same name or who have been places they have been, and so forth. So these connections in common may in fact be important to the reader but not important to understanding the text. To help the reader decide, we use a three-column form headed My Connection/Important to Me/Important to Understanding the Text. Kids record their connection in the first column and then decide if it is important to the reader or important to understanding. In this way, we are not telling readers that their thinking doesn't matter, but rather that their thinking matters a great deal and that it is their responsibility to decide about the importance of their connection in relation to understanding the text.

Will Any Connection Do?

We watch carefully for authentic connections that support understanding. Kids are terrific teacher-pleasers and may think that any connection is better than no connection at all. Sometimes, particularly when kids are new to the practice, they go overboard making connections just for the sake of it. Younger kids often get so excited about writing on sticky notes that they write down just about anything that comes to their mind. "It reminds me of when I went down on a sinking ship," third-grader Jake wrote while reading Robert Ballard's *Exploring the Titanic*. When his teacher quizzed him privately about this connection, he sheepishly admitted that he had never really been on a sinking ship.

After the untimely death of a class pet, Michelle Meyer read her first-grade class *The Tenth Good Thing About Barney*, Judith Viorst's picture book about the death of a beloved pet and the family's attempt to gain closure after the incident. After reading the story, Michelle encouraged the kids to write down their connections in their notebooks. Katie was clearly moved by the story and wrote prolifically about her similar past experience (see Figure 8.5). And although Daniel wrote less, a smile crept across Michelle's face as his honesty burst through (see Figure 8.6). Sharing Daniel's connection with the class as well as Katie's shows how Michelle values authentic, honest connections.

Figure 8.5
Katie's Connection Response to *The Tenth Good Thing About Barney*

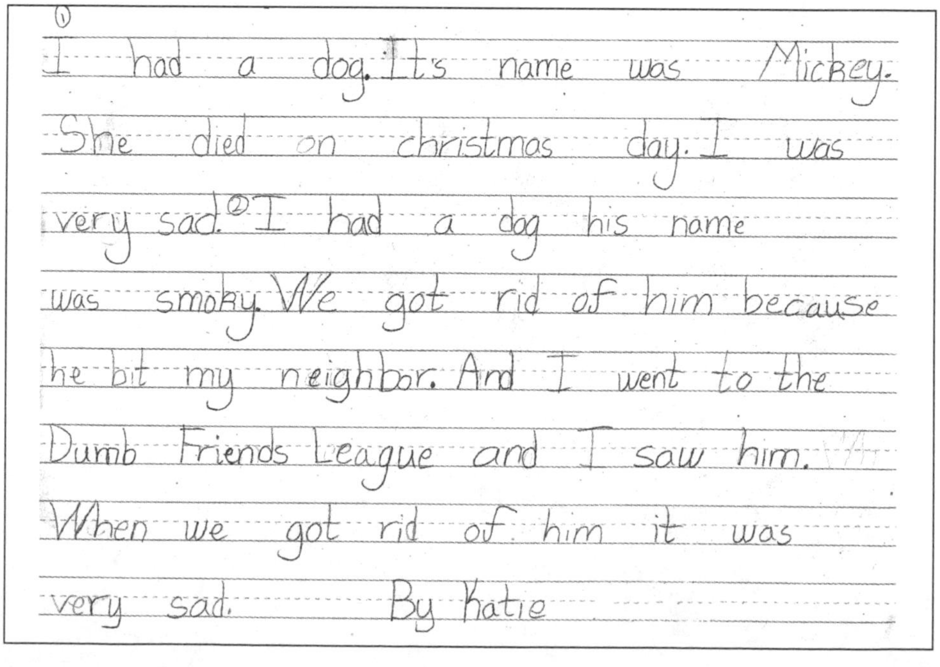

(1) I had a dog. It's name was Mickey. She died on christmas day. I was very sad. (2) I had a dog his name was smoky. We got rid of him because he bit my neighbor. And I went to the Dumb Friends League and I saw him. (4) When we got rid of him it was very sad. By Katie

Figure 8.6
Daniel's Connection Response to *The Tenth Good Thing About Barney*

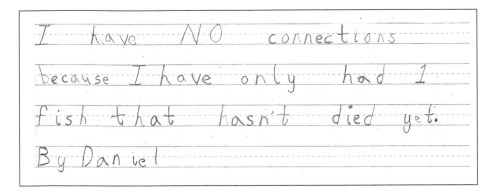

I have NO connections because I have only had 1 fish that hasn't died yet.
By Daniel

How Does That Connection Help You Understand?

One day Steph conferred with Allison, a seventh grader reading *Mirette on the High Wire* by Emily Arnold McCully, the story of a brave little girl who helps an aging tightrope walker overcome his fear. She noticed Allison's sticky note coded *R* for *Remind* that said, "I get really scared in high places just like Bellini does."

"Tell me about that," Steph nudged.

"Oh, I don't know. I just get scared looking down from tall buildings or standing on the edge of a cliff," Allison explained.

"That's interesting. So how does that connection help you understand the story?" Steph asked.

"I don't know," Allison replied. She hadn't even thought about it because she was so busy reading and writing down her connections.

"It seems to me that you have a leg up on understanding the character of Bellini because you, too, have a fear of heights. You bring your own experience to the character, and you know better how that character feels and even how he might react. Better than me, for instance, because although I have plenty of fears, heights isn't one of them," Steph said.

Steph and Allison agreed that the next time Allison made a connection, she would stop and ask herself how the connection helped her understand the story. Although children may initially have trouble articulating more significant connections, with teacher and peer modeling and plenty of time they gradually begin to refine and focus on connections that deepen their understanding and engagement.

Teaching with the End in Mind: Assessing What We've Taught

Activating, Connecting to, and Building Background Knowledge

Based on the lessons in this chapter, we look for evidence that

1. *Students make connections to their own lives to further their understanding of events, characters, problems, and ideas in realistic fiction.* We look for responses that illustrate insight into characters' problems, actions, and motives or that demonstrate that kids have understood ways to meaningfully connect to books.

2. *Students make connections to stories, short pieces, or poems. They demonstrate these connections through responses, including their personal narratives, poems, and illustrations.* We look for responses that show rather than merely tell. (We also check to see that illustrations and writing are complementary.)

3. *Students activate and build knowledge as they read informational text.* As teachers we ascertain kids' background knowledge on topics and observe the ways in which they build their knowledge. We look for evidence of the ways they merge their background knowledge with new information.

Suggestions for Differentiation

Reading picture books with clear illustrations that complement the vocabulary and language of the text builds kids' background knowledge and scaffolds their understanding as they learn about new topics. When introducing a new subject or topic, we take a few minutes to make sure kids link the text's language and vocabulary with the illustrations so that ELLs, especially, won't be lost as they listen to the story.

As one class launched their study of pioneers and the journey west with *Red Flower Goes West*, by Ann Turner, Anne wanted to make sure all the kids understood vocabulary words and ideas, including *pioneers, covered wagon, oxen,* and *crossing the river.* She decided to put up pictures of these terms on a chart and work with the class to label them. This would support some of the English language learners, but Anne also wanted to make this time worthwhile for kids who already had some background knowledge of this topic. So she asked the kids to turn and talk about what they already knew about pioneer times and going west in a covered wagon. They wrote down and illustrated their background knowledge and put it up on the chart as well.

Before beginning to read the book, the kids quickly shared their information and illustrations. Children who were new to these words and ideas could refer to the pictures and labels as they listened to the story. Kids who had some background knowledge were enthusiastic about teaching others what they already knew. In short, this preview engaged all the kids regardless of their background knowledge. It got them "warmed up" and eager to listen to the story and ready to participate in the interactive read-aloud.

Activating and Connecting to Background Knowledge Assessment Commentary

Sticky notes related to the big ideas in *Each Kindness* from the lesson "Surfacing Big Ideas with Personal Connections"

▾ These students sorted their sticky notes according to some of the big ideas that they discussed from the story. Their notes related to their experiences of being judged by others and reflect the theme of paying closer attention to what's inside of people rather than what can be seen on the outside.

As we read Each Kindness, we made connections to our own lives + experiences. Some important ideas + themes surfaced.

I was tesed at frst but then kids wer nice.

Judging others...

Don't act like this to others becaus you whont to be trite lik you trite others.

Looking at what's "outside" not what's "inside" a person.

Nobody was nice to Maya. They just looked at her old cloths. They did not look at her hert.

When I moved here, girls I was trieing to impress, regreted being mean to me, and started to be my friend. Then, her friends became my friends too.

I think Maya was being jued by the way she looked.

This book made me feel sad, mad and confoused. Why did the girls deselut Maya? I think the girls should not be mean to Maya because she is nice. When I came here it was hard for me to make friends so I feel just like Maya did. Then my friends get to know me.

Independent reading sticky notes from the lesson "Noticing and Thinking About New Learning," which uses Stephen Kramer's *Avalanche*

L) WOW! Cocoa beans are one of the most important crops in the world becaus they are used to make chocolate.

L) Shrubs are a short word for bushy plants News to me!

L) Oh my gosh! I never knew lighting can go through people, and they still survive.

NO) I did'nt know whiskers help cats feel it's way through the dark

◀ These sticky notes show how readers wrote down new information and merged their thinking with it. The readers used words like *Wow, Oh my gosh, News to me, I didn't know,* or *I never knew* to shape the new information into their own thought. That is exactly what we are shooting for when we teach this lesson.

▶ These two sticky notes were done by a student who was reading a book about the sun. We can see that she cleared up some big misconceptions by stopping and thinking about the information. She used to think the sun was solid and not a star, but after the reading, she has changed her thinking. She still has a lot to learn about the sun, but it is likely she will never forget this information since she thought of it herself and really owns the new thinking. We are thrilled when kids clear up their own misconceptions through reading!

L) Wait but how could the sun be a star because stars come out at night I never knew that.

L) That's so cool. I thought the sun was solid. But actualy it is boiling and bubbling.

Notes that do not demonstrate understanding and need clarification and intervention

> The dwarf goby is smaller than your fingernail.
>
> wow!!! scientists thought coelacanth had been extinct for 65 million years Then in 1938 one was found in a fishing net.

◄ The first sticky note is copied directly out of the text. This is very common when kids first begin to jot down new learning. We would form a small group with anyone who copied directly from the text and show how we merge our own thinking with the information, using starters such as *I never knew, I didn't know, I learned.* That would be the first step in supporting kids to put the information into their own words and shape their own thought.

▸ The second sticky note merely says *WOW!* No content here. We would meet with kids who do this and ask, "What is so Wow?" And then we would encourage them to write that information.

▸ The third sticky note shares a misconception that the moon is a planet that circles the earth. When we see this, we confer with kids as soon as possible, as misconceptions get a choke hold on us, and we want to help kids revise them. Reading kids' sticky notes is one of the quickest and best ways to clear up misconceptions.

> The moon is a planet that crcls the earth

Independent notes about using reading strategies while viewing a video

▾ This student made good use of the strategies outlined in the anchor chart titled Thoughtful Readers. His questions are authentic, and he notices that the details are confusing, so he tries to focus on the big ideas. His enthusiasm shines through.

Toothpaste ingredients Elijah
Oct 10, 2016, 9:35 AM

Thoughtful Readers...

→ ask questions before, during, and after reading.

→ Connect parts of the text together to get the big picture.

→ take time to separate big ideas and details, understand the important parts.

→ Make inferences about things not said, use the text to support their inferences.

→ Stop and ask—does this make sense?

Thoughtful readers

I never thought about what was in my toothpaste. I wonder what kinds of things they put in their.

I am very shocked that he is talking about krushed bones and poomis rocks. Did people use that stuff?

I never new there was so much stuff in toothpaste.

I think all these ingredients are giving me a lot of detailes that is confusing me. I am trying to focus on the big parts to understand.

He is making the ingredients into categories: abrasives, humectants, sweeteners, flavors, and foaming. I think these are the important parts to know. Also thickers and Floride I know

that's important from the dentist.

Can he really make his own? Cool!
Chalk! Eeeewwww 😲

I thought this was an interesting video but also a little hard to understand because there were a lot of words that I did not know. I used reading strategies like asking questions to help me try to find answers and understand. I figured out there were a lot of little things I could not know and just try to focus on the big ideas. I understood better when he made his own toothpaste I thought that was really cool and I would like to try that at home can we try that in class ?

Chapter 9

Questioning: The Strategy That Propels Readers Forward

Curiosity spawns questions. Questions are the master key to understanding. Questions clarify confusion. Questions stimulate research efforts. Questions propel us forward and take us deeper into reading. Human beings are driven to find answers and make sense of the world. The Nobel Prize–winning physicist Richard Feynman referred to this need as his "puzzle drive" (Feynman 1985). He couldn't not search for answers to those things that confounded him, those things he didn't understand.

The teachers portrayed in this book encourage this same puzzle drive in their students. Matt, a space lover, began writing what he knew and was learning about his favorite topic. But his curiosity got the better of him, and halfway into a letter to his teacher, his questions burst forth and hijacked his response (see Figure 9.1). Matt reminds us that good questions spring from background knowledge. Matt knew about and loved space; hence he could ask terrific questions. It's

125

Figure 9.1
Matt's Response, Full of Questions

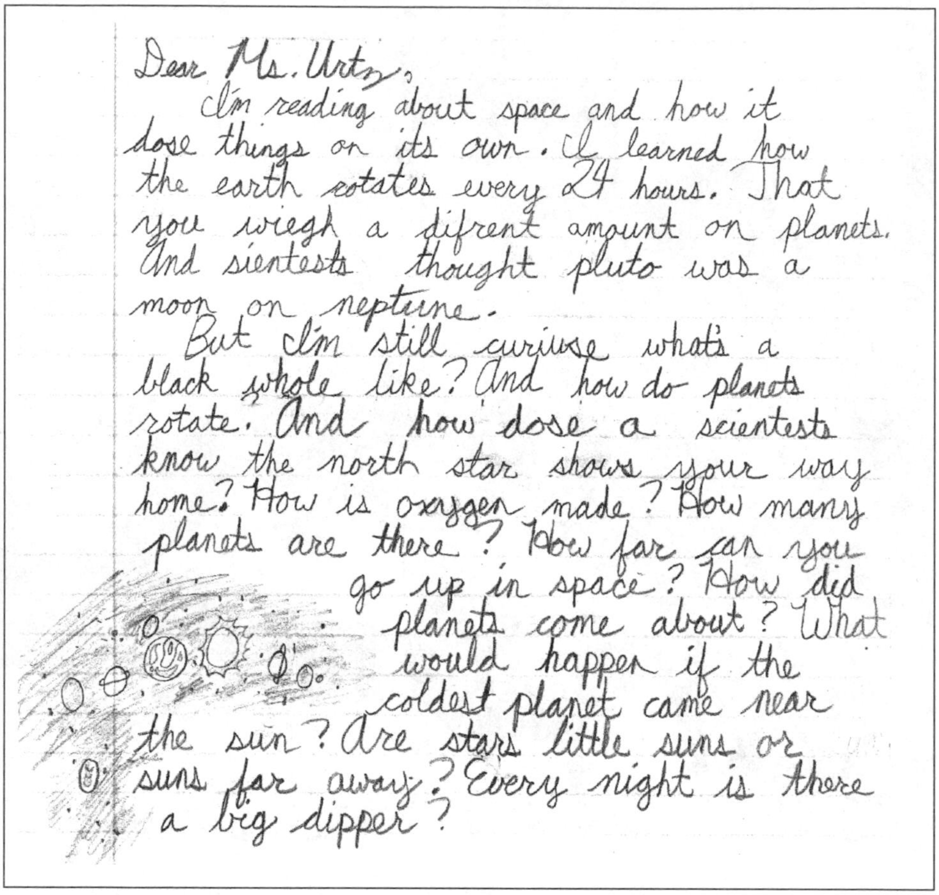

Dear Ms. Urtz,

I'm reading about space and how it dose things on its own. I learned how the earth rotates every 24 hours. That you wiegh a difrent amount on planets. And sientests thought pluto was a moon on neptune.

But I'm still curiuse what's a black whole like? And how do planets rotate. And how dose a scientests know the north star shows your way home? How is oxygen made? How many planets are there? How far can you go up in space? How did planets come about? What would happen if the coldest planet came near the sun? Are stars little suns or suns far away? Every night is there a big dipper?

tough to ask a substantive question about something we know or care nothing about.

As adult readers, we question all the time, often without even thinking about it. When we first began to pay attention to our thinking as we read, we were stunned at the number of questions we had, many of which were inspired by relatively small amounts of text. Kids don't grow up knowing that good readers ask questions. In fact, schools often appear more interested in answers than in questions. So now we teach kids to think about their questions before, during, and after reading. We encourage them to stop, think, and record their questions throughout the reading process. And we always remember to ask them if they have any lingering questions after they read. Those are the most important questions, the ones the reader has.

Our students need to know that their questions matter. They need to see us asking questions as well as answering them. Asking questions engages us and keeps us reading. A reader with no questions might just as well abandon the book. When our students ask questions and search for answers, we know that they are monitoring comprehension and interacting with the text to construct meaning, which is exactly what we hope for in developing readers.

Strategy Lessons: Questioning

Share Your Questions About Your Own Reading

Purpose: **Using adult text to show the questions we have when we read**
Resource: **The novel *All the Light We Cannot See* by Anthony Doerr**
Responses: **Sticky notes coded with ?; follow-up group discussion**
Audience: **Intermediate and middle**

The next time you read a piece of adult text, pay close attention to the questions that surface and share those questions with your kids. Let them know that all readers—even adults—have questions. When introducing questioning to a group of sixth graders, Steph shared an excerpt from the novel *All the Light We Cannot See* by Anthony Doerr, a book that moved her deeply, so much so that she continues to ponder, ask questions, and think about it to this day.

She gathered the kids in front of her and talked about how the text raised questions for her. She wrote her questions on sticky notes, placed them next to the passages that spurred them, and coded them with a question mark. She pointed out that some of her questions were answered in the text and others were not. She explained that her sticky note marked with "I love the title, but why is it called *All The Light We Cannot See*?" did not become apparent until quite late in the book. The answer to her question "What is a windburned corsair?" could be inferred by reading on when the writer followed up with information from the text. When she read on and inferred the answer, she moved her sticky note to the spot where the question was answered, wrote the answer on the sticky note, and recoded it *A* for answered.

When she was mired in confusion, she coded a sticky note *Huh?* to note that meaning had broken down for her. This code signaled her to reread or read a few sentences ahead to try to make sense of the text before going on.

At the conclusion of this mini-lesson, Steph invited the kids to talk about questioning in reading. Robbie commented that he never knew a teacher could have so many questions about her reading. He seemed to be saying, "If she can have questions, so can I."

Some Questions Are Answered, Others Are Not

Purpose: **Listing and categorizing questions to promote understanding**
Resource: **The picture book *Charlie Anderson*, by Barbara Abercrombie**
Responses: **Chart with list of kids' questions; codes for categories of questions, including *A* for answered, *BK* for background knowledge, *I* for inferred, *D* for discussion, *RS* for research, *C* or *Huh?* for confused**
Audience: **Primary and intermediate**

When we begin teaching the strategy of questioning, we simply share the questions we have before, during, and after reading, and talk about them. All written text gives rise to questions, but sometimes we find a book that spurs questions from start to finish. Barbara Abercrombie's *Charlie Anderson* is just such a book. It tells the story of a cat who moves surreptitiously between two homes, living with one family by day and another by night, unbeknownst to the two separate owners. This story line parallels the lives of the two young characters, Sarah and her sister, Elizabeth, who move between their divorced parents' homes, as many kids do. This is a terrific book for kids who share this lifestyle. In fact, we have noticed that kids who spend their time in two different homes are more likely to pick up on the parallel theme. Alternatively, many young kids never even notice the divorce angle but seem to enjoy the simple story of a mysterious cat who disappears each night and returns home each morning.

Listing Questions

For all kids, however, we have found this to be a useful book to teach questioning, since they brim with questions when they read it. Second-grade teacher Mary Lawlor read *Charlie Anderson* to her class. The text is sparse, with fewer than five or six sentences per page. When she reached the end of each page, she solicited kids' questions. A parent volunteer recorded their questions on a piece of chart paper as Mary read. Their numerous questions emerged from the cover illustration and the prereading discussion as well as from the text and pictures during the reading. At the end of the story, the chart included the following list of questions:

Why is the book called <u>Charlie Anderson</u>?—A

Who is that cat in the yard?—A

Why was the door open just a crack?

Do cats really like french fries?

Where does the cat go every morning?—A

Are these girls twins?

Does Sarah get jealous that he likes Elizabeth's bed best?

Why did he get fatter and fatter every day?—A

Did they miss Charlie when they went to their dad's on the weekends?

Do they like their dad's house better?

Why didn't Charlie come home one night?—A

Is he going to be all right?—A

How come Anderson looks just like Charlie?—A

Which family does Charlie like better?

As Mary read through the questions, she asked the kids to come up and put an *A* for answered next to the questions that were explicitly answered in the text. After reviewing and coding the questions, the class discussed them. In most cases, the unanswered questions were the more intriguing ones, the questions that dug toward deeper themes and bigger ideas. The question about where the girls preferred to live sparked a lively conversation. We have discovered that unanswered questions often stimulate the most stirring discussions.

Categorizing Questions

We can start helping kids categorize questions in primary grades. As we move up through grade levels, we can add different categories of questions. Some question categories and corresponding codes are listed here:

- Questions that are answered in the text—*A*
- Questions that are answered from someone's background knowledge—*BK*
- Questions whose answers can be inferred from the text—*I*
- Questions that can be answered by further discussion—*D*
- Questions that require further research to be answered—*RS*
- Questions that signal confusion—*Huh?* or *C*

The endearing question about whether cats eat french fries would likely require further research, although someone may have the background knowledge to provide an answer. As we look at the questions, we can work together as a class to code them. After kids have had some time to practice together, they practice on their own in their independent reading.

Collaborating on Questions

Purpose: **Viewing classmates' questions using a digital tool**
Resources: **A picture book that is read aloud, devices with Internet capability, and a digital chat tool like TodaysMeet**
Responses: **Collaborating digitally on asking questions**
Audience: **Intermediate and middle**

In this lesson we use a document projector to share the pages of a picture book so that students can examine images and words carefully. This is also done to keep students together as they move through the discussion—sharing their questions about each section.

Teacher Michelle Scott starts her lesson by asking students to go to a TodaysMeet chat room that she has created for them. She models how to go to the link, type her name, and add a question. She asks students to try it and then post a simple greeting to the group in order to confirm that they are all able to participate. (If students are working in pairs or trios, they need to be sure to include all of their names.) By ensuring that kids are ready to go on the tech tool at the beginning of the lesson, Michelle saves valuable class time and will be able to maintain the flow of her lesson.

> *Class, today we're going to do something special. Normally when we read, I would ask you to keep track of your questions by annotating the page or jotting your thinking. But today we're going to share our questions on a web tool that will allow you to see everyone else's questions too! We're going to see if being able to see what your classmates are thinking as they read helps us think about the text in a new or different way. Consider this a little bit of an experiment in a new way to think about our reading.*

She asks students to flip their tablets facedown and give their full attention to the projection screen so that they can listen and view with attention. Michelle is careful to explicitly teach kids how to tune in and tune out when needed, a necessity in today's technology-rich classrooms. She begins reading and viewing, asking questions aloud as she goes, then pauses and demonstrates how she considers each of her questions and determines which one she thinks would be best to add to the group chat.

> *I see that my first question was answered quickly as I read, so I think I'm going to add my second question, which is a little more detailed and harder to come up with an answer to.*
> *I think the class would benefit from this question because it will give us something to think and talk about.*
> *I have many questions, but I think I should share my most important thinking with the group.*

After a few modeled questions, students begin to participate, stopping to type their own questions. Michelle provides clear directions for how to interact on the tool. The purpose is to gather as many questions as possible.

As the teacher reads through the book on the document camera, she stops occasionally to have students turn and talk or share their questions. She finds that mixing these two strategies gives all students an access point to the lesson and keeps it engaging and energetic.

She continues through a few images and paragraphs, pausing to model her thinking or ask students to share. As students stop to type and share, she quickly scans the document to see who is able to share their questions and which students might need a quick conference.

When she finishes reading from the text, she asks students to stop and take a few minutes to go back and reread some of the questions that their classmates came up with. Students meet in small groups to discuss answerable questions or clarify misunderstandings about the text. The teacher then asks students to conclude the lesson by selecting a few questions that they found to be especially interesting, or that pushed them to think about the text in a new and different way.

Because the chat has archived everyone's ideas, it is easy to go back and look at them more carefully. From here Michelle has many options. She might

- have students meet to discuss questions in small groups as she did above,
- sort and analyze the questions as a whole class,
- do a quick-write about the questions, or
- archive them for a later date.

Finally the teacher asks students to take screenshots of the questions they would like to respond to and use an app to record themselves talking about each screenshot—why they chose each question and how it challenged their thinking as a reader and viewer.

Building in Time, Routines, and Structures for Asking Questions, Wondering, and Searching for Answers

Purpose: **Creating a variety of spaces, places, and routines for kids to record their questions and hold their thinking**

Resources: **Assorted nonfiction trade books, articles, blog posts, websites, and so on**

Responses: **Wonder Books, Wonder Walls, Wonder Boxes, Genius Hour**

Audience: **Primary, intermediate, and middle**

We don't have to teach curiosity. Anyone who has ever taught pre-K or kindergarten knows what we're talking about. Young kids burst into the room brimming with questions. In fact, they might drive us crazy with all of the questions if they weren't so charming. Why is the sky blue? Why are the tigers and zebras the only ones with stripes? and on and on. Unfortunately, by fifth grade they aren't asking as many questions, and by eighth grade even fewer. Conventional schooling seems to drive the curiosity right out of them. We need to build in daily rituals, routines, and structures that continue to fan that curiosity flame rather than snuff it out.

Wonder Books

Fifth-grade teacher Eleanor Wright begins the year by sharing her own questions, those things she wonders about and longs to explore further. She jots them down in a notebook called a Wonder Book. She puts these notebooks on the supply list. At the beginning of the year, she models her own curiosity by jotting her questions, some from the curriculum and others from anything she wonders about, and then encourages her students to share their own questions, wonders, and discoveries in these precious books. After modeling her questions, Eleanor asks students to choose at least three things they wonder about and jot them down. As you can see, Cassie is nothing if not curious! Eleanor invites Cassie to share her question list with the class (see Figure 9.2).

Figure 9.2
Cassie's List of Questions

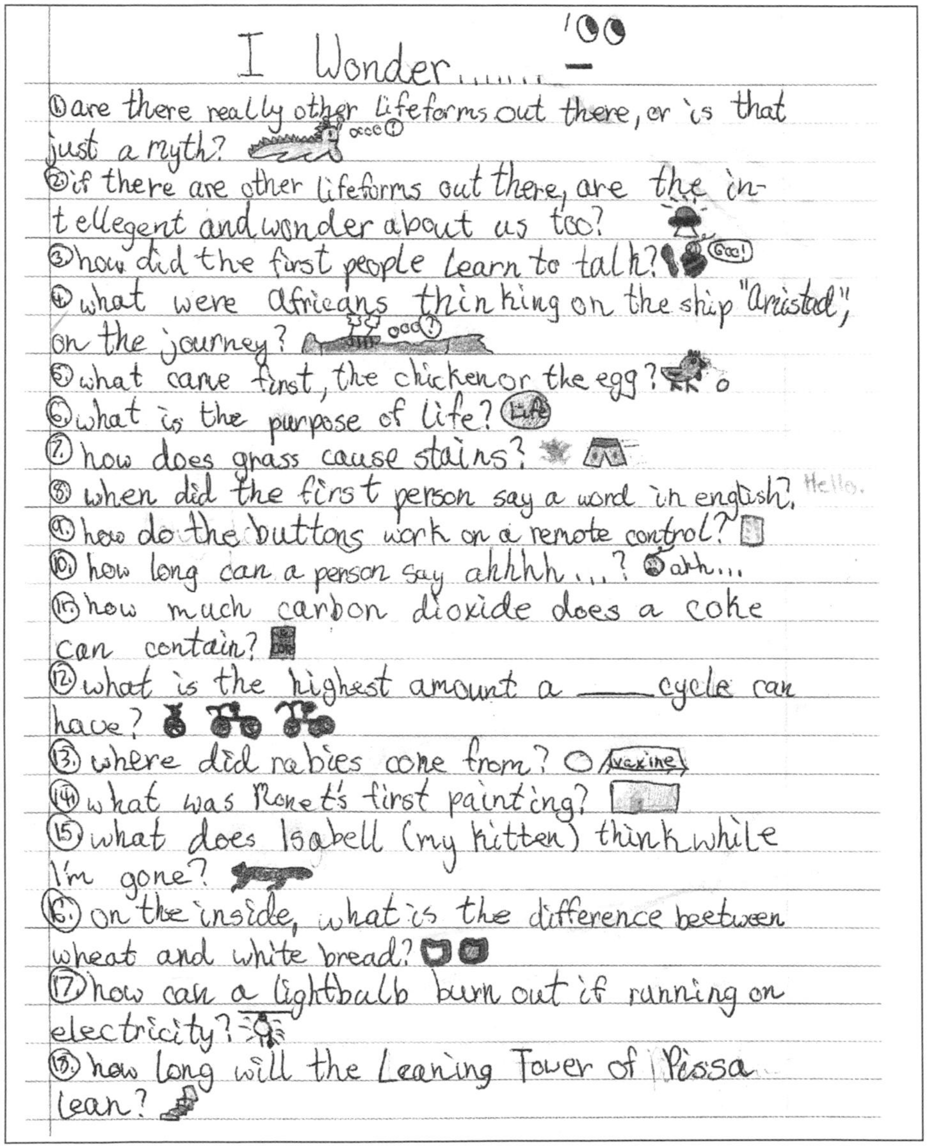

Questions and curiosity are contagious. We have noticed that kids who are struggling to come up with a question may just catch the wonder bug from other kids like Cassie, so we make sure to share as many questions as we can. In classrooms that value wonder, kids come up with terrific questions. These Wonder Books give kids a formal place to jot those questions, hold their thinking, and research answers (see Figure 9.3).

Figure 9.3
Amanda's Questions and Answers in
Two-Column Format

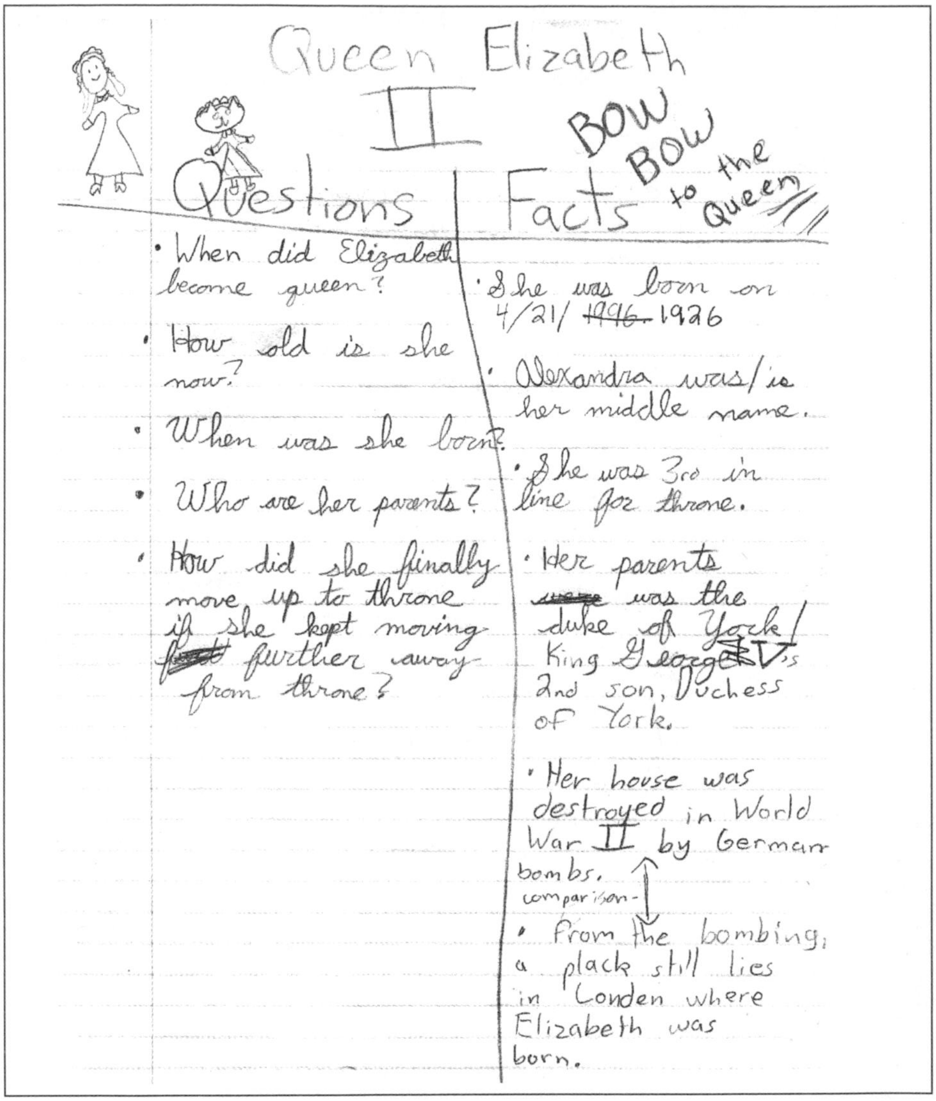

Wonder Walls

Second-grade teacher Brad Buhrow has a board on a wall in his room dedicated solely to kids' questions. Brad begins the year by jotting some of his questions on sticky notes and then placing them on the Wonder Wall. As kids' questions pop up, they learn to jot them down and post them on the Wonder Wall. Brad builds in time throughout the week for kids to address, investigate, and answer their questions. He makes a habit of checking the questions out and gathering similar ones together on the Wall so that kids who have related queries can collaborate when investigating them. Sometimes his Wonder Wall is reserved for the content they are studying (see Figure 9.4) and other times for the myriad questions kids often have.

Wonder Boxes

Debbie Miller, educator, author, and teacher extraordinaire, came up with the notion of Wonder Boxes for her first graders. She added small recipe boxes to the supply list—you know the ones, plastic or metal boxes with alphabetic tabs and note cards behind each letter tab. Then she modeled questions she had and drew and wrote them on a note card, placing it behind the appropri-

Figure 9.4
Wonder Wall of Questions for a Class Study of Insects

ate letter; puppies went behind *P*, bikes behind *B*, and so forth. The kids went crazy for these Wonder Boxes, jotting and drawing their questions, researching them, and drawing or jotting the answers on each card. It is a teaching 10 when you can work grapho-phonics into something as much fun as Wonder Boxes. Kids get to investigate those curiosities they care about, learn a lot, and get more experience with beginning letter sounds to boot.

Genius Hour

When your school schedule is packed as tightly as most are, establishing a time each day or week to investigate a topic of interest needs to be built into the schedule, or it simply won't happen. Daniel Pink, author of *Drive: The Surprising Truth About What Motivates Us* (2011), writes that "The secret to high performance and satisfaction—at work, at school, and at home—is the deeply human need to direct our own lives, to learn and create new things, and to do better by ourselves and our world." Teachers we know who value curiosity set aside one hour or other fixed period a week for kids to investigate their own questions and pursue their own interests. (Some teachers even set aside a half hour to an hour a day to build in even more time for kids to ask their own questions and direct their own learning.) We build in this time to encourage our students to pursue their own passions and questions, study something of interest to them, and learn something new on their own or with their buddies. We leave a few minutes at the end of this time for them to share their hot topics and burning questions. Because kids love it so much, many teachers we know who have launched Genius Hour in their classrooms find themselves building in more time each week for this kind of exploration. Most kids can't get enough of this time to explore their interests and curiosities. For more information on Genius Hour, check out #geniushour on Twitter. Twitter is a hotbed for inquiry-based learning and #geniushour is a good place to start.

Asking and Answering Questions in Seesaw

Purpose: **Sharing questions online**

Resources: **Seesaw app and *Seeds and Seedlings* by Elaine Pascoe, or any other nonfiction book**

Response: **Shared questions on Seesaw app**

Audience: **Primary**

The students in Mrs. Kinnaman's first-grade class had been reading about apples and how apple trees grow, so extending our learning to read *Seeds and Seedlings* was a natural. As the class read, they recorded their questions in Seesaw, an interactive app in which students can see one another's thinking in real time on the class screen, "like" it if they want to, and leave comments. Students are represented by animals for easy reference, particularly helpful for the most emergent readers. Literacy coach Jen Burton reports that primary teachers love this app because it is so easy to use. It also allows teachers to share kids' work with parents or the whole class. See Figure 9.5.

Figure 9.5
A Student's Comment (Enlarged) in the Seesaw App

The More We Learn, the More We Wonder

Purpose: **Wondering as we learn new information**

Resources: **Books on topic of study, in this case, Antarctic animals**

Responses: **Gather information, record it, and wonder about it**

Audience: **Primary**

By the end of the year, Kristen Elder-Rubino's kindergartners knew how to do research. They'd studied African people, cultures, and animals. They'd explored photographs, artifacts, and books. So when Kristen asked them if they were interested in another adventure, this time to the vast, frigid continent of Antarctica, they were ready to put on their mittens!

As the kids learned information through videos, photographs, picture books, and other sources about life in this inhospitable climate, they asked a lot of questions. Questions are natural for curious five-year-olds, but for the entire year Kristen had encouraged the kids to stop, think, and wonder about what they were learning.

After Kristen modeled ways to record information and questions on an I Learned/I Wonder chart, the resulting list of questions demonstrated that thinking and wondering had become second nature to her students. As the kids worked with Kristin and librarian Melissa Oviatt in small

Antarctica Research

Topic: Leopard seals

What do leopard seals eat?

Leopard seals eat penguins. Seals can't catch penguins on the land because the penguins can get away. So seals catch and eat the penguins in the water.

Figure 9.6
Students Present Their Questions and the Answers They Find by Reading

groups to do animal research, Melissa used this same format to record their thinking. Frankie, Eduardo, and Leah, who were researching leopard seals, learned that leopard seals eat penguins, and Melissa recorded this information for them. A picture of a swimming leopard seal capturing a fleeing penguin confirmed that leopard seals catch penguins in the water, and they recorded this information on their chart too. But then they noticed a picture of a leopard seal on the ice, with a few penguins standing some distance away. Leah offered, "I learned leopard seals and penguins are on the ice." Of course, a question was not far behind. "Wow," Frankie wondered, "is that leopard seal going to catch those penguins?"

I Learned	I Wonder
Leopard seals eat penguins.	Do they eat the feet?
Leopard seals catch penguins in the water.	Can penguins swim faster than leopard seals?
The leopard seals and penguins are on the ice.	Is that leopard seal going to catch those penguins?

Frankie was still thinking about that question when he noticed a caption under the picture of the leopard seal and penguins on the ice. After the group read the information, Frankie responded, "I get it. When they are on the ice, leopard seals can't move very fast, so they can't catch the penguins." When Frankie shared this information, he noticed the concerned looks on his classmates' faces. "Don't worry," he said. "Penguins are safe when they're on the ice." (See Figure 9.6.) These kindergartners do a great deal of talking as they think through, draw, and begin to write down the information they are learning. Learning new information, wondering about it, and answering their questions prepares them for more independent research in first grade. (See more examples of kids' work in the assessment section at the end of this chapter.)

Reading with a Question in Mind

Purpose: **Taking notes on information to expand thinking and answer questions**
Resource: **"What's the Fuss About Frogs?," an article in *Odyssey* magazine by Laurie Ann Toupin**
Response: **A two-column think sheet headed Notes/Thinking**
Audience: **Intermediate and middle**

As readers read informational text, they are frequently overwhelmed by the sheer volume of information. Modeling how we read with a question in mind is one way to help readers cut through the dense text and zero in on important information. Steph joined Jeff Osberg's science class to help his eighth graders read with a question in mind, take notes on related information, and merge their thinking with it as they engaged in a study of global warming. Steph brought in an article titled "What's the Fuss About Frogs?" from *Odyssey*, a science-oriented magazine for intermediate and middle-grade kids. The article explored the recent decline in amphibian populations throughout the world, some possible reasons for their disappearance, and some suggestions about what can be done about it.

Steph passed out the article and a think sheet headed Notes/Thinking and asked the kids to skim the article and then turn and talk about what they knew about this topic and what they wondered about. A number of them shared that they noticed that frogs were disappearing and wondered why. Several inferred that their disappearance might be related to global warming, which they had been studying. After several students had shared their thinking, Steph explained that readers can sometimes better understand what they read and pick out the most salient information if they read with a question in mind. So she wrote the question, "Why are these frogs disappearing?" in the Thinking column. The kids, with their think sheets on clipboards, jotted that question down as well.

Steph explained that as she read, she would keep her question in mind and jot down information that related to that question in the Notes column. In addition, she shared that simply jotting the facts by themselves was not enough and that readers need to merge their thinking with information to make sense of it. As she read the first few paragraphs of the article, she took notes on the information that related to her original question in the Notes column and merged her thinking in the Thinking column. Through her reading, she discovered that all amphibians are in great decline, that they are an important food source, that they slow the greenhouse effect by eating insects that normally contribute to decomposition, and that they are the canaries in the ecological coal mine.

As she modeled, she didn't write just any fact in the Notes column, but only information that related directly to her question. In this way, the process of note taking didn't become cumbersome and unwieldy, but instead contributed to her understanding. She also showed how she used the Thinking column to help her when she became confused. She would simply jot down the page number and paragraph that didn't make sense so she could clarify the confusion later on. She shared how sometimes one question leads to another. As she read, she noted several questions in the thinking column, including a big one: Why does it matter if amphibians are declining? From that point on, she kept that question in mind as well as her original question. Her Notes/Thinking two-column form follows here:

Notes	Thinking
All forms of amphibians are in decline, not just frogs.	Why are these frogs disappearing?
Frogs, toads, newts, salamanders, and caecilians are all amphibians.	Don't get this part—what is decomposition? (p. 15 3rd para.)
Slows down greenhouse effect	Why does it matter if amphibians are declining?
Because they are the canaries in the ecological coal mine	Miners used to take canaries into coal mines to test the air, and if the canaries died, it meant they had to get out right away.

After modeling and engaging the kids in guided practice, Steph reminded them once again that the Notes column was to jot down information related to their question and the Thinking column was a place for them to "work out their thinking" and try to make sense of the new information. Then she sent them off to try this with a partner, having them take turns reading and talking about the section they read, keeping the big question in mind, and filling in the think sheet in response to their question. Shoko's think sheet is shown in Figure 9.7. Her last comment in the Thinking column illustrates how she merged her thoughts with the information and expanded her thinking after reading.

Figure 9.7
Shoko's Think Sheet About Frogs

Name _Shoko_ Date _1/10/07_ 6° Science

Notes	Thinking
·brooding frogs- unusual reproduction	*Why are these frogs disappearing?*
·no one knows why they disappearing	·are frogs fresh H₂O or sea H₂O animals?
·all forms of Amphibians are disappearing	·Global Warming plays BIG role
·important food source + pest control (ex. mosquitoes)	·encroachment + predators
·slows down greenhouse effect	·frogs + amphibians warn effects of global warming - indicator species
·"canary in ecological coal mine"	·someday, somehow, the bad things we do to our environment is going to affect _us_.
→THIN SKIN-POROUS causes them to be vulnerable	

Reading with a Question in Mind When Reading Digitally

Purpose: Keeping a question in mind while exploring online nonfiction articles on current events

Resource: "Breathe and Give It All You've Got: How Mindful Athletes Raise Their Game," an article from Newsela, or any digital text

Responses: Questions organized into a question web

Audience: Intermediate and middle

We often help students set a purpose for their work by asking them to read with a specific question in mind as in the previous lesson, because having a focus helps them to gather essential information from the text as they work to answer their question. This powerful strategy is perfect for online reading. The increased distractions kids encounter as they engage in online reading makes teaching them strategies for thinking and annotating online essential. It's essential that we teach students to apply these strategies to online reading, especially if they have no way to mark up the text or jot their thinking, as is often the case.

In Katie Muhtaris's fifth-grade classroom, students are used to using a variety of strategies to capture, organize, and analyze their thinking about text. Today they've been split into partners and small groups, armed with a large piece of paper, markers, and classroom devices. She opens the lesson by asking students to preview the article without reading the entire thing. Students know this means to skim and scan, checking out the title, any subheadings, or other text pieces that pop out so they can ready their mind for the topic. She then launches the lesson and sets the students to work.

Readers, today we're going to read this article that I found during our nonfiction reading time. You already know that when we read online, we have to work double-

time to apply our good reading and jotting strategies in order to follow the text closely. I thought today we could use our question-web strategy. [Katie points to an anchor chart in the room that holds a list of tried-and-true strategies that the class has been working on recently.] What big question could we ask to help guide our reading and thinking today?

The class works to brainstorm some big questions, turning and talking, sharing ideas, building on one another's thinking, and coming to a consensus within their small group. After a few ideas are offered, the teacher refines student ideas into one big question and models placing it in the center of the question web. In this case, "How can athletes be mindful and up their game at the same time?"

Readers, this is a great question to guide our thinking today. Now as you read with your partners or in groups, you can be looking for clues to help you answer all or part of this question. Let's keep all that great thinking on our web so we don't lose any of it.

Katie reads the first few paragraphs, stopping to note an important point in the text. She adds this and a few relevant details to her question web that she is projecting using a document camera. She flips between this and projecting the article so that students can see the text she is reading as well as the work that she is doing. Next, students break off into small groups, taking their own large paper and markers to flexible seating areas in the classroom (see Figure 9.8). Some groups move off to the sides; they will continue this work independently, using one of the class tablet devices to read the article. Katie keeps a few groups with her at the carpet to continue working together in order to provide more support. (See example of kids' work in the assessment section at the end of the chapter.)

Figure 9.8
Students Work on a Question Web

At the conclusion of the article students take a few minutes to review their web and come to a consensus about what the answer to their question is. In this case Katie asks students to hang their question webs around the room, and students do a silent gallery walk so that they can share and see what work their classmates have done. They end the lesson back at the carpet to reflect on the strategy, discuss why and when they would want to apply this strategy to Internet reading, and share any lasting ideas or questions from the reading of the day.

Thick and Thin Questions

Purpose: **Differentiating between large global questions and smaller clarification questions in a content area**

Resources: **Science textbook, nonfiction trade books**

Responses: **Thick questions on the front of 3-by-3-inch sticky notes; thin questions on the front of sticky flags; attempted answers on the reverse sides of the sticky notes and flags**

Audience: **Intermediate and middle**

Horace Mann Middle School teacher Margaret Bobb uses many different types of texts to teach seventh-grade physical science: newspaper and magazine articles, websites, blogs, trade books, and, yes, the dreaded science textbook. She knows that textbooks don't usually go deep enough to give kids the background they need to understand important science concepts, so she surrounds her kids with science print of every type. But she also knows that her students will likely be steeped in textbooks, both print and digital, for years to come and she would be doing them a disservice if she ignored teaching them how to read these bastions of American secondary education.

A technique she uses that helps her students sift large global questions from smaller clarification questions is the thick and thin question approach. Thick questions in Margaret's class are those that address large, universal concepts and often begin with "Why? How come? I wonder . . ." Or they address large content areas, such as "What is photosynthesis?" The answers to these questions are often long and involved, and require further discussion and research.

Thin questions are those primarily asked to clarify confusion, understand words, or access factual content. Questions that can be answered with a number or with a simple yes or no fit into this category. "How far is the earth from the sun?" is an example of a thin question. The answers are typically shorter than those for thick questions.

Kids in Margaret's classroom code for thick and thin questions in trade books and articles as well as in textbooks. For thick questions, they use the 3-by-3-inch sticky notes, mark them with the word *Thick*, and write the question on the front. For thin questions, they use the skinny, sticky flags with room only for small questions. In both cases, Margaret encourages her students to take a stab at the answer on the back of the sticky note. They may have no ideas about the answer, which is fine. But if they do, they can attempt an explanation on the reverse side of the sticky note.

Margaret has noticed that the visual marker of the large sticky notes for thick questions and the small sticky flags for thin questions has an immediate impact and helps students categorize questions more quickly than before. In the content areas, particularly, these question categories, which separate broad concepts from smaller issues of clarification, seem to guide students down the path to further insight.

Reading to Answer a Question:
Asking Questions to Gain Information

Purpose: **Reading to find answers**
Resources: **A variety of nonfiction texts, images**
Responses: **Discussion and short written summaries**
Audience: **Intermediate**

When Carole Suderman brought her third graders together to discuss what they had learned about Native Americans during their study of early Colorado history, she asked the kids if they had any lingering questions. The class had spent some weeks studying the Plains Indian way of life, especially during the time when they depended on the buffalo for their food, clothing, shelter, tools, and other needs. Charlie thought for a minute and raised his hand.

"I wonder," he said, "whatever happened to the Plains Indians?" Charlie's question prompted a flood of questions from the other kids. "Did they disappear when all the buffalo got killed?" "Where did the Native Americans go if they didn't live on the plains anymore?" "Did the settlers live on the Indians' land without asking permission?" Often, we notice that the more kids learn, the more questions they have. Charlie and the other students were eager to pursue these lingering questions. So Carole and the kids hightailed it down the hall to meet with the librarian and enlist her help as the kids read to find some answers.

They began by putting Charlie's question squarely in the center of a large piece of paper. As the kids shared their additional questions, Carole listed them, and then the group searched the library for books that might contain some answers. First, Carole modeled how to check for relevant information in a book, skimming the table of contents and the index for key words related to a particular question. Next, Carole and the librarian read aloud several promising subtitles and sections of texts to show kids how they found the information in the text that answered a question. Then Carole demonstrated how to read and paraphrase the information, write up a short paragraph to summarize it, and add it to the chart. Finally, the kids went off to try this same process with their own questions.

When they came back together, the kids placed their answers on the large paper. Some children found information about the diseases that settlers brought to the plains and that killed many of the native people. Others wrote about the overhunting of the buffalo and how this destroyed the Plains Indians' source of food, shelter, and tools, effectively forcing those remaining tribes and nations to find their way to reservations. (See examples of students' work in the assessment section of this chapter.) After reading and writing the answers to their questions, the kids came together to summarize and share what they had learned. During the share session, Irania raised her hand. "So what's happening to the Plains Indians right now?" Carole and the librarian looked knowingly at each other and then smiled at Irania's next question—"Can I go back to the library to find out?" (See examples of kids' work in the assessment section at the end of the chapter.)

Thinking Beyond the Book:
Creating a Line of Research Questions

Purpose: **Investigating questions to build knowledge**
Resources: ***The Journey That Saved Curious George* by Louise Borden; online and text resources about the beginning of World War II**
Response: **Related questions for further research into a specific topic**
Audience: **Intermediate and middle**

Sophisticated picture books not only engage older kids, but often introduce them to unfamiliar topics about which they are eager to know more. *The Journey That Saved Curious George*, by Louise Borden, chronicles the remarkable story of the creators of the Curious George stories, H. A. and Margret Rey, as they escaped (with their manuscripts in a bag) from Paris on bicycles in 1940, as World War II began. Their story is suspenseful, fascinating, and complex, filled with engaging illustrations as well as letters, photographs, telegrams, diary entries, and other primary sources that help readers understand the unfolding saga. The purpose of the primary source documents, we tell kids, is to give the reader a sense of history and enhance the narrative by making both the Reys' journey and the historic time period come alive.

The riveting story line makes readers feel smack in the middle of the City of Light just before the Nazi occupation, so kids mostly understand what is going on even though they know very little about the time period. The amazing illustrations, Louise Borden's engaging text, and the extraordinary collection of historical documents are irresistible and were just what was needed to whet kids' interest in the events surrounding the beginning of World War II. Once these sixth graders got started asking questions about the historical events that were unfolding, they couldn't stop. They got into small groups to research those questions and topics that most interested them, discussing events and formulating questions they planned to investigate.

One small group returned to the information about the week of May 10, 1940. "On the northern French border, the Nazi tanks moved like lightning. It was a *blitzkrieg*" (2005). They thought about this information and then began taking notes and posing a line of questions to try to find some answers.

Events in History	Our Questions
Tanks—moved like lightning	What is a blitzkrieg? (maybe tanks moving like lightning)
News from the front was grim . . .	Which countries had surrendered to the Germans? Why? What is a front?
Belgian king had surrendered	What happened to the people in countries taken over?
British army and 100,000 French rescued at Dunkirk	What happened at Dunkirk? Why were men rescued?
English Channel—filled with boats and ships trying to save armies, taking them to England	Why would the defeated armies go to England?

Another small group had different questions, which led them to brainstorm a line of specific questions to research:

Why were so many people fleeing Paris and other parts of France?

Where would everyone go?

Why did they feel they had to leave their homes? How long did they stay away?

Did they just abandon their homes? Did they ever return?

If the Germans were coming, what were they going to do to people who lived in France? Were people living in towns captured?

It said the Reys were Jewish; what would have happened if they had been caught by the Germans?

Could the Germans just go in and arrest Jewish people once they took over? When did the concentration camps begin?

Why did Hitler hate the Jews so much?

While questions such as these may not have simple answers or answers that are easy to find, researchers nowadays can take advantage of a variety of books and online sources that feature maps, text, photographs, videos, and time lines that support kids to build their knowledge about World War II. Too often kids find history boring—and yawn through the facts and details they are expected to remember, or worse, memorize for and then immediately forget after Friday's quiz. Not these junior historians. Giving them plenty of time and latitude to come up with their own authentic questions shows they are eager to take the lead, delving into not just the what and how but the whys of history.

Questioning That Leads to Inferential Thinking

Purpose:	**To teach that asking questions may lead to making inferences**
Resource:	***Waiting* by Kevin Henkes**
Response:	**Sticky notes with questions and inferences**
Audience:	**Primary and Intermediate**

Readers don't read with one strategy in mind. When readers read, they integrate strategies. We plan instruction on a single strategy so that readers get an idea of how the strategy works when they read and how they can use it as a tool for understanding. But the truth is, readers use a small repertoire of strategies in combination as they read. For instance, in most cases, the moment we ask a question when reading, an inference follows quickly on its heels.

In this lesson, we show how asking questions often leads to inferential thinking and how some questions are answered in the text and others have to be inferred. Inferring involves taking our background knowledge and merging it with clues in the text to come up with a reasonable idea of what is going on. We let kids know that inferring involves a dialogue with the author and an inference must be based on evidence from the text. Inferring connects to what the author has in mind.

We also share the difference between an inference and a guess. Guessing does not have to be related to the text. Guessing takes our background knowledge and often relies on our imagination to come up with an idea that may or may not be found in the text. But we don't tell kids that they are not allowed to guess! Guessing is derived from their imagination, and we wouldn't want to limit that. We just need for them to understand the very important difference between inferring and guessing. After they have asked questions and made inferences, we ask them to see if their questions were answered and their inferences were confirmed.

Steph joined fourth-grade teacher Kai Johnson to do this lesson on how asking questions often leads to making inferences, using Kevin Henkes's *Waiting*. Steph led the lesson on the first day, and Kai followed up on the second day, rereading the text to see whether students' questions were answered in the text or had to be inferred. The book is highly inferential. It features five toy animals on a windowsill who, the text says, are waiting there for something. It naturally spurs questions and inferences throughout.

Steph begins by sharing that when we read, we have questions and sometimes those questions are answered directly in the text. But other times, those questions are not answered, and we have to use the text clues to infer the answers to them. Through an interactive read-aloud, Steph models her own thinking by looking at the cover picture with all five toys and the title and saying, "I wonder what they are waiting for. I have to view the pictures very closely to get a reasonable idea." She explains that this book has very little text and that most of the information can be inferred from the pictures, so close viewing will be a big help to understanding. She notices that three of the animals are holding something: the pig has an umbrella, the dog has a sled, and the teddy bear has a kite.

"I wonder why the pig has an umbrella," she says, and jots that down on her sticky note. "The umbrella is a clue that makes me infer that the pig might be waiting for rain. So I'll jot that down and mark it with an *I* for Infer."

She has the kids turn and talk about anything they wonder and then jot down their questions. They have lots of questions and some inferences as well, particularly related to what these animals are waiting for. When she turns the page, the text actually says what they are waiting for, except for the rabbit, which is "not waiting for anything in particular." So kids who asked about the other animals got answers in the text and their inferences were confirmed, and they marked those questions with an *A* for *answer*. But kids who asked what the rabbit was waiting for didn't get that question answered and can't actually infer the answer from the text or picture. Here is a place where kids might guess what's going on with the rabbit since the text holds no clue whatsoever, a good spot to illustrate the difference between inferring and guessing.

Steph continues with the interactive read-aloud, sharing her thinking occasionally as kids jot down their questions and inferences (see Figure 9.9). Soon the images show the toy animals still on the windowsill but in different positions—lying down, bending over, and so on. One child asks why they are changing positions.

"Wow, interesting question; jot down what you are inferring about that question, and then share your inference with a partner," Steph suggests.

Kids are bursting with thoughts and can't wait to share. Most have inferred that someone is moving them, probably the kid whose room it is, which appears to be the author's point. Yet some kids think it might be a magic story, and there is evidence to suggest that could possibly be fantasy, since the animals stand or lie in certain

Figure 9.9
Sticky Notes with Questions, Answers, and Inferences

positions that would not be feasible even if they were moved by someone. At one point, a Russian nesting doll joins the group. Kids who have background knowledge about them notice the line in the middle and infer that there will be more dolls within. This is a classic example of how our background knowledge can lead to reasonable inferences.

Kai rereads the book the following day, and kids realize that some of their questions were clearly answered, whereas others had to be inferred. But the conversation continues since there are some questions that can't even be answered with reasonable inferences. *Waiting* is a terrific book to demonstrate how asking questions leads to inferential thinking. But since some questions are not answered and can't be reasonably inferred, some readers may still be left pondering what is actually going on. The kids decide that they would like to write to Kevin Henkes and see what he says in relation to their unanswered questions. This is a great idea for those kids who are still curious about ideas in a text after reading it several times.

Lingering Questions

Whenever kids finish reading or listening to something, or thinking about something they've read, we ask them to jot down any remaining questions they have. These lingering questions extend kids' understanding beyond the text. Some lingering questions come up when there is no clear resolution to a story and the reader is left up in the air. Sometimes a good story requires the reader to draw his or her own conclusions about what happened or consider varying interpretations of the characters' actions and the unfolding events. When readers finish a book like *Charlie Anderson* (Abercrombie), questions may remain. These lingering questions encourage kids to consider the many possibilities raised by an ambiguous ending. It's these kinds of questions that prompt discussion and debate or keep us up at night pondering the twist at the end of a great novel.

Kids also ask lingering questions in science, social studies, and history. It is these questions that often become researchable questions. Students may come up with important questions as they read magazines and newspapers about current events. Sometimes, these significant questions spur kids to ask "why" or "how" questions—questions that may not be answered by simply amassing more information. Lingering questions in history move into the realm of speculation—"what-if" questions that consider how things might have turned out differently. Or lingering questions can extend a child's understanding of a topic or issue as he or she grapples with new ideas or empathizes with different perspectives. When reading about a Syrian refugee child and her difficult life in a war-torn country, Megan asked, "I wonder what it would feel like to live where there is a war going on." Megan's empathy for a young girl in difficult circumstances pushed her thinking further. Second graders read newspaper accounts of recent hurricanes, and as the enormity and tragic nature of the events sank in, they asked, "How could we help the victims?" In response to their question, they brainstormed things they could do. We encourage kids to engage in further conversation about a great read or take action in response to compelling information, so we constantly model and encourage kids to ask and consider lingering questions.

Authentic Questions or Assessment Questions

P. David Pearson (2010) says that "the questions a student asks after reading a text are a better assessment than the questions a student can answer about that text." What an interesting take on assessment. And we couldn't agree more. When we were in school, the teachers asked the questions, and we supplied the answers, or tried to anyway, whether we knew them or not. The teachers knew the answers to the long list of questions they asked or that appeared at the end of the story in our basal readers or science textbooks. Teachers asked these questions to check on us, to see whether we had done the homework, read the chapter, or memorized our facts. Those were the only questions we remember in school. Our own questions, important or not, were reserved for recess, walking home after school, or the dinner table that night. School was not to be mucked up with a lot of tangential kid questions.

But, as David Pearson points out, the questions that really give us information are those that students have *after* reading, listening, or viewing. Those are the most important questions and the most revealing as well. We can really learn from kids' questions—what they understood or didn't, what they know, what they learned, what they want to learn, what they predict, and so forth. So we pay particular attention to their questions after they have read, listened to, or viewed something. Those questions can drive our teaching and help students go further.

Fortunately, in the classrooms portrayed in this book, authentic student questions are encouraged and valued. Authentic questions, whether asked by students or teachers, have the following characteristics:

- Prompt thinking
- Don't always have one right answer
- May have multiple answers
- Cause us to ponder and wonder
- Dispel or clarify confusion
- Challenge us to rethink our opinions
- Lead us to seek out further information
- Are subject to discussion, debate, and conversation
- Often require further research

Many tasks we ask kids to do in schools involve what we have to come call *assessment questions*. Assessment questions are questions that we teachers know the answers to and that we ask primarily to check or monitor our students' knowledge. Now, before launching a full-frontal attack on assessment questions, we recognize that we are teachers and that we have both the right and the responsibility to ask assessment questions to monitor our kids' progress. Asking assessment questions represents one way to measure academic growth. But do we need to ask so many? Right now, most of the questions asked in schools fall into the assessment category. Curiosity-driven questions are still rare in classrooms. We need to balance this by allowing more time for kids and teachers to ask and explore authentic questions.

We explain the difference between authentic questions and assessment questions to the kids. Why fake it? When we ask assessment questions, we might tell our students, "This is an assessment question. I know the answer. Here comes the question." With younger primary kids, we might call these *checking questions*. "I know the answer to this question. I'm asking it to check and see if you do." When we consider authentic questions, our response is something like, "I don't know the answer, but let's see if we can find out."

Peter Johnston (2004) lists a number of ways that teachers can ask students authentic questions that prompt thinking. Authentic questions are typically open-ended and encourage divergent thinking rather than one right answer. Some that we use frequently include the following:

- What makes you think that?
- Why do you say that?
- Can you elaborate on that?
- Can you tell me more about your thinking?
- How did you come up with that?

When all is said and done, these kinds of questions have an authentic feel. We ask these kinds of questions to probe and find out about what kids are thinking, not to check whether or not they did their homework. Authentic questions such as these, whether asked by kids or adults, are more likely to encourage new thinking and prompt new insight. In his enthusiastic response to his teacher Eleanor Wright, fifth-grader Brandon reminds us how questioning helps him in both reading and life (see Figure 9.10). We think that's terrific!

Figure 9.10
Brandon's Opinion About the
Questioning Strategy

How Has Questioning Helped Me

The format you have taught me has helped me in many ways. When I write down a question, it makes me wonder why. It helps me think of multiple possibilities. It makes me wonder what was the author thinking. They help me in real life. Now, if I have a question on anything from computers to military aircraft, I want to know the answer. I wonder how I would act if I were to be the character. For short it helps me in many wonderful multiple ways, and it's the next best thing since sliced bread.

Teaching with the End in Mind: Assessing What We've Taught

Questioning

Based on the lessons in this chapter, we look for evidence that

1. *Students stop, ask questions, and wonder about their reading.* We look for evidence that students are stopping to think about their reading and record their questions.

2. *Students ask questions to clarify confusion.* We look for evidence that students are monitoring their understanding and stop and ask a question when they are confused.

3. *Students read to gain information and answer questions.* We look for evidence that students are reading with questions in mind and noting when they find information that answers them.

4. *Students consider lingering questions to expand thinking and spark investigation.* We look for evidence that students are asking inferential and interpretive questions that encourage discussion, debate, and further research.

Suggestions for Differentiation

Anchor charts make comprehension strategies concrete and can be invaluable for our English language learners and children just learning to read. We keep anchor charts of kids' questions about a text, a topic, an issue, and so forth posted on the walls and refer to them frequently. In addition to written questions from both the teachers and the kids, we encourage kids to illustrate their questions with a visual image that helps them keep their question in mind. They also write or illustrate answers as they find them.

Another anchor chart that we co-construct focuses on how questioning helps us understand and ways kids can use questions in their reading. For instance, the chart might begin with a statement such as "We ask questions to . . ." and go on to finish the statement with "make sense of what we read," "find information," and "answer our wonders." Kids then draw themselves on large sticky notes doing these things—answering questions, finding information, and so on—and place their pictures on the appropriate place on the chart.

We can create anchor charts such as these for a variety of strategies. Incorporating drawing is one of the best ways for kids to make their thinking visible.

Questioning Assessment Commentary

Stopping to wonder and think about pictures and information. Independent work from the lesson titled "The More We Learn, the More We Wonder"

As young children learn from pictures and listen to the teacher reading informational text, they often stop, think, and wonder about the information.

◀ In this series of drawings, a young child draws and writes in her own invented spelling the questions she asked as she learned about penguins. Among her questions are "I wonder why penguins fall down," "I wonder why the egg is on his feet," "I wonder if they eat fish," and "I wonder what else they eat." Our next step would be to teach her to keep her questions in mind as she continues to learn about penguins. In this way, she could find answers to her questions.

▶ As kids learn more information, they sometimes find the answers to their questions. Young children's drawings often illustrate very specific information that we need to talk to them about in order to see whether they are making sense. This question and its answer are part of a kindergarten class's research on Antarctica. We recorded and typed the child's language, and she illustrated the information. In this case the drawings accurately depict both the question and the answer.

Antarctica Research

Topic: Penguins

I wonder how penguins eat fish underwater.

I learned that penguins swim and catch fish!

Creating question webs to address and answer questions from the lesson "Reading with a Question in Mind"

By: Sui Yee, Nina

"They accept them and learn to behave better, in sports & in life"

"A lot of teams are interested in being mindful"

I helps athletes to stop worring about the game by teaching lessons about mindfulness and doing yoga.

Mindful people are able to give full attention to do something. Try to block but worries & fears.

doing yoga can help the athlets be midful

How do mindful athletes raise their game?

Players were able to concentrate more on like playing the game with less stress.

"he prefers to do it in the morning: "it wakes you up"

They had a goal to teach athletes lessons about mindfulness to help them.

Helps them stay relaxed. The team members reported feeling more relaxed and mindful.

Players learn breathing exercises, to help.

"It was good to add the yoga" grandsay

▲ Sui Yee and Nina address the central question of how athletes raise their game through mindfulness. They use information they found in the text, including direct quotations, as evidence for their thinking. The power of creating a web like this requires kids to discuss the information, shape it into their own thoughts, and jot it down.

Researching answers to questions from the lesson "Reading to Answer a Question"

The Government made the Indians move because the settlers took their Land so they moved them to reservations.

When kids have lingering questions, we take the time to read to answer them. Charlie's question, "Whatever happened to the Plains Indians?" provided an opportunity for kids to extend their thinking about this topic.

◄ When kids read to answer their questions, they often come up with information that answers the question but may need additional explanation to clarify the answer. This response summarizes information that answers the question, but in order to make sure the child understands the information he's found, we would confer and discuss what he means by "the government" and see if he could tell us what happened as the Native Americans moved to reservations. Then we would work with him to elaborate on his answer to the question.

The Plains Indians got sick because they got germs from the white people.

◄ ◄ When we do research with the whole class, it's all about differentiation. This response clearly describes what happened when the Plains Indians caught diseases from settlers. An English language learner, this child's illustration of an Indian in poor health lying on buffalo robes demonstrates her understanding.

▶ This illustration succinctly sums up what happened to the Plains Indians over time. Incorporating many of his peers' responses, this child asked to put his response at the end of the class chart—a thoughtful synthesis of everyone's learning.

The settlers' animals ate the grass on the prairies. Settlers cut down trees for making fires. They killed lots of buffalo. American Indians could not survive without the buffalo—they sometimes begged for food from the settlers. Some Americans Indians attacked wagon trains because they knew the settlers were taking the land, their food and they had no way to live.

◄ This detailed answer summarizes many aspects of what happened as settlers moved west. The child synthesized information from several sources and wove it together to explain what happened to the Indians as well as why they began to try to defend their lands from settlement.

Chapter 10

Visualizing and Inferring: Making What's Implicit Explicit

A number of years ago, Steph walked into a staff developers' meeting and mentioned that she was in search of a picture book to teach visualizing. Our colleague and friend Chryse Hutchins suggested Estelle Condra's *See the Ocean*, a beautiful book filled with stunning watercolor illustrations, striking poetic words, and a moving narrative.

It is the tale of a little girl who travels to a beach house with her parents and her brothers each summer. As we read through the story, we soon notice that something is different about Nellie. She never begs to sit near the window in the car, she describes the ocean as an old white-bearded man, and she asks her parents endless questions. Near the end, we discover that she is blind. As Steph read through it, she, too, had endless questions.

"I wonder why Chryse recommended this for visualizing," she said to Anne the next day. "I think it's perfect for questioning." Anne read it and commented that she thought it was just what she was looking for to teach inferring. When we talked with Chryse later, she said that from her perspective the poetic language, metaphoric writing, and stunning imagery best lent itself to teaching visualizing.

Different readers rely on different strategies to help them gain better understanding. We mention this because, as we have said, well-crafted picture books can be used to teach and practice just about any strategy. To gain understanding of *See the Ocean*, readers are likely to activate several strategies, including visualizing, questioning, and inferring.

Many teachers we know introduce this book after their students have spent considerable time practicing different strategies. They encourage their kids to think about which strategies they are using to make sense of *See the Ocean* and to mark sticky notes with whatever strategy seems to help them gain meaning. Veronica's sticky notes show how this eighth grader activates all three of these strategies and more as she reads and thinks through the book (see Figure 10.1). These sticky notes provide strong evidence of her flexibility with strategy use. She activates multiple strategies to comprehend.

Figure 10.1
Veronica's Sticky Note Responses for *See the Ocean*

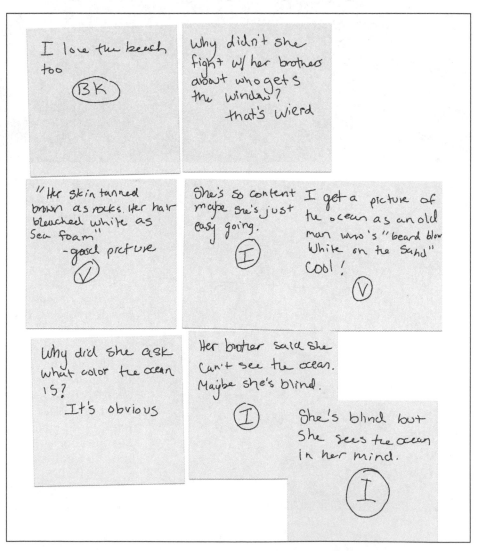

We discuss visualizing and inferring in one chapter because they are closely related. Visualizing strengthens our inferential thinking. When we visualize, we are in fact inferring, but with mental images rather than words and thoughts. Visualizing and inferring don't occur in isolation. Strategies interweave. Inferring involves merging background knowledge with text clues to come up with an idea that is not explicitly stated in the text. Inferring is the proverbial reading between the lines.

A variety of mental processes occur under the umbrella of inferential thinking. When we teach kids to infer, we might teach them to draw conclusions or make predictions. Predicting is related to inferring, of course, but we predict outcomes, events, or actions that are confirmed or contradicted by the end of the story. Prediction is one aspect of inferential thinking. To help our students understand the difference, we encourage them to consider the outcome of an event or action each time they make a prediction and notice whether there has been a resolution.

Inferring also involves using the context to figure out the meaning of unfamiliar words or noticing a character's actions to surface a theme. Our colleague Judy Wallis created a visual that describes the multifaceted nature of inferential thinking. She chose an umbrella to represent the many aspects of inferring. We have adapted it here to show the different ways readers use inferential thinking to enhance understanding. (See Figure 10.2.)

Figure 10.2
The Inferring Umbrella

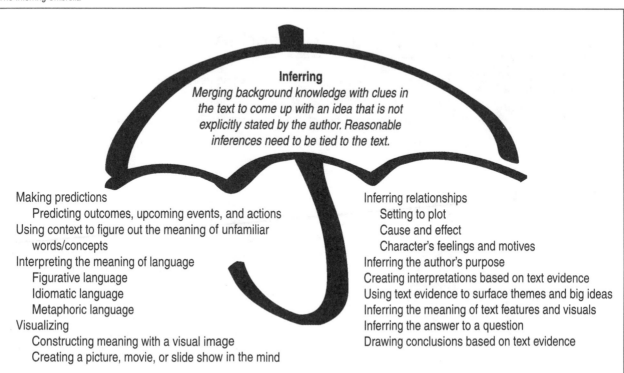

Inferring
Merging background knowledge with clues in the text to come up with an idea that is not explicitly stated by the author. Reasonable inferences need to be tied to the text.

Making predictions
　　Predicting outcomes, upcoming events, and actions
Using context to figure out the meaning of unfamiliar
　　words/concepts
Interpreting the meaning of language
　　Figurative language
　　Idiomatic language
　　Metaphoric language
Visualizing
　　Constructing meaning with a visual image
　　Creating a picture, movie, or slide show in the mind

Inferring relationships
　　Setting to plot
　　Cause and effect
　　Character's feelings and motives
Inferring the author's purpose
Creating interpretations based on text evidence
Using text evidence to surface themes and big ideas
Inferring the meaning of text features and visuals
Inferring the answer to a question
Drawing conclusions based on text evidence

Visualizing: Movies in the Mind

Visualizing brings joy to reading. When we visualize, we create pictures in our minds that belong to us and no one else. As more and more books are routinely churned into movies, we are not surprised that most people prefer the book over the movie, kids included. One problem inherent in transforming text to film is that Hollywood routinely takes a four-hundred-and-fifty-page novel and converts it into a one-hundred-page script. Not surprisingly, depth and texture suffer. Another common complaint relates to the characters. Steph could never sit back and enjoy the film *Seven Years in Tibet*, based on one of her favorite books by Heinrich Harrer, because Brad Pitt, no matter how cute he was, did not jibe with her image of the book's protagonist.

When we visualize, we create our own movies in our minds. We become attached to the characters we visualize. Visualizing personalizes reading, keeps us engaged, and often prevents us from abandoning a book prematurely. When we introduce visualizing, we are likely to facilitate a conversation about books and movie adaptations in an attempt to make the strategy concrete. Kids relate and quickly weigh in with their own thoughts.

Strategy Lessons: Visualizing

Drawing to Respond to Reading

Purpose: Creating images to better understand the text
Resource: *The Watcher* by Jeanette Winter
Response: Drawings on the iPad using the Drawing Pad app
Audience: Primary

Kids love responding to read-alouds using iPad apps such as Drawing Pad. Artistic responses such as these reflect children's visualizations as they listen to text being read aloud. With young children, their drawings of their ideas and images often give us far more information about what they are thinking than what they can write in words. Teacher Marisol Payet's second-grade students are flexible; with only a few iPads in the classroom, kids use sticky notes and pencils as well as devices. As Marisol read *The Watcher*, by Jeanette Winter, a book about Jane Goodall and how she studied and lived with chimpanzees, the kids were chock-full of mental images of every sort.

Whether they had sticky notes or iPads, the children had many responses. As his drawing indicates, Egan wondered if Jane watched the chimps at night. (See Figure 10.3.) Kids were amazed to find out a few pages later that she slept in trees, just like the chimps, to observe their nighttime and early morning behavior. Giselle wondered if Jane was friends "of" the chimp. (See Figure 10.4.) This led to a class discussion of whether or not humans can befriend chimps. As they looked back in the text to answer this question, kids noticed that first Jane observed the chimps from a distance, becoming more familiar with them as they became used to her presence. These drawn representations of their mental images allowed the kids to better understand and remember what they were listening to or viewing, enriching their reading experience.

Figure 10.3
Egan's Question About Jane Goodall

Figure 10.4
Giselle's Question About Jane Goodall

Visualizing from a Vivid Piece of Text

Purpose: **Merging prior experience and the text to create visual images**
Resource: **The lead to Chapter 3, "Escape," in *Charlotte's Web*, by E. B. White**
Response: **Drawing visual images with small groups**
Audience: **Primary and intermediate**

We work on and practice strategies with small groups. A group of six fourth graders had chosen to read E. B. White's *Charlotte's Web* in their book club. Steph saw this as a great opportunity to talk to them about visualizing because E. B. White writes in such a strikingly visual way.

Chapter 3, "Escape," begins with a vivid, detailed description of the barn where Charlotte, the magical spider, lives with all of the other animals in the story. The passage describing the barn is about a page and a half long and is filled with specific nouns and compelling descriptions:

> The barn was very large. It was very old. It smelled of hay. . . . It smelled of the perspiration of tired horses and the wonderful sweet breath of patient cows. . . . It smelled of grain and of harness dressing and of axle grease and of rubber boots and of new rope. . . . It was full of all sorts of things that you find in barns: ladders, grindstones, pitch forks, monkey wrenches, scythes, lawn mowers, snow shovels, ax handles, milk pails, water buckets, empty grain sacks, and rusty rat traps. It was the kind of barn that swallows like to build their nests in. It was the kind of barn that children like to play in.

Steph read the passage out loud to the group and asked them to close their eyes and visualize the scene. When she finished, she said to them simply, "Tell me about your barn." Jon said that the barn was rickety and old and in need of a coat of paint. Jessica said she visualized a red barn with white trim. Jason mentioned beautiful green pastures with cows and horses grazing peacefully. Others mentioned farmers pitching hay and kids jumping from the hayloft. E. B. White had not explicitly written these details. The kids' comments reflected the movies running through their minds.

After about ten minutes of discussing their images of the barn, Steph asked them to sketch their barn. Each drawing was unique. The drawings included kids swinging on tire swings, riding the horses, and driving tractors. Some of the barn roofs were rounded; one was pointed with a rooster weathervane on top. Some pictures had farmers working and birds flying in and out of a small opening on top. Others had no people or animals. Some included wheat and corn fields. One was a detailed drawing of the interior of the barn loaded with mousetraps, milk pails, and water troughs. In some cases, none of the items drawn were mentioned in the text. As the kids shared, it became clear that many of their pictures came from their own prior knowledge of barns combined with the words of E. B. White.

This is what visualizing is all about—taking the words of the text and mixing them with the reader's background knowledge to create pictures in the mind. Good writers like E. B. White act like old-time movie projectionists who crank up the projector with their vivid words and then sit back as the reel runs unfettered for the viewer. The movie becomes the reader's own. In this case, if we were raised on a farm, we have the most detailed movie of all. If we live around farms or have seen pictures of farms, we pick up on those. Combining the author's words with our background knowledge allows us to create mental images that bring life to reading.

Visualizing and Sketchnoting Using Digital Tools

Purpose: **Harnessing the power of digital tools to capture thinking in images for archiving or sharing with a wider audience**

Resources: **A drawing app and the article "You Can Grow Your Intelligence" (Mindset Works 2014), or any text to read aloud**

Responses: **Drawings on a drawing app**

Audience: **Intermediate and middle**

In this lesson, fifth-grade teacher Katie Muhtaris uses sketchnoting to help her students explore a different way to capture their thinking and learning. Sketchnoting is the use of doodling to capture ideas, information, and thoughts while listening to a story or lecture. If you'd like to learn more about how sketchnoting is being used in classrooms, you can visit Kathy Schrock's website (http://www.schrockguide.net/sketchnoting.html).

Katie explains to her class that sketchnotes use colors, drawings, and words to help hold information. As she talks about her example, she shows students how she's taken information and put it into visual form using little images and codes for herself. She also shares that instead of trying to type everything that she was hearing, she worked to listen, think, and then represent that new learning with a few key pictures or words that would trigger her memory. (See Katie's example of sketchnotes in Figure 10.5.)

Figure 10.5
Katie's Example of Sketchnoting in Color

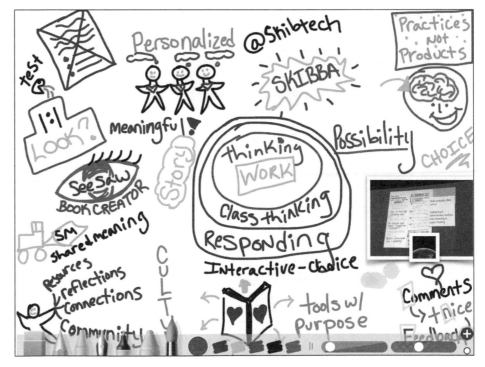

Before having students begin, Katie shares a few tips on sketchnoting:

- It doesn't need to be perfect! Don't dwell on the details, so you can keep up with the reading.
- Share ideas for "codes." Use codes you already know from reading.
- Use color to highlight important information, but don't go overboard.
- It's okay to use words and pictures.

Katie gives students the option to do their sketchnotes by hand or on a digital tool. While most students prefer to try the tablet first, because they know the power of being able to quickly share and add audio, some choose markers and paper, which is fine. Either works.

Katie pauses frequently as she reads to enable students to internalize this new skill. She starts by showing the article "You Can Grow Your Intelligence" (Mindset Works 2014) on the projector so that students can refer to the text if needed. She reads the first two paragraphs aloud and then pauses to give students time to quickly sketch their ideas. She encourages them to draw quickly and not erase too much, so that they can keep up a quick pace. As students work, Katie draws on Drawing Pad, pausing to show her work to any students who need help. Throughout the lesson, she asks students to turn and talk, share what they've done, and tell their partner what their sketches help them remember.

Students continue reading in partners, pausing to stop and sketch as they go, until they finish the article. When students have completed their drawings, they come back together to share with the class, talk about what they learned from the text using their sketchnotes, and debrief about the process. Katie asks the class a few questions: "Is this something you would like to try more of? How did it help you learn?" Students also start a classroom chart of ideas for symbols to use as they sketch, including codes they have used before as well as those new to the repertoire, for example, a brain for thinking and up arrows to show growth or positive ideas.

Katie wraps up the lesson by sharing how students might use an app called Explain Everything to do more with their sketchnotes. She shows how she uses this app to go back and record her voice talking about each part of her image while pointing to it with a digital arrow. When she finishes, she reflects that she is surprised at how much she remembered about the article from just a few pictures and words.

Visualizing with Wordless Picture Books

Purpose: **Visualizing to fill in missing information**
Resource: ***Good Dog, Carl* by Alexandra Day**
Response: **Drawing what you visualize**
Audience: **Primary and intermediate**

We teach visualizing in many different ways, but one surprising way is through wordless picture books. One might think that when a book has only pictures with no written text, visualizing is rendered unnecessary. Not so. We take the clues revealed in the illustrations and combine them with the missing pictures we create in our minds to make meaning.

Alexandra Day's picture books about Carl, the babysitting rottweiler, are wonderful examples of wordless books that kids love and that we can use for the purpose of teaching visualizing. *Good Dog, Carl* tells the story of a household adventure in which Carl leads the baby on a romp through the house while the mother is out shopping.

Midway through the book, we find a picture of the baby sitting in front of a laundry chute with Carl standing right behind her. The picture on the very next page shows Carl dashing down the stairs, and when we get to this point, the kids' expressions are priceless. Many students erupt with laughter. We ask them what they visualize between the two pictures and then have them draw, write, or talk about their response. Angie Carey's first-grade class visualized an array of scenarios, including the baby falling down the laundry chute, the baby sliding down on purpose, and Carl pushing the baby down.

Cristina and Max had different mental pictures, but both had the baby headed down the chute, which is exactly what happened one way or another. Cristina visualized an elaborate floor plan of the house in relation to the laundry chute (see Figure 10.6). Max created a less complicated image but used the phrase "shot down the laundry shoot" to convey how the baby got down (see Figure 10.7). As with all comprehension strategies, we bring our schema to our mental images to make sense of things. Both Cristina's and Max's images make perfect sense.

We can alert ourselves to misconceptions by looking at student work. For instance, if a drawing had the baby sprouting wings and flying into the clouds, we would talk to the child about whether that was reasonable given the context of the story. We don't want kids to go too far afield because the purpose of visualizing is to help them better understand the actual text. One student in Angie's class drew a picture of Carl carrying the baby down the stairs. While this was closer to reality than a baby sprouting wings, it was still a misconception. The first picture clearly showed the baby at the edge of the laundry chute followed by the next picture of Carl running down the stairs, no baby on his back. In either case, we would confer with the child to help clear up any misconceptions.

Visualizing with wordless books helps readers build meaning as they go. Visualizing with text does the same thing. This lesson might become an anchor to help kids remember how visualizing helps them better comprehend. Although the examples here are from first graders, we have used wordless picture books for teaching visualizing with older kids as well, to give them a concrete sense of the strategy and how it works. They are frequently amazed at how their notion of visualizing is clarified when we show them wordless picture books.

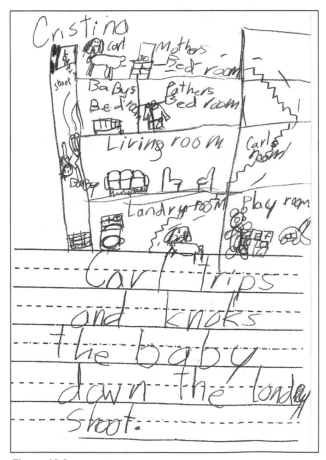

Figure 10.6
Cristina's Response to *Good Dog, Carl*

Figure 10.7
Max's Response to *Good Dog, Carl*

Visualizing in Reading, Showing Not Telling in Writing

Purpose: **Creating images with compelling nonfiction**

Resources: **Baseball, the American Epic series, including *Shadow Ball: The History of the Negro Leagues* (Ward, Burns, and O'Connor 1994) and *Who Invented the Game?* (Ward, Burns, and Walker 1994)**

Responses: **Class discussion; charting of responses**

Audience: **Intermediate and middle**

Some years ago, hordes of American baseball fans switched their channels from ESPN for several nights and glued themselves to their local public broadcasting system affiliate to watch documentary filmmaker Ken Burns's series titled *Baseball, the American Epic.* Later, much to our delight, Knopf published a series of nonfiction trade books based on the compelling documentary programs.

The print series includes *Shadow Ball* and *Who Invented the Game?* and comprises one of the most comprehensive young adult trade book accounts of baseball history. We love both books, but *Shadow Ball: The History of the Negro Leagues* stands out as one of the finest pieces of narrative nonfiction that we have ever encountered. It is striking not only for its content but also for the quality of the writing.

This book is multifaceted. We have used it to build background knowledge about the black experience in America, to develop a greater sense of the American civil rights movement, and to teach questioning and inferring. But above all, we have found it to be a terrific model for writing. *Shadow Ball* is written in such a vivid and compelling way that readers can't help but create stirring visual images in their minds when reading it. It begins this way:

> The crowd stirs with anticipation as the Indianapolis Clowns, an all-black team, take the field for their warm-ups. The second baseman's glove snaps back when he snags a quick peg from first. He hurls the ball to the third baseman, whose diving catch brings the fans to their feet. Then a batter steps to the plate. The pitcher sets, gets his signal, winds up, and throws. The batter swings. He hits it! The shortstop leaps to his right and makes a tremendous backhand stab. He jumps up, whirls, and throws to first just ahead of the sprinting runner. The low throw kicks dirt up by the first baseman's outstretched glove. The runner is out! The crowd roars.
>
> But wait! There's no ball in the first baseman's glove. The batter didn't really hit it. The Clowns were warming up in pantomime—hurling an imaginary ball so fast, making plays so convincingly, that fans could not believe it wasn't real.
>
> They called it shadow ball—and it came to stand not only for the way the black teams warmed up, but the way they were forced to play in the shadows of the all-white majors. Many black ballplayers were as good—if not better—than the big leaguers. All that kept them out was the color of their skin.

After overcoming our surprise at the pantomime warm-up and the rich shadow-ball metaphor, we can't get over the compelling writing. This is a terrific piece to point out how active, visual verbs and specific nouns enhance writing quality and paint pictures in our minds. After discussing the content, we reread it and ask the kids to close their eyes, visualize the scene, and then comment on what makes this scene come alive for them. We write their comments on a large chart:

The running
The sliding
The kicked-up dirt
The outstretched glove
The tremendous backhand stab
Snagging a quick peg from first
Hurling the ball

In this excerpt from *Shadow Ball*, all of these images and more combine to create a realistic movie in the mind. Carefully chosen nouns and verbs give writing its life. We label the nouns and verbs and ask kids to think about how these parts of speech bring such striking visual imagery to the piece. Before we finish, we encourage them to think about this vivid piece the next time they try to recount a true event in writing.

Beyond Words and Pictures:
Musical Response to Literature

Purpose: **Using the senses to interpret literature**
Resources: **GarageBand app and *Harry Potter and the Sorcerer's Stone* (Rowling)
              or other literature**
Response: **Creating sounds and songs with GarageBand**
Audience: **Intermediate and middle**

Picture a class of fifth-grade students assembled around the classroom: huddled in pairs, headphones shared; sprawled on the carpet; perched on the edge of their chairs; spread across tables. Copies of *Harry Potter and the Sorcerer's Stone* by J. K. Rowling rest open next to iPads. A constant din of quiet conversation and finger taps on glass screens fills the room. Kai Johnson had asked his language arts students to compose a musical score for a scene in *Harry Potter* by using the GarageBand app. He envisioned this as an activity for students to read closely and immerse themselves in the text, and the class quickly took the project in directions he had not imagined.

First, Kai demonstrated a few aspects of the app: starting a project, picking an instrument, "playing" the instrument. The class immediately lost interest in his explanation, browsing on their own through the variety of instruments available. Especially popular were cacophonous drumbeats and sound effects for the electric guitar.

Lesson learned: giving students fifteen minutes of unstructured time to simply explore allows them to learn about an app and find their own path in using it. Consider our own learning experiences with technology; who doesn't need to try things out to see what works? More often than not, we discover something new as we explore.

After students had ample time to explore and become familiar with the app, Kai brought the class back together and asked students to share what they discovered. Kids suggested different approaches and ideas, and Kai jotted down some guiding questions to focus their music-making:

- *What is the mood of this section?*
- *What scene do you visualize in your mind, and what are the characters feeling?*
- *If you were the director making this movie, how would you want your audience to feel? What music would you use to evoke those feelings?*

The kids carefully reread parts of the text, chose a scene, and brainstormed ideas in pairs or small groups; Kai met with them to troubleshoot technology issues. In some cases, Kai prompted the students to dig deeper into the text to explore more fully their understanding of the scene and mood.

Kids flipped through the pages to find a spot in the book that would highlight the right note of drama or terror or levity. One group placed their iPad near the classroom door to record its swoosh and creak, using the sound to highlight a particularly suspenseful moment in the corridors of Hogwarts. Two boys asked to go into a quiet room so that they could record the dialogue through a dramatic reading, later revealed to include faux British accents. Dialogue between characters was recorded again and again to get the pacing and expression just right. A student with a background in piano composed an original melody and set the bright, upbeat song to the scene when Harry is on his first train ride to Hogwarts. She explained that her idea was to capture the mix of excitement and anxiety that children know so well from starting a new year at school. The engagement and depth of thinking was impressive; kids' creativity and ingenuity with a brand-new tool surfaced interpretations of the text that Kai hadn't anticipated.

This simple activity transformed how Kai thought about the role of technology in his classroom. Students worked collaboratively, with focus and energy, motivated entirely by their own interest and engagement rather than a teacher's external prodding. Importantly, the audience for their work widened; it could now be easily shared not just with the teacher, but with their peers and families. Students moved beyond the typical responses of written words and illustrations and were expressing their understanding in an entirely novel way that allowed multiple entry points for those with a variety of learning styles. But what really surprised Kai was that students were intrinsically motivated to reread and think more deeply about the text. A "fun activity" to integrate music and technology ended up deepening kids' reading and understanding in powerful ways.

Steps to Integrate GarageBand Meaningfully into Your Reading Lesson

1. Before the lesson, download the app onto students' iPads.
2. Plan five minutes to model opening the app and selecting an instrument.
3. Give students fifteen minutes of unstructured time to "play" in the app to help them learn how to navigate it and explore options for their work.
4. Enlist the support of students already familiar with the app to go around and help their peers who are novices.
5. Take out books and model rereading to find an interesting scene.
6. Brainstorm with students key words to describe the mood in different scenes.
7. Model key questions to help them think more deeply about the section they select.
8. As some students begin to add music, encourage the ones who are finished to record their voice reading the book, partner with another student to act out multiple characters, and record sound effects to add into their musical score.
9. Differentiate by letting students work at their own pace, and allow for a range of complexity. If one group finishes quickly by recording a brief song, ask them to extend their first try, select another scene, or add other elements to their work.
10. Give an opportunity for students to stop and share their work in progress as a way to bolster collaboration and creativity. Let the ingenuity of the class emerge, and be sure to highlight and share creative strengths and ideas to deepen the activity.

Inferential Thinking: Reading Between the Lines

Inferring is the bedrock of comprehension, not only in reading. We infer in many realms. Our life clicks along more smoothly if we can read the world as well as text. If our boss looks grumpy in the morning, it might not be the best day to ask for a raise. If a kid's lips are quivering, it might be a sign to give him or her a hug. To help students understand the nature of inferential thinking, we might feign a terrified look and ask them what they can infer from our facial expression. If they mention scared or frightened, they've made an accurate inference. Inferring is about reading faces, reading body language, reading expressions, and reading tone as well as reading text.

Strategy Lessons: Inferring

Inferring Feelings with Kindergartners

Purpose: **Helping kids to better understand their own and others' feelings**
Resources: **A feelings chart and a card with the word *sad* written on it**
Response: **Clues to how students feel when their feelings match an emotion written on a card**
Audience: **Primary**

Kindergarten teacher Sue Kempton organizes a game with a twofold purpose. She wants her students to have an opportunity to explore feelings, and she hopes to help them begin to get a handle on the notion of inferential thinking. Every few days, Sue introduces a new emotion and writes it on a card. At this point, the kids have *mad, sad, happy, disappointed,* and *frustrated* in their repertoire of cards. Sue reviews the nature of these feelings and then chooses one of the cards. She pins it on the back of a class volunteer; on this day Andrew wears the card. Andrew stands in the middle of the circle and turns around several times slowly so that everyone has an opportunity to see his card. He doesn't know which card he wears on his back.

"Who has a clue for Andrew?" Sue begins. Kids raise their hands and give clues that might help Andrew figure out what word he is wearing on his back. Each student begins with "I felt that way when . . ." and completes the clue:

> . . . my sister hit me with a golf club
> . . . my dog died
> . . . my mom said we couldn't go to the Children's Museum
> . . . my dad didn't let me go to the movies
> . . . my grandpa Nick died

After five or six kids have shared their clues, Sue asks, "Okay, Andrew, can you infer what the feeling is?"

"Sad," Andrew answers triumphantly.

"Good thinking, Andrew. How did you know?" Sue asks.

"Because people get sad when animals and grandparents die," Andrew answers.

And he was right, of course. The kids love this game. As they play more often, they clarify their feelings and predict which situations might lead to one feeling or another.

Kindergartners Get the Message

Purpose: **Understanding the text and inferring the big ideas in fiction**

Resources: ***Oliver* by Birgitta Sif**

Response: **Short written and illustrated responses on sticky notes**

Audience: **Primary**

Kindergartners in Kristin Elder-Rubino's class love to hear stories—and they eagerly gather on the rug each day to listen to a picture book. Birgitta Sif's *Oliver*, a story about a little boy with a huge imagination who lives in his own world, has humorous illustrations and important messages that kids can understand and connect to. When he finds a friend at the end of the story, kids are relieved and happy to see that someone so different from everyone else finds a best friend. As they read and stop to talk about the book, they also learn that stories have many ideas that are worth discussing with your friends.

Early in the year, Kristin launches an interactive read-aloud by giving kids plenty of practice with routines such as turning and talking about the story. Rather than emphasize the talker during this routine, Kristin reminds kids that the most important job is probably to listen to what one's partner is saying, encouraging kids to take turns talking and listening to each other.

Kristin begins by thinking out loud as she reads the story, writing her thoughts on the chart. She comments and writes that Oliver does not seem to notice what's going on around him and creates his own world using his imagination. Kids chime in that Oliver is happy playing by himself with his stuffed animals, and many make a connection that they love to do that, too. When, at the end of the story, Oliver accidentally meets a little girl just like him, the kids get it. Gina comments, "Maybe they'll be friends so he doesn't have to keep playing with his stuffed animals all alone." After they talk about the ending, kids rush back to sticky notes at their tables, eager to draw and write their thinking.

While kids are encouraged to write their thoughts in invented spelling, Kristin occasionally jots a longer and more complex idea to capture a child's thinking. When she conferred with Michael, he asked her to write: "The book *Oliver* reminds me of *Corduroy*, when Lisa got to bring him home and hugged him and became friends." He and Kristin discussed the idea that both main characters in these stories found friends in unusual places. Cullen chimed in on the conversation, showing Kristin and Michael his drawing of two houses, one Oliver's and one Olivia's. He asked Kristin to write "I'm glad they found each other." At the end of the lesson, the kids eagerly put their sticky notes on a big chart (Figure 10.8), coming up to share their thoughts and the big ideas in the story: that having an imagination is great, but it may be even better to have friends.

Figure 10.8
Students' Responses to *Oliver*

Making Inferences in Media

Purpose: **Applying inferring skills to images and media in order to become critical viewers as well as readers**

Resources: **The image of an elephant rampaging through a city in India from the *New York Times* (2016) website "What's Going On in This Picture?" or any other image**

Responses: **Annotating images and sharing using digital tools**

Audience: **Intermediate and middle**

We've long known that students gain important information from images in a text. Learning to examine, evaluate, and infer from images is a skill that all students benefit from. Now in a digital world filled with images this lesson becomes even more critical.

Teacher Arlene Amonte uses this lesson across the curriculum in her fourth-grade classroom. She offers a variety of images for students to examine and evaluate—to teach students how to make thoughtful inferences, to help launch a unit of study, and as a way to give access to all students in her class. When digital tools are available, she uses them to provide high-quality color images for students to examine carefully and closely. In classrooms with many devices it is easy to give students digital copies and have them use any number of apps to type, write, circle, or highlight on the image. Without devices you can provide printed copies, perhaps to small groups, and annotate by hand. Either way, the power comes in sharing the thinking. Students might do a gallery walk or share on a personal blog so that they can write about their ideas. Today Arlene is asking students to post to Padlet, an online bulletin-board website.

Arlene projects her first image on the screen to pique student interest as the kids gather materials and come to the carpet. "What do you see in the image and what does it make you think?" she asks as students gather. "Today we're going to make inferences based on evidence in the images."

Arlene first models this process, showing how she is sure to find evidence in the image for each inference she makes. She displays a few images to the entire class, using a projector, and uses explicit language:

> *I see . . . which makes me infer . . .*
> *I'm inferring that . . . because I notice . . .*
> *These details here make me think . . .*
> *I infer . . . because when I look at the image, I see . . .*

The students join in, using the language of inferring as they work in partners discussing, reflecting, and sharing with the class. Once students have demonstrated that they understand the challenge of the day, they move off to practice in partners to annotate a new image with their thinking. Arlene works with small groups, pairs, or individuals, depending on the needs of her students.

While students work, Arlene listens carefully to ensure that students are applying the inferring strategy with ample evidence for their thinking.

> *Jeremy, I notice that you say you're inferring that this image is from a desert. What makes you think that? Could it also be someone at the beach? What evidence do we see for each theory? Let's look carefully at the details so that we make sure our inferences are really grounded in the image we are looking at.*

The powerful piece of this lesson is that all of Arlene's students have access to the image regardless of reading ability. This access allows all kids to participate in the discussion and have thoughtful conversations with each other, while reinforcing that inferences must be based in evidence from the text.

One strategy that Arlene uses with today's lesson is to have students share their thinking on a digital bulletin board. For this she uses the Padlet website (https://padlet.com). There, students follow the link to the online bulletin board she has created and are able to share their thinking with the entire class (Figure 10.9). This quick snapshot of student thinking serves several purposes: it gives kids a wider audience for their work, provides a view of the work of the entire class, and acts as formative assessment data for the teacher. Students find this medium engaging and interesting and benefit from being able to read and respond to one another's ideas on a larger scale.

Additional resources: For images or media clips for making inferences check out pics4learning.com; the *New York Times* What's Going On in This Picture? website, or a daily student news outlet like Time for Kids. For media clips, The Kid Should See This has a variety of thought-provoking videos.

Figure 10.9
Students' Responses in Padlet

Nate
I see people running away. They are running up the stairs. This makes me think the elephant is dangerous.

Heidi
I see an elephant crushing bikes with his feel which makes me think he is on a rampage through the street. I see people running away and watching him. I think that they are scared because I would be scared if I saw a mad elephant in the street.

Sara
I see lots of bikes. Is this a place where people park their bikes? I see bags, it makes me think this is a market of some kind.

I see a lot of people up on the things behind fences does that mean they are watching a show?

Laura
I see things being destroyed. I'm inferring this elephant escaped from a zoo or something.

Inferring and Visualizing with Poetry

Purpose: **Constructing the meaning of a poem through inferential thinking**
Resource: **The poem "Celebrations of Earth" by Stuart Franklin (2000)**
Response: **Annotations on a poem**
Audience: **Intermediate and middle**

Poetry is both a highly visual and inferential genre. Poems are often loaded with figurative language, and poets try to paint pictures with their words. So inferring and visualizing are two strategies that are very helpful to us when we are reading and understanding poetry.

Steph models this lesson with a poem from *National Geographic Magazine*:

> *Celebrations of Earth*
> A small planet in a modest solar system
> a tumbling pebble in the cosmic stream
> and yet . . .
> This home is built of many mansions,
> carved by wind and the fall of water,
> lush with living things beyond number,
> perfumed by salt spray and blossoms.
> Here cool in a cloak of mist
> or there steaming under a brazen sun
> Earth's variety excites the senses and exalts the soul.

She begins by explaining that poets often search for words that represent ideas in ways that prose does not, and that poets really try to paint pictures with their words so that the reader can visualize what the poem is saying. Poems are often shorter than most prose, and poets try to capture meaning with minimal text, which requires us to think inferentially when constructing meaning in poetry.

As she shares this poem, she thinks aloud and annotates it so kids can see how she goes about making meaning. She infers that the first line, "A small planet in a modest solar system," probably refers to Earth, especially since the title is "Celebrations of Earth." She has the kids turn and talk about what they think that line in the poem means and what they are inferring as she continues thinking aloud and annotating.

As she moves to the next line, "a tumbling pebble in the cosmic stream," she shares how she infers that the pebble is the poet's way of seeing Earth as it orbits the sun. She continues to share how she visualizes Earth as a place with canyons carved by the wind, and oceans giving off salt spray. She codes her inferences with an *I* and her visualizations with a *V*. Throughout her think-aloud, she continues to have kids discuss the poem and talk about what they are inferring and visualizing. Her annotated version of the poem is shown in Figure 10.10.

Figure 10.10
Steph's Annotations of "Celebrations of Earth"

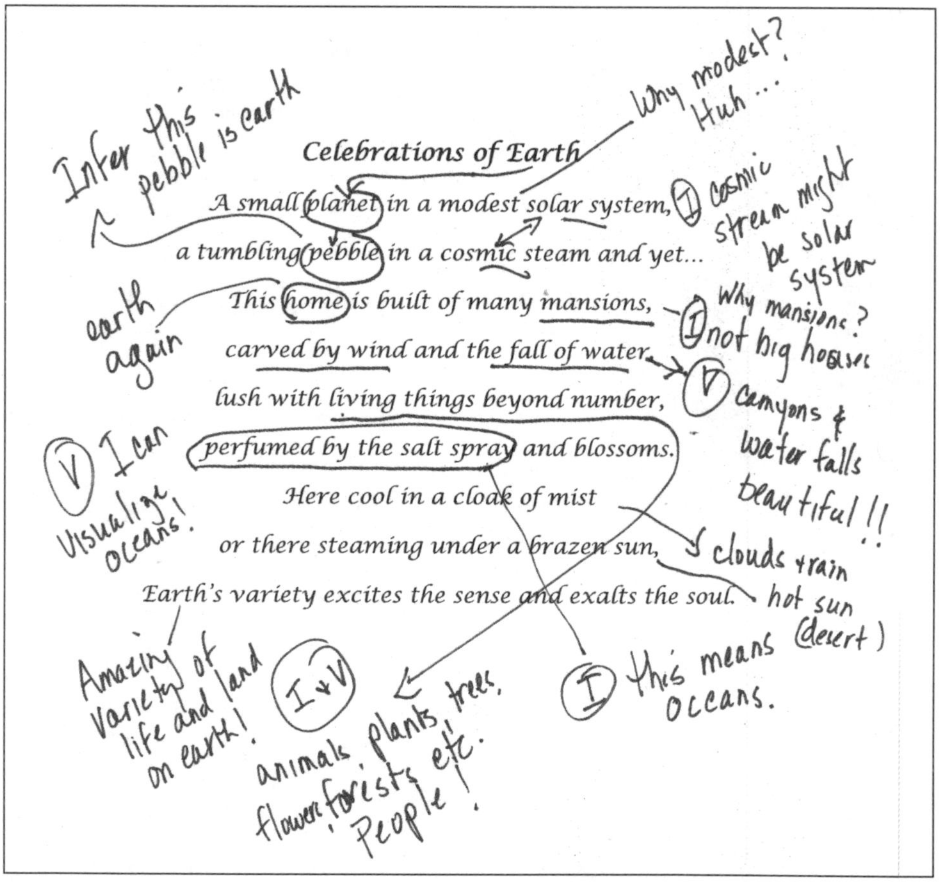

After modeling, she hands out several poems to these fourth graders, including "He's Still Here," written by a wonderful teacher (and poet) Holly Occhipinti. Gabriel and Rachel choose Holly's poem and work together to reason through it. They infer and visualize to understand it, as well as make connections as they read. They annotate the poem like Steph did as she modeled (see Figure 10.11).

We need to share much more poetry with our kids. They love the sound, the flow, and the puzzle of it. And inferring and visualizing offer a key to unlocking the meaning.

Figure 10.11
Gabriel and Rachel's Annotated Poem

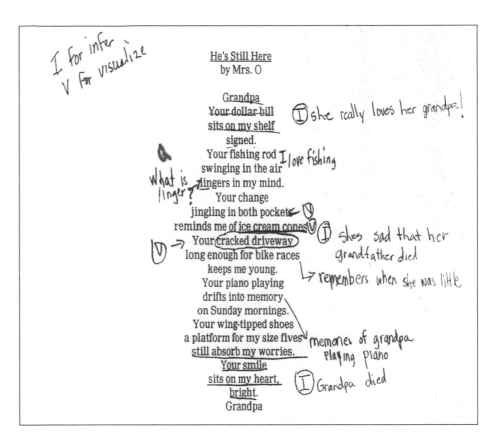

Inferring from Images and Text in Nonfiction

Purpose: **Using images, features, and simple text to infer information**

Resources: **Simple nonfiction books with vivid photographs, various features, and text**

Responses: **Drawings and explanations inferred from the text and images**

Audience: **Primary and intermediate**

Teachers often ask how kids use inferential thinking to gain information in nonfiction. In fact, inferential thinking is one of the primary ways that children access and learn information. Show kids a photograph of a great white shark and have them turn and talk about what they can learn simply from viewing the photo. "Must be a carnivore," a child may quip after noticing the sharp teeth. Ask them what makes them think that and most will shout out, "The teeth!" Show them a diagram of a volcano erupting and someone will almost certainly infer that anybody living close is in trouble. This is inferring at its simplest and most useful.

In fact, we do it so frequently that we may not even notice that we are inferring. We need to teach kids explicitly to read and view closely so they can use their inferential skills to more fully understand the information derived from illustrations, photos, maps, diagrams, close-ups, and, of course, text. We often ask kids to illustrate and/or explain any information they inferred from viewing features and reading text. And we don't just do this lesson one time only. Viewing and analyzing features is a practice that we engage in every time we read for information. So inferring is one of the most powerful avenues we have for learning information.

Analyzing Infographics: Understanding and Interpreting Visual and Text Features

Purpose: **Inferring about words, illustrations, and features to learn from infographics**

Resources: **Loreen Leedy's *The Shocking Truth About Energy***

Response: **Organize information, inferences, and conclusions on a chart**

Audience: **Intermediate and middle**

Infographics barely existed when we wrote the previous edition of *Strategies That Work*, and now they are ubiquitous. The short text, engaging illustrations, vivid colors, and sheer variety of visuals make infographics appealing to young readers. Once we begin to dig into the array of visuals and text, however, the information and ideas on these popular graphics may be more complex than is apparent at first glance. We teach kids to slow down, pay careful attention to the visuals, and merge their thinking with many different kinds of clues to fill in gaps that the author or illustrator may not have fully explained.

Engaging and informative, Loreen Leedy's book *The Shocking Truth About Energy* makes an often-complicated topic fun for kids to learn about. Packing a lot of information and concepts into each infographic, Leedy makes the often-abstract science behind energy sources such as solar power, wind power, and geothermal power concrete and comprehensible for kids. To get the full meaning of the infographics in the book, Jeanette Scotti's fifth graders needed to fire up their detective skills to infer and draw conclusions about the catchy but complex illustrations and text. Kids worked together to closely read sparse text, interpret visuals, and pool their collective background knowledge as they plumbed the meaning of arrows, diagrams, and other nonfiction features.

In the first part of this lesson, the class analyzed an infographic about fossil fuels. Although they had quite a bit of background knowledge, students had to slow down when they came to unfamiliar information describing how fossil fuels were formed to closely view and read the visuals and the text. To make the process of reading and interpreting the infographic more visible, Jeanette guided the kids to create a class chart explaining how they pulled out important information and made inferences about it. Then kids turned and talk about their conclusions, referring to the infographic for evidence.

How We Read, View, and Interpret Infographics

Visuals/Features/Text	Information	Inferences/Conclusions
Arrows show a process; illustrations clarify this.	How coal, oil, and natural gas formed in prehistoric times	If coal and oil were formed a long time ago, we infer that this isn't happening anymore. But is it?
Illustration and a thought bubble	Takes a long time for fossil fuels to form	If it takes so long for these to form, must be using up coal, oil, and natural gas.

Once kids reached the conclusions, shown in the chart, their inferences sparked lingering questions. Those questions were the perfect segue to explore another infographic in the book—one that explained the science behind global warming. Jeanette projected the infographic titled "Earth is getting hotter because of Global Warming." on the document camera—and posted versions of the kids' questions up on the screen:

- What is global warming?
- How is it related to fossil fuels and pollution?
- What will happen to the earth as a result of global warming?

As Jeanette introduced this infographic, the class noted a play on words: "It's a hot topic." They immediately interpreted this to mean that there is a lot of talk about global warming and that the topic is controversial. They also discussed the big idea of the infographic, "The earth is getting hotter because of global warming." As they noticed various features on the infographic, kids realized that it was explaining a process: how and why the earth is getting hotter. Small groups continued to interpret the text and visuals and draw inferences and conclusions, creating their own charts as they analyzed the infographic. As Jeanette wrapped up the lesson, the kids voiced their amazement at how much information they had learned from a single infographic.

Figure 10.12
The Global Warming Infographic

Inferring the Meaning of Unfamiliar Words

Purpose: **Using context clues to crack open vocabulary**

Resource: ***Fly High! The Story of Bessie Coleman* by Louise Borden and Mary Kay Kroeger**

Responses: **A four-column think sheet titled Word/Inferred Meaning/Clues/Sentence and a chart with the same titles**

Audience: **Intermediate**

Readers are frequently frustrated when they meet unfamiliar vocabulary words as they read. Jumping up and grabbing a dictionary takes time and wrests readers out of the text. Asking the teacher can be time consuming as well. One of the quickest and most effective ways of dealing with unfamiliar vocabulary is through inferential thinking. To figure out the meaning of unfamiliar words, readers need to take what they know and gather clues in the text to crack the meaning of vocabulary. They need to consider the context to understand what they read.

James Allen, a third-grade teacher, introduced his students to a four-column think sheet headed Word/Inferred Meaning/Clues/Sentence to help them figure out the meaning of unfamiliar words. James modeled this lesson with the picture book *Fly High! The Story of Bessie Coleman*, the gripping story of an extraordinary woman who has the distinction of having been both the first woman and the first African American pilot. James created a four-column lesson chart with headings identical to the ones on the think sheet. As he read the story aloud, he asked kids to raise their hands when he came to a word that they had never heard before. Several pages into the story, he read the sentence "Bessie's brother Walter had moved to Chicago years ago when Bessie was little. Now Walter was a fine Pullman porter." Hands waved in the air. Few, if any, of the kids knew the meaning of the term *Pullman porter*.

So James wrote *Pullman porter* in the first column on the chart and then thought through how he could crack the meaning of that term. He first tried to read on, but to no avail. Then he tried rereading and that didn't help either. Luckily for him, there was a picture at the top of the page of a gentleman in a uniform carrying a suitcase and helping a young woman off the train. So James shared his thinking of how he inferred that a Pullman porter was a railroad worker who carried bags for people as they boarded and disembarked the train. He then proceeded to fill in the chart with the word, the inferred meaning, and the clue that helped him infer (which was the picture in this case). Then, together with the kids, he wrote a sentence in the final column. James explained that the purpose of writing the sentence was to demonstrate understanding of the word. As James continued reading, the kids raised their hands at different points in the text, and together with their teacher they co-constructed the following anchor chart:

Word	Inferred Meaning	Clues	Sentence
Pullman porter	Railroad worker who carries bags and helps passengers	Picture	The Pullman porter helped the woman onto the train.
manicurist	Someone who trims nails	Reading on	A manicurist trims nails.
The Defender	The name of something	Capital letters	The Defender was a Chicago newspaper.

After James modeled this lesson for the whole class, he gave them each their own think sheet and asked them to practice this in their own reading. So they jotted down unfamiliar words and used the context to infer the meaning. This became a regular practice in James's classroom and provided ongoing support to his kids as they came across unfamiliar words and tried to discern the meaning.

Recognizing Plot and Inferring Themes

Purpose: **Differentiating between plot and theme, and inferring the big ideas or themes**

Resource: ***Teammates*, by Peter Golenbock**

Responses: **Class discussion; chart of themes; theme boards**

Audience: **Intermediate and middle**

Literature, both fiction and nonfiction, is rife with themes. Books and articles rarely promote just one main idea but rather several for readers to ponder and infer. When we talk to students about themes, we help them discern the difference between theme and plot. We explain that the plot is simply what happens in the narrative. The themes represent the bigger ideas of the story. The plot carries those ideas along. To demonstrate plot, we choose a simple narrative that everyone is likely to be familiar with. We might recount the plot of *Goldilocks and the Three Bears* by summarizing the events of the story as follows. A girl named Goldilocks was wandering through the forest and entered an unfamiliar, empty house. She tasted porridge that didn't belong to her, broke a chair, and slept in a bed that wasn't hers. She was caught when the bears returned, and she ran out of the house scared to death.

We explain to our students that themes are the underlying ideas, morals, and lessons that give the story its texture, depth, and meaning. The themes are rarely explicitly stated in the story. We infer themes. Themes often make us feel angry, sad, guilty, joyful, frightened. We tell kids that we are likely to feel themes in our gut. To help students more clearly understand the difference, we might ask, "What are the bigger ideas in *Goldilocks and the Three Bears*?" Kids tend to identify taking things that don't belong to you, selfishness, thoughtlessness, and so on. They have experienced these notions and they understand them.

A nonfiction picture book we have used to demonstrate inferring themes is Peter Golenbock's *Teammates*. It is the moving story of Jackie Robinson's courageous breakthrough into the all-white major leagues. It goes beyond the history and describes the personal relationship between Jackie and his white teammate Pee Wee Reese. Pee Wee was the only player on the Brooklyn Dodgers team who supported Jackie's quest.

To continue their study of inferring, Steph demonstrated a think-aloud with *Teammates* to the fifth graders in Jennifer Jones's class the day after taking them through the Goldilocks exercise. After describing the difficult, segregated life of players in the Negro leagues, Golenbock writes that life was much better for players in the major leagues. They were paid well, and many were famous all over the world. Steph coded her sticky note *I* for Inference while noting that this kind of racial inequality might breed anger. She suggested that both racial inequality and anger might be themes in the story even though the writer hadn't written those very words. So Steph created an anchor chart headed Evidence from the Text/Themes. Under Evidence from the Text, she wrote *Words, Actions, Pictures* and explained that we can infer themes from the words in the text, the actions of characters, and the pictures and illustrations. All of these provide evidence that supports the bigger ideas and themes we infer in a narrative.

When Curtis heard that Branch Rickey, the manager of the Brooklyn Dodgers, was looking for a man who "would have to possess the self-control not to fight back when opposing players tried to intimidate or hurt him," he suggested that self-control might be a theme. Steph concurred and added it to the chart and pointed out that Curtis was using evidence from the text. When Steph finished reading the story, she facilitated a discussion about the bigger ideas in the narrative based on text evidence.

"Jackie was alone without a single friend. No one would sit near him or talk to him," Chantal mentioned.

"Good noticing, Chantal. Why didn't he get mad about that?" Steph asked.

"Because he had a lot of self-control. The manager wanted a man who wouldn't fight back, no matter how mad he got, and Jackie never did."

"Chantal, that is exactly how we use evidence to infer a theme. Let's put your thinking up on the chart," Steph suggested. She wrote *self-control* in the Themes column and then *Jackie never fought back* in the Evidence column.

"So, what might be another theme?" Steph asked.

"I know how he felt. When I moved here, I didn't have one single friend. I felt really lonely," Rogers said. So Steph added *loneliness* to the chart and cited Rogers's evidence.

"But Pee Wee was his friend," Jaquon added.

"So, is friendship a theme?" Steph asked.

"Sort of, but most of the team would not be his friend because he was black," Jaquon continued.

"That's racist," Curtis added.

"It sure is racist, Curtis. Are racism and friendship both themes in *Teammates*?" Steph asked.

The kids nodded, and Steph added both of those themes to the chart along with the evidence for them. And so the discussion went for nearly forty-five minutes, culminating in a long list of themes and evidence for them. Some of the themes that surfaced included racial inequality, segregation, anger, taking a stand, and bravery.

Steph reiterated that all of these themes represented the bigger ideas in the story and that most of them evoked strong feelings. We have noticed that kids are more likely to remember important themes when they derive the ideas themselves and feel them deeply. It is our role to help draw students out through engaging discussions about the bigger ideas in the story. Often, the kids used their prior knowledge to infer themes and better understand the narrative, as Rogers did when he mentioned being the new kid on the block. As students talk about the bigger ideas, it is our responsibility to help them label the ideas, articulate the themes, and cite text evidence. Inferring after all is about taking what we know, our background knowledge, and combining it with clues or evidence in the text to draw a conclusion or, in this case, surface a theme.

On the following day, Steph handed out a think sheet that matched the chart, with the headings Evidence from the Text/Themes. The kids went back and reread and reconsidered *Teammates*. They cited evidence from the text and recorded themes they discovered during the first read as well as themes that surfaced on their second reading and reviewing of the text. (See some of their think sheets in the assessment section of this chapter.)

Distinguishing Between Major Themes and Minor Themes

Purpose: **Rereading to notice the preponderance of evidence and understand more deeply**

Resource: ***Teammates* by Peter Golenbock**

Response: **Two-column chart titled Major Themes/Minor Themes**

Audience: **Intermediate and middle**

After several days of small groups working together to infer themes in *Teammates*, Steph thought it might be a good idea to help the fifth graders in Jennifer Jones's class distinguish between major themes and minor themes. She and Jennifer had taught them that as long as there was evidence for a theme in the words, actions, or pictures in the text, kids could identify it as a theme. This is true, of course. But writers often give more credence to some themes above others. They dedicate more words to the themes that are most important to them, and they allot more space to those major themes. Steph decided it might be helpful for kids to begin to discern the difference.

As she brought this up, she explained that some themes seemed to have more evidence in the text than others. She suggested that those themes the author wrote most about might be considered major themes. She noted that those with less evidence, while still important themes, might be considered minor themes.

As Steph modeled her own thinking, she began with the title. "I know something about titles," she said. "Writers spend a lot of time thinking about the best title. Sometimes it is really hard to come up with one, but they often try to assign a title that synthesizes one of the most important ideas in the book. The cover is important too. So I'm thinking that the picture of both Jackie and Pee Wee on the cover and the title of *Teammates* suggests that being true friends and teammates might be one of the major themes in this book. Turn and talk. What do you think after having read this several times?" The kids agreed with Steph so she jotted *Teammates and Friendship* under the column for major themes.

"Now, besides the title and cover, another way writers try to let us know what they think are the most important themes is the amount of space they devote to that theme. Sometimes we call this real estate, meaning the more pages alloted to one idea, the more likely that is to be a major theme. And the fewer pages devoted to an idea, the more likely that is to be a minor theme."

Steph continued paging through the story and asking kids to discuss what each page was mostly about and what themes the writer seemed to give the most attention to. The kids quickly noticed that the first five pages were almost exclusively about racism, prejudice, and segregation. They all concurred that the writer gave a lot of real estate to these themes and that they were definitely major themes in the book. They also found a good deal of evidence for *courage*, on the parts of Branch Rickey, Jackie, and Pee Wee and *determination* in Jackie. They decided that there was less evidence for *anger*, although there was enough to call it a minor theme. And so it went as they paged through the book.

It's important to note that readers of this age would likely have difficulty distinguishing between major and minor themes on a first read. Rereading closely with a purpose such as this takes readers to a deeper, more complete understanding of text. And Steph made sure that kids understood that the minor themes were not necessarily less important to the reader, but that the writer was more concerned with the themes he gave the most attention to. She reminded them, however, that the reader writes the story and what matters most to them is also very important.

Theme Boards: Hey, What's the Big Idea?

Jennifer continued to work on surfacing themes throughout the year. She reported that her students became quite adept at inferring themes as well as labeling them and distinguishing between major and minor themes. They even began to notice when certain ones appeared over and over in a wide range of texts. To reinforce theme identification and the connections between themes in one text and those in another, Jennifer established a theme board headed Hey, What's the Big Idea? Each time the class read a book, they developed a theme list and added the list to the theme board.

Understanding Graphic Novels: Inferring and Visualizing for Deeper Comprehension

Purpose: **Inferring from the illustrations and text in a graphic novel**

Resource: ***El Deafo*, by Cece Bell**

Response: **Jotting and sketching on sticky notes**

Audience: **Intermediate and middle**

Graphic novels are increasingly popular in classrooms around the country. Although many students enjoy the genre because they resemble comic books, graphic novels challenge students to use inferring and visualizing as well as other strategies to explore complex ideas. They're not as easy or straightforward as they appear to be.

El Deafo uses the subject of disability as a springboard to address more universal themes of friendship, school, and coming-of-age—issues that kids find engaging. Cece Bell's memoir about her childhood is a particularly vivid mix of themes and events that tell her incredible life story. Due to an illness when she is very young, Cece loses most of her hearing. Her life is filled with challenges—new schools, new friends, her family's move—all while learning how to read lips and fit in with hearings aids. In a profound realization, Cece eventually comes to think of being deaf not as a disability, but a superpower. With a special school hearing aid, she is privy to all manner of secrets throughout the school day. How's that for turning disability into possibility? (For more information, listen to an interview with Cece herself at http://www.npr.org/2014/12/14/369599042/el-deafo-how-a-girl-turned-her-disability-into-a-superpower.)

Graphic novels present their own particular challenges for the reader. Each page is a series of panels resembling a movie storyboard. The space limits of each panel on the page means the illustrations and the text leave much unstated. Readers have to fill in the gaps, making inferences about events, actions, and feelings. Students must build the scene and story in their minds, visualizing and inferring what's not explicit in the illustrations or words on the page.

This requires a different approach to reading, and students need instruction in ways to decipher the visuals and text in order to get the most out of the text. Once kids understand that the reader has to make inferences and create mind pictures even with lots of illustrations right there in the text, kids often get hooked on the genre. Emergent readers often become the genre's most fervent fans.

Teacher Kai Johnson thought out loud about the first few pages of the book, showing what he did as a reader to make sense of the text. Kids immediately began chiming in with their observations.

One child said, "Look, that bubble seems different—it looks like a cloud—it must be a thought bubble!" Kids paid close attention to this comment—and they began distinguishing between "thought bubbles" that show the characters' inner conversations and "speech bubbles" that capture what characters actually say. Other students noticed the different font colors in certain speech bubbles at the beginning of the text and drew inferences that helped them analyze how challenging it would be to go through the world without clear hearing.

Guiding the kids, Kai asked them to find a page with both a speech and a thought bubble and discuss in partners what Cece thinks to herself, comparing this with what she actually says to others. Conversations erupted as students found examples and made connections to the multiple instances in their own lives. They dug deeper into the challenges Cece faces as a young kid trying to fit in: can she always say what's on her mind? Students observed that "we all say things that are different from what we are thinking," especially when it comes to our friends.

Kids went off to read with a partner or independently, and Kai conferred with one pair. When kids made inferences, a question usually wasn't far behind. They also sketched their insights about the characters' interactions. As the students drew inferences and created their own images detailing Cece's many challenges, they wondered: "Will she have a 'normal' childhood? How much does she understand about what is happening to her? Why don't the other kids understand what she is going through?"

Students reviewed the sticky notes they created while reading the story and selected a scene they wanted to explain in depth. After snapping a quick photo, the students synthesized their thinking into a verbal narrative of the scene. They explained what occurs on the page but also offered their insights about what is on Cece's mind on that page. See examples of their interpretations in the assessment section at the end of this chapter.

From his experiences with students who loved *El Deafo*, Kai discovered many ways to encourage students to infer based on their own experiences and insights. Students who were strong visual learners loved the opportunity to build understanding by filling in the missing pieces with their own interpretations and mental images. Students who typically resist reading dense text eagerly devoured page after page of panels, reading closely while feeling their confidence grow as they finished the book in a matter of days. Students internalized some of the illustration techniques and used them in their drawings throughout the year. Storyboard panels become a great way for students to visualize to explain their understanding. (See kids' work examples in the assessment section at the end of the chapter.)

Inferring and Visualizing to Understand Historical Concepts

Purpose: **Inferring and visualizing to understand ideas and concepts in historical fiction**

Resource: ***Encounter* by Jane Yolen**

Responses: **Inferring and visualizing to analyze and interpret big ideas and messages**

Audience: **Intermediate and middle**

Powerful picture books bring ideas and concepts in history to life, so we use them whenever possible to provide a thoughtful introduction to topics from far away and long ago. The compelling illustrations and evocative language in Jane Yolen's *Encounter*, a fictionalized account of Columbus's encounter with the Taino people, is told from the perspective of a Taino child.

The book's message is that history is all about different perspectives, and it sparks larger questions about what it means to "discover" a new land. The important historical concepts are brought to life with the story of this encounter between colonizers and indigenous people, whose very survival was threatened with the arrival of the Europeans. The essential question teacher Hilary Barthel posed was "What does it mean to discover something?"

Kids in Hilary's fifth-grade class are bilingual in English and Spanish. The complex language of the English version of this book is challenging because the young Taino boy telling the story has never seen Europeans, so their clothing, weapons, and actions are strange to him. The language he uses to describe what is happening is grounded in his view of the world and his unique perspective, so the reader has to carefully infer from and interpret both the words and illustrations in the text.

Before introducing the story, the kids' had gained some background knowledge about the topic by reading about the Taino culture in Spanish. Introducing the inferring equation,

Background Knowledge + Text Clues = Inference, Hilary modeled her own thinking and showed kids how to use their prior knowledge about the Taino culture to interpret and infer from the words and illustrations.

Kids were hooked as they read about the Taino child's dream that foreshadowed Columbus's ships arriving at their island; they became reading detectives, piecing together the visual and text clues to understand what happened.

As they read the end of the story, when the young Taino boy is now an old man reflecting on the tragic changes that this encounter brought to his land and people, the kids truly understood what had happened. They inferred from his last words, "So it was we lost our lands to the strangers from the sky. We gave our souls to their gods. We took their speech into our mouths, forgetting our own." The kids inferred that the Taino people had lost their culture amidst the coming of many Spanish to their lands; students noticed that in the illustration, the old man's feet were disappearing into the sea, which prompted Diego to infer that the man was forgetting his identity and realized his people and their way of life were disappearing. As the story came to its sad end, the kids' sobering conclusions about the reasons for the demise of the Taino culture spurred them to want to investigate further the original essential question "What does it mean to discover something?" They had a whole list of questions: "What other people and cultures did this happen to? Could this happen today? Has this ever happened in our country?" Coming to understand different perspectives, in this way, sparked kids' interest in history and motivated them to want to find out more. (See student work in the assessment section at the end of this chapter.)

Rereading to Clear Up Misconceptions

When we come across information that surprises us, such as Nellie's blindness in *See the Ocean* or the phantom baseball game in *Shadow Ball*, we can't help but flip back through the pages and search for the clues we missed that might have led us to draw a more accurate inference earlier in our reading. Readers need to stay on their toes to make meaning, checking for misconceptions as they go. And teachers need to look closely at student work and listen intently to student comments to nip misconceptions in the bud.

As a little girl, whenever Steph heard the Christmas carol "Silent Night," an image of a large, round Friar Tuck sort of character appeared in her mind. It wasn't until later that she realized that this misconception had originated in her confusion about the words of the song. Where it actually said "round yon Virgin," Steph had always heard it as "round John. . . ." She visualized a fat, jolly monk. This misconception disrupted meaning and kept her from fully understanding the carol.

Encourage your kids to go back through the text to check their mind pictures and inferences, and remind them to check their thinking with someone else if it doesn't seem to make sense. A good reality check can go a long way toward keeping Friar Tucks at bay. Visualizing and inferring are strategies that enhance understanding, but if ill conceived, they can just as easily hinder understanding. Rereading is one of the best ways to check for meaning. It all makes so much sense the second time through.

Teaching with the End in Mind: Assessing What We've Taught

Inferring and Visualizing

Based on the lessons in this chapter, we look for evidence that

1. *Students visualize and create mental images to make sense of what they read.* As students listen to and read text, we look for evidence that they draw and write about their mental images or mind pictures to support understanding.

2. *Students infer the meaning of unfamiliar words.* We look for evidence that students are using the context to figure out the meaning of words and concepts that elude them.

3. *Students use text evidence to infer themes and big ideas.* We look for evidence that students are merging their background knowledge with clues in the text to surface themes and big ideas.

4. *Students infer and draw conclusions from many different texts and genres.* They also infer from a variety of text features, including infographics, diagrams, illustrations, and so on. We look for evidence that students enhance their understanding and build knowledge in all genres.

Suggestions for Differentiation

Visualizing and inferring lend themselves to differentiation. We cannot overestimate the importance of drawing as a means to understanding. When kids draw to clarify understanding, they are constructing meaning. Sensory imaging is about more than just visualizing. Kids taste, touch, feel, and smell their way through books as well as through experiences. So we model using all of our senses to understand what we read, hear, and view. Many times kids can express through drawing what they may have difficulty articulating in oral or written words.

We teach inferring in many contexts outside of text. Playing charades is a wonderful way for kids to get a concrete idea of what it means to infer. Role playing and drama also encourage kids to act out their understanding of what they read. Sharing unfamiliar items and objects like kitchen utensils, old-fashioned tools, and so forth require kids to use inferential thinking to make sense of them and infer their purposes. All of these activities give kids a more concrete idea of what it is to infer.

Visualizing and Inferring Assessment Commentary

Two-column think sheets on inferring themes using text evidence from the lesson "Recognizing Plot and Inferring Themes"

Evedance from the text (words, pictures, ideas)	Themes
Pee Wee looked into his tzanates bold, painced eyes.	caring
He had done nothing to be taonted. He just wanted to be equal.	equality
PeeWee smiled at Jakie and he smiled back.	kindness
Pee Wee put his arm around Jakie's sholdurs	frendship
The crowd gasped when Pee Wee put his arm wrouned Jakies	astonishment

Josh

◀ Josh's think sheet about *Teammates*, by Peter Golenbock, shows a good understanding of using evidence to infer themes. In each case, Josh used the pictures, the words, and/or ideas as evidence for themes.

Evidence from the Text Luke (Words, Pictures, Ideas)	Luke Themes
• Couldn't drink from same water fountain, " "	• Fairness/Unfairness
	• segregation
• didn't challenge segregation	• fear
	• apathy
• Branch R. believed seg was unfair and wanted to give everyone the same chance	• resistence to change
	• equal opportunity
• Brave by joining on all white team	• violence
• taking abbuse	• brave
• not fighting back.	• self control
	• Friendship
• Friendship with Pee wee	• Lonelyness
	• Pain on the outside
• Sitting alone	• Pain on the inside
• kicking him	• anger
• People threatning him would make mad	not kind words against jackie
	• hate
	• race, ism

▲ Luke also was able to use text evidence to surface themes. Although he has a good understanding of the story and some terrific ideas, we would confer with him regarding his organizational style. One of the purposes of a graphic organizer is to organize thinking, and his is a bit all over the page. He does draw arrows, but if he were to reread for information, he might struggle finding which piece of evidence relates to a given theme.

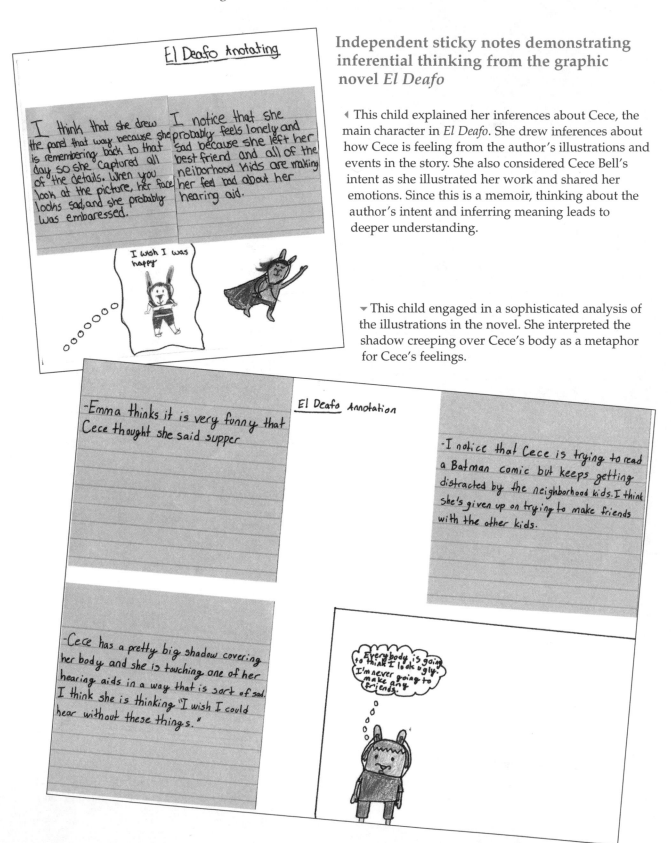

Independent sticky notes demonstrating inferential thinking from the graphic novel *El Deafo*

◂ This child explained her inferences about Cece, the main character in *El Deafo*. She drew inferences about how Cece is feeling from the author's illustrations and events in the story. She also considered Cece Bell's intent as she illustrated her work and shared her emotions. Since this is a memoir, thinking about the author's intent and inferring meaning leads to deeper understanding.

▾ This child engaged in a sophisticated analysis of the illustrations in the novel. She interpreted the shadow creeping over Cece's body as a metaphor for Cece's feelings.

Illustrated think sheet about the picture book *Encounter* from the lesson "Inferring and Visualizing to Understand Historical Concepts"

▾ Fourth-grader Osvaldo demonstrates how he inferred from the words, events, and illustrations. He included salient quotes and events from the text; his elaborate inferences and succinct illustrations are a great example of the deeper understanding kids develop as they delve into the text language and ideas.

Chapter 11

Determining Importance in Text: The Nonfiction Connection

Many years ago a large footlocker arrived at Steph's door. Her parents, their kids grown, had sold the house where she had grown up and moved to another. In the move, they boxed all of her remaining possessions and sent them out to Steph in Denver. As the padlock clicked free, the top of the trunk burst open and childhood treasures of every imaginable size and shape poured out. Stuffed animals, glossy black-and-white photographs of Hollywood movie stars, her collection of Nancy Drew books, a well-loved Raggedy Andy doll, a 1954 edition of Dr. Seuss's *If I Ran the Zoo*, and even her kindergarten report card cascaded over the sides.

As Steph peeled away the layers of her life, she came upon several hulking college textbooks lining the bottom of the trunk. When she opened a tome titled *Modern European History*, a blast of yellow blinded her. Page after page of white space and black print had been shaded neon yellow, the result of Steph's bout with mad highlighting disease! Throughout her education, teachers had instructed Steph to highlight the important parts. But no one had shown her how. She assumed that if the writers of these massive textbooks had written it down, it must be important. So she highlighted just about every letter of print. Highlighting is easy; determining what to highlight is the challenge.

For years in schools, students everywhere have been asked to pick out the most important information when they read, to highlight essential ideas, to isolate supporting details, and to read for specific information. This is easier said than done. When we read nonfiction, we can't possibly remember every fact, nor should we. To expand our understanding, we need to focus on information and merge it with what we already know about a topic. We remember facts and details better when we link them to larger concepts. We separate what's important from what's interesting. We distinguish between what we think is most important and what the writer most wants us to get out of the text. Only after we sort and sift details from the important information can we arrive at a main idea.

The strategy lessons in this chapter are designed to help readers sift and sort information and make sense of the barrage of information that crosses their radar screens every day.

The Link Between the Strategy of Determining Importance and the Genre of Nonfiction

When we teach the strategy of determining importance, we often introduce it in nonfiction. They go together. Nonfiction reading is reading to learn. Simply put, readers of nonfiction have to decide and remember what is important in the texts they read if they are going to learn anything from them.

When readers determine importance in fiction and other narrative genres, they often infer the bigger ideas and themes in the story, as the kids in Jennifer Jones's fifth grade did when they read *Teammates* (Golenbock; see Chapter 10). Getting at what's important in nonfiction text is more about gaining information and acquiring knowledge than discerning themes. Nonfiction is full of features, graphics, text cues, and structures that signal importance and scaffold understanding for readers. These features, specific to nonfiction, provide explicit cues to help readers sift essential information from less important details when they read expository text. We explicitly teach readers how to use these cues to extract salient information. But first we need to ensure that they have a wide range of nonfiction at their disposal.

Steph and Anne both have wonderful memories of having been read aloud to in school. We can still hear the words of *Black Beauty* (Sewell) and *The Secret Garden* (Burnett) as our teachers lured us in from recess for read-aloud time. And we loved those books. But neither of us can ever recall having had a piece of nonfiction read aloud to us or even seeing it in school. It was as if the genre didn't exist—outside of textbooks, that is. And that was true for years. Nonfiction was an absent genre.

This has changed dramatically since this book was first written. The advent of Common Core Standards and other 21st-century standards has brought with it a tsunami of nonfiction reading. These new standards call for 50 percent of what kids read in elementary school to be nonfiction and 70 percent by the end of high school. We have advocated for more nonfiction for years, so in many ways we are thrilled! Steph's first book, *Nonfiction Matters*, written in 1998, is a testament to our belief in the genre. We still view nonfiction as highly engaging, intriguing, and informative. But we worry now that fiction is taking a back seat. So, as always, balance matters. Flood your kids with all genres. Nonfiction, fiction, and poetry all matter.

But this chapter is about nonfiction because it is the genre that requires us to think about what is important. It is also the genre that pumps kids up! Nonfiction picture books, websites, videos, magazines, and newspapers fire kids up. There's nothing like a photograph of the jaws of a great white shark clamping down on the front end of a surfboard to spark kids' interest in ocean life. Interesting authentic nonfiction fuels kids' curiosity, enticing them to read more, dig deeper, and search for answers to compelling questions. When kids read and understand nonfiction, they build background for the topic and acquire new knowledge. The ability to identify essential ideas and salient information is a prerequisite to developing insight.

Distilling the Essence of Nonfiction Text

In *Nonfiction Matters* (Harvey 1998), Steph wrote about overviewing and highlighting the text to help students determine important ideas and information while reading.

Overviewing

When students read nonfiction, they can be taught overviewing, a form of skimming and scanning the text before reading. Reading comprehension researcher Jan Dole suggests focus lessons on the following to help students overview the text:

- Activating prior knowledge
- Noting characteristics of text length and structure
- Noting important headings and subheadings
- Determining what to read and in what order
- Determining what to pay careful attention to
- Determining what to ignore
- Deciding to quit because the text contains no relevant information
- Deciding if the text is worth careful reading or just skimming

A careful overview saves precious time for students when reading difficult nonfiction text. The ability to overview eliminates the need for them to read everything when searching for specific information. Overviewing represents an early entry in the effort to determine importance. Teachers can model these components of overviewing in their own reading and research process.

Annotating, Coding, Underlining and Even Highlighting

To effectively make sense of text, readers need to read the text, think about it, and make conscious decisions about what they need to remember and learn. They can't possibly remember everything. They need to sort important information from less important details. They need to pick out the main ideas and notice supporting details, and they need to let go of ancillary information. But it's not enough to simply run that yellow highlighter over the text. In order to remember important information, we teach kids to jot their thoughts in the margin or on a sticky note right next to the information they deemed important. They might highlight or underline the words in the text, but jotting thoughts is what seals the information in the brain. We encourage students to consider the following guidelines when they read nonfiction, and we provide explicit instruction in each of these points:

Guidelines for Annotation

- Look carefully at the first and last line of each paragraph. Important information is often contained there.
- Highlight, circle, or underline only necessary words and phrases, not entire sentences, and jot thoughts next to the highlighted segments.
- Jot notes in the margin or on a sticky note to paraphrase the information, merge your thinking with it, and better remember it.
- Don't get thrown off by interesting details. Although they are fascinating, they often obscure important information.
- Code the text with symbols, such as an *L* for new learning, a ? for a query, an ! for surprising or compelling information, an *I* for important information. These codes help when kids go back and review.
- Note signal words. They give cues about what's to come and are almost always followed by important information.
- Pay attention to the vast array of nonfiction features that signal importance.
- Pay attention to surprising information. It might mean you are learning something new.

Nonfiction Features That Signal Importance

When a word is italicized, a paragraph begins with a boldface heading, or the text says "Most important, . . ." readers need to stop and take notice. This may sound obvious, but it's not. No one ever taught us to pay attention to these nonfiction conventions. Steph was so textbound as a young reader that to this day she still skips over the title to get to the text. This is a shame. Titles, headings, framed text, and captions help focus readers as they sort important information from less important details. Nonfiction is one of the most accessible genres for reluctant and less experienced readers because the features scaffold the reader's understanding. A photograph and a caption sometimes synthesize the most important information on the page, rendering a complete reading of the text unnecessary. Nonfiction features are user-friendly. Some that we teach follow.

Signal Words and Phrases

Nonfiction writing often includes text cues that signal importance. Signal words and signal phrases (sometimes referred to as cue words or phrases), like stop signs, warn readers to halt and pay attention. Proficient adult readers automatically attend to these text cues. Less experienced readers don't. We need to remember to point these signal words out to readers. For instance, when a writer says, "most important," readers need to stop and pay attention. As students come across signal words or signal phrases, they can add them to a classroom chart headed Signal Word or Phrase/Purpose, with the signal word or phrase on the left and the purpose on the right. Kids and teachers co-construct these charts to help readers navigate difficult expository text. Standardized tests as well are full of signal words and phrases, and familiarity with these cues may boost scores.

Signal Word or Phrase	**Purpose**
Surprisingly	Signals something unexpected
Importantly	Signals the need to stop and pay attention
But	Cues a change to come
However	Prepares for a change
Likewise	Cues a similarity
Consequently	Signals a cause and effect
In other words	Restates the intent
Before, after, next, finally; first, next, last, then, now	All show sequence
In conclusion	Synthesizes the big idea
In sum	Same
Overall	Same
There are several factors	Gives information; the first factor or last is most important
There are several reasons	Same
There are several purposes	Same
As opposed to	Signals a contrast
On the other hand	Signals a change or contrast
In addition to	Adds another factor
Because of	Signals a cause and effect

As with any list, the signal word and phrase list is far from finite. Feel free to add any words or phrases that you view as signals to important information.

Fonts and Effects

Teachers can note examples of different fonts and effects, such as titles, headings, boldface print, color print, italics, bullets, captions, and labels, that signal importance in text. We can remind kids that font and effect differences should be viewed as red flags that wave "This is important. Read carefully."

Illustrations and Photographs

Illustrations play a prominent role in nonfiction to enhance reading comprehension. Nonfiction trade books and magazines brim with colorful photographs that capture young readers and carry them deeper into meaning.

Graphics

Diagrams, cut-aways, cross-sections, overlays, distribution maps, word bubbles, tables, graphs, and charts graphically inform nonfiction readers of important information.

Text Organizers

Teachers cannot assume that kids know concepts such as index, preface, table of contents, glossary, and appendix. When kids are surveying different texts for information, knowledge of these text organizers is crucial for further research.

Text Structures

Expository text is framed around several structures that crop up in both trade and textbook publications and standardized test forms. Understanding different expository text structures gives readers a better shot at determining important information. These structures include cause and effect, problem and solution, question and answer, comparison and contrast, and description and sequence. If students know what to look for in terms of text structure, meaning comes more easily.

Strategy Lessons: Determining Importance

In the classrooms portrayed here, teachers at various grade levels surround their students with nonfiction trade books and other materials to help them build background knowledge of the genre, to see how certain features signal importance, and to model interesting as well as accurate writing. The first three lessons that follow illustrate these goals.

As we have understood for years, nonfiction writing does not have to be boring. All we have to do is pick up a newspaper, look through a *National Geographic*, check out a scientific website, or read a nonfiction best seller to see that nonfiction writing can be rich in voice. Indeed, it is so compelling that sifting important information from the overall text can be challenging. Readers are likely to become so engrossed in authentic nonfiction that they may get carried away by the rich details and miss the essence of the text. But the first purpose of real-world nonfiction is to convey factual information, important ideas, and key concepts. The remaining strategy lessons in this chapter show how teachers help students read to extract important information and essential ideas from nonfiction text.

Determining Importance in Digital Media

Purpose: **Applying the ability to determine big ideas in text to media**

Resources: **Media clip and short videos. For this lesson we've used several clips about the Albuquerque Balloon Fiesta.**

Responses: **Discussing and analyzing big ideas in a media clip, jotting on sticky notes, and sharing on Padlet**

Audience: **Intermediate and middle**

Media clips can offer a wow factor that engages our students and gets them thinking. We love to use media because all students can access it and participate in high-level thinking and discussion. We also feel that this is an essential medium to practice critical thinking in, as students are flooded with media every day.

Pam Parsons starts each school day with a "soft start." Students enter, chatting quietly as they ready themselves for the day. The predictable structure of the classroom allows kids the autonomy to start their day in a peaceful way. As students begin to make their way to the carpet, Pam turns on the time-lapse video of balloons launching from the Albuquerque Balloon Fiesta. Students are captivated by this artistic wonder, and the rest of the class hurries to finish preparing for the day so they can join the excited conversation at the carpet.

Pam prompts the class, when ready, with a few simple words to get them thinking: What do you notice? What do you wonder? Then she asks the students to share their thinking with a buddy at the carpet. She prompts the class to share their questions about this clip and then offers them the chance to explore more by showing a newscast that details the how, what, when, where, and why of the event. Pam tells the class that as they view, they are going to pay careful attention to the information and try to determine what's most important.

Students grab a clipboard and sticky notes so that they can jot thinking as they watch. Pam has planned where she will stop and ask students to turn and talk or jot. As they view together, Pam models using prompts like What is the most important information? and What is the author trying to make sure we understand? She also mentions that sometimes information is really interesting but may not be the most important. After modeling and guiding them for a few minutes, Pam asks the kids to get into small groups and try their hand at the strategy using a different video clip about the same topic. Students repeat the process of viewing, pausing, talking, and jotting as Pam moves about the room conferring with them. At the end of the lesson the class comes together to create a "chart" that cements the work of the day. Pam uses the online tool Padlet and titles the chart Important Ideas about the Albuquerque Balloon Fiesta. Students type in the most important information they've gathered from the day, then read the chart on Padlet to compare their thinking with classmates'. See Figure 11.1 to see students' responses.

Figure 11.1
Padlet Responses to a Web Page Image

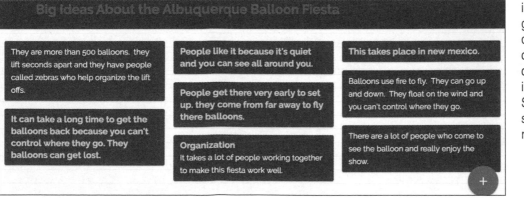

Recording Important Information Through Real-Time Observations

Purpose: **Observing and learning from online, real-time sources of information**

Resources: **Online science sites with webcams, such as the Cornell Lab of Ornithology's (www.birds.cornell.edu)**

Response: **Recording observations, questions, and thinking on an observation form**

Audience: **Primary and intermediate**

Each morning, Brad Buhrow's second graders rush into the classroom, curious to check on what's happened overnight to the raptors and other birds they've been observing on a daily basis. Checking the webcams at the Cornell Lab of Ornithology's Feeder Watch and other bird cams throughout the day, these junior ornithologists experience what it's like to be scientists studying bird behavior in the field. Keeping an eye on the webcam, they grab their field notebooks, ready to record the ongoing action, beginning with the location, temperature, and time of their observation.

During researcher's workshop that day, Brad and these second graders review what information is important to record. As the class observes a barred owl, Brad summarizes the process of writing in their field notebooks on a chart:

- Write down what you see happening by observing closely.
- Ask questions and jot your thinking.
- Write down and draw only the most important information.

The webcam zeros in on an owl mother with two owlets, and Brad writes his observations on a chart, showing kids how they can record their observations in their own notebooks. Brad is careful to demonstrate how he observes the bird behavior and writes down exactly what is happening:

- Two owlets in the nest
- Mother owl is perched on the edge of the nest
- Mother has a curved beak
- Mother feeds the owlets, putting her beak into the owlets' mouths

He adds a question about this observation: "What is the mother feeding the babies?"

As the kids continue to watch closely, Ari realizes what's going on. "Look, I can see that the mom is feeding the babies a rabbit." The kids follow Brad's lead and record what they have observed in their notebooks. They discuss their observations as evidence of how the owl feeds her babies. Now the kids are all set to record what they view on their own.

Watching a red-tailed hawk one day, Maddie wrote and drew in her observations, shown in Figure 11.2.

She is ripping apart her food.
The chicks have gotten bigger.
It is eating a rabbit.
She is feeding the babies.

Figure 11.2
Maddie's Observations of a Red-Tailed
Hawk

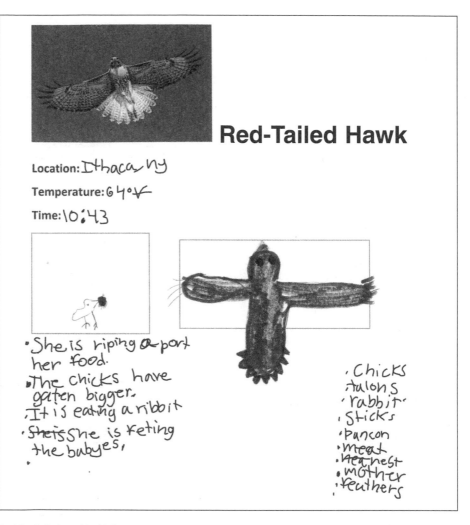

In this digital world with instant access to a wide array of online resources, real-time observations are no longer limited to a walk around the neighborhood or an occasional field trip. Real-time experiences such as webcams and other resources from scientists working in a variety of fields exponentially expand the opportunities for these young ornithologists to broaden their knowledge. (See another example in the assessment section at the end of the chapter.)

Building Background Knowledge of Nonfiction Features

Purpose: **Building background knowledge of nonfiction features by creating books that illustrate them**

Resources: **Tons of nonfiction books with a wide variety of features**

Responses: **A different nonfiction feature on each page; a two-column class chart headed Feature/Purpose, which serves as a record for all of the kids**

Audience: **Primary and intermediate**

Figure 11.3
Cover of a Nonfiction Features Book

Figure 11.4
Catie's Illustration of a Comparison in Nonfiction Text

To help her first graders become aware of the features of nonfiction, Michelle Meyer had them create nonfiction feature books. These little booklets were made up of six sheets of 8-by-11-inch paper folded over and stapled together with a construction-paper cover. The kids wrote the title "Nonfiction Features" on their books and decorated them (see Figure 11.3). To help build her students' background knowledge of nonfiction features, Michelle filled her room to capacity with nonfiction books and read them aloud each day, pointing out various nonfiction conventions as they came up.

The first feature Michelle presented for these nonfiction feature books was captions. She pasted a photograph of her and her cat, Madison, on the first page and wrote the following caption under the picture: "Here I am with Madison wearing her princess look as she drapes herself over the pillow while lounging on my bed." Then Michelle labeled the page "Caption." Later, the kids each brought in a photograph, pasted it on the first page, wrote a caption under the picture, and labeled the page "Caption." (Michelle had a digital camera for those kids who were unable to come up with a photograph from home.) The photograph and the caption made for a very appealing page to begin the nonfiction feature books.

Each day as she read a nonfiction book out loud, Michelle added a new feature to her own book. The kids joined in the search, and when they came across an unfamiliar nonfiction feature, they shared it with the class and added it to their booklets as well as to a large two-column class chart headed Feature/Purpose. Along with Michelle, the kids recorded the new nonfiction features in the first column and indicated their purposes in the second column.

One day Catie found an illustration of a whale shark stretched across the roof of a bus, a visual marker of its great size. Michelle suggested that Catie teach the other kids about this new feature, called a comparison. Catie drew the whale shark on top of a school bus and labeled her new page with the heading "Comparisons" (see Figure 11.4). The next day she taught the class about the notion of comparisons by sharing her illustration. Michelle reinforced this by reading a written example of a size comparison between a Tyrannosaurus tooth and a banana.

Michelle pointed out to the class that Catie and Sean used different words to compare these items. Catie wrote *a little bit bigger than* and Sean wrote *as big as*. The class discussed the difference in these phrases and their meanings because Michelle wanted them to begin to notice the language of comparison. Just telling kids about the special features and language of nonfiction is not enough. But having them search for their own examples and talk about nonfiction characteristics scaffolds their nonfiction reading and enhances their understanding of the genre.

Becoming Familiar with the Characteristics of Nonfiction Trade Books

Purpose: **Acquiring information about an interesting topic, asking some questions, and designing pages based on authentic pages in nonfiction trade books**

Resources: **Nonfiction trade books, students' own nonfiction feature books, paper, and markers**

Responses: **Prior-knowledge form; Questions form; 11-by-17-inch paper for page design**

Audience: **Primary and intermediate**

Slavens Elementary teacher Barb Smith led her second graders through a nonfiction study. After surrounding them with nonfiction material, teaching them about nonfiction features, encouraging them to choose a topic for exploration, having them read for information and write down what she called WOW facts (striking information that makes one say Wow!), Barb helped her students design nonfiction pages that looked very much like the pages we find in nonfiction trade books.

Barb thought about having her students write nonfiction picture books, but wisely decided to have them create single pages instead as a first effort. These pages included both factual content about a chosen topic and the nonfiction features that kids had noticed in trade books. These topics ran the gamut from Sherman tanks to the life of Elvis Presley.

Barb asked her students to begin their research by recording what they already knew about their topic. Turner listed five things he already knew:

Research Topic: Elvis Presley
Prior Knowledge: Write down facts that you already know about your topic.

1. Elvis was the king of Rock and Roll.
2. He was very famous.
3. He sang many great songs.
4. He was very tall.
5. He died of drugs.

Next, Barb asked her students to record their questions on a Questions form. After thinking through what he already knew about his topic, Turner made a list of questions:

Research Topic: Elvis Presley
Questions I have before I begin my research are . . .

1. Did Elvis have any other jobs?
2. Did he have children?
3. Did he have brothers and sisters?
4. What were his parents' names?
5. What instruments did he play?

An additional sheet asked the kids to list five new facts they learned as they conducted their research. In their final form, these nonfiction pages included interesting factual information, answered questions, resembled published nonfiction, and were visually striking (see, for example, Figure 11.5).

Figure 11.5
Turner's Nonfiction Page

This was a terrific project that helped build background knowledge about the genre of non-fiction as well as demanding that kids sift through interesting information and choose what they deemed most important to include on their page. This would serve as an important step in creating nonfiction picture books at a later date.

Determining What's Important When Writing Information

Purpose: **Becoming a specialist on a favorite topic, choosing what is important to include in a piece of writing, and writing informational teaching books**

Resources: **Nonfiction trade books, magazines, and former students' work; 8-by-11-inch construction-paper booklets containing about twelve pages folded and stapled**

Responses: **Teaching books that replicate authentic nonfiction trade books, features and all, either in print or digitized. The writers write about their specialties, something they know about, care about, and would like to teach someone.**

Audience: **Primary and intermediate**

On a visit to Jacqueline Heibert's third-grade classroom at Crofton House School in Vancouver, British Columbia, Steph worked with the students on writing important information about a topic of choice in the form of a "teaching book." Jacqueline had surrounded her third graders with non-fiction trade books, and they were becoming increasingly knowledgeable about the characteristics of the genre. When Steph arrived, she encouraged them to flip through nonfiction books, magazines, and examples of former students' teaching books and note the features and the writing. After they perused the resources for twenty minutes or so, Steph talked to the kids about writing books whose purpose is to teach something. "Everyone is a specialist in something," she told them as she wrote the following on a large chart:

A specialist is someone who

- cares a lot about a topic and is passionate about it;
- knows a lot about the topic; and
- wants to teach someone about the topic.

She then made a list of several topics she knew and loved. Her list of specialties included the following:

- Teaching and learning
- Reading and writing
- Her family
- Snorkeling
- Snow skiing
- The country of Tibet
- Hiking in the Colorado mountains

Figure 11.6
Hillary C.'s Teaching Book Page on Skiing

After sharing the topics she specialized in and choosing snorkeling for further exploration, she asked the kids to think of at least three specialties of their own. She asked for at least three in the belief that one will almost always emerge, even from more reticent kids, and that three or more would be a welcome bonus. The kids jotted down their specialties and shared them in pairs.

Next, Steph modeled writing her own teaching book. She wrote different information on each page of a construction-paper booklet containing about twelve pages of paper, lined on the bottom half and unlined on the top for illustrations. She explained that since the purpose of nonfiction writing is to teach something, writers need to choose the most important information to include in the writing. To do this, writers ask themselves, "What information will best help my reader understand the topic?"

Steph began with snorkeling equipment on the first page, wrote about getting into the water on the next page, and followed with safety, coral, fish, and hazards on subsequent pages. Writing these parts on a page served as a preamble to later paragraphing. Steph explained that she chose these particular components of snorkeling because she felt they represented the most important information she could teach on the topic. She illustrated each page and included some nonfiction features, such as labeling her illustrations and marking each page with a heading.

The kids leapt at the chance to share their considerable information in the teaching-book format and filled them with interesting content as well as an array of nonfiction features, including illustrations. Creating these nonfiction books gave kids opportunities to draw as well as write. Hillary C. used labeling to enhance her informational book about skiing (see Figure 11.6), and Hillary W. headed each section in her manatee book with a pertinent question, which she answered on

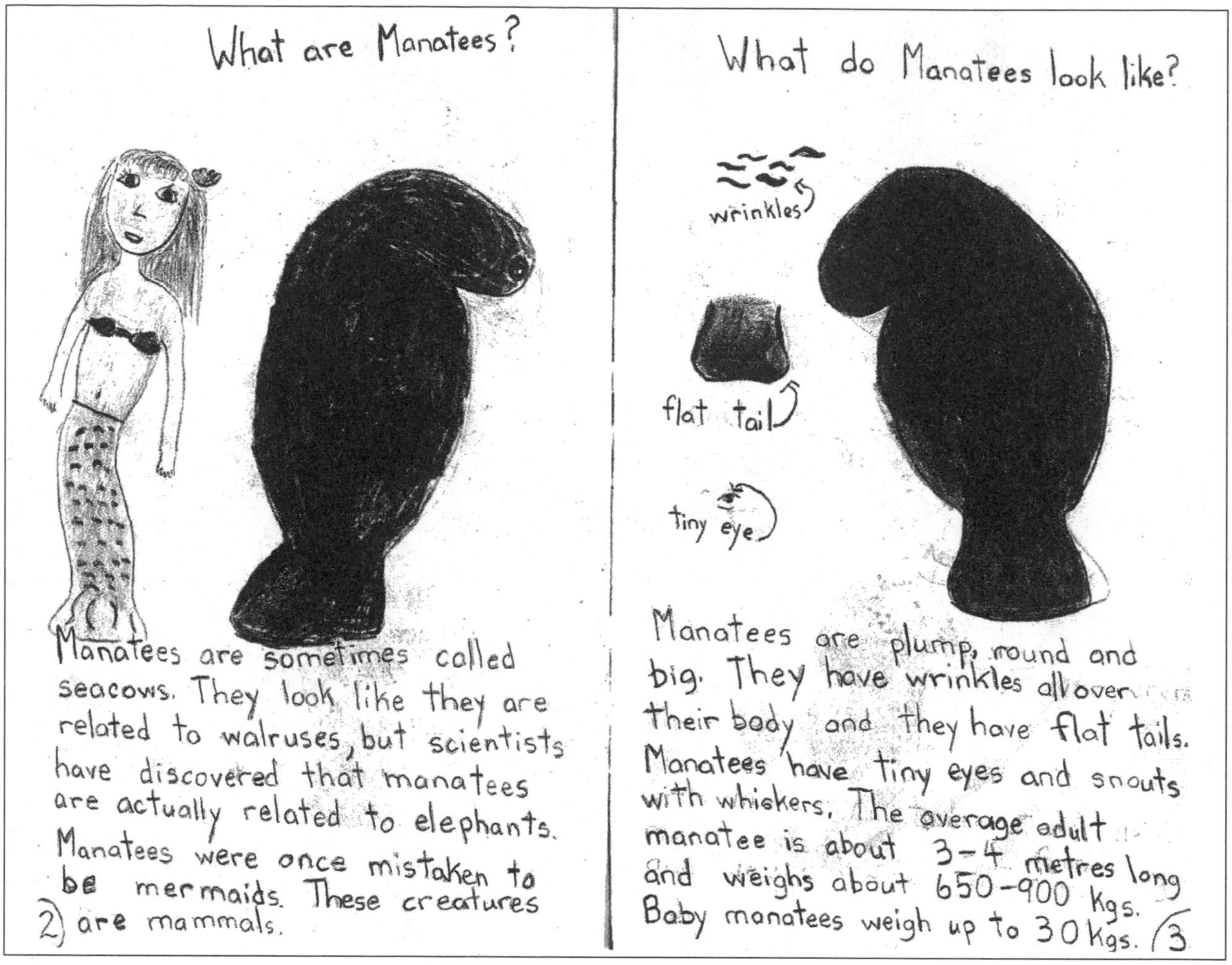

What are Manatees?

Manatees are sometimes called seacows. They look like they are related to walruses, but scientists have discovered that manatees are actually related to elephants. Manatees were once mistaken to be mermaids. These creatures are mammals.

2)

What do Manatees look like?

wrinkles

flat tail

tiny eye

Manatees are plump, round and big. They have wrinkles all over their body and they have flat tails. Manatees have tiny eyes and snouts with whiskers. The average adult manatee is about 3-4 metres long and weighs about 650-900 kgs. Baby manatees weigh up to 30 kgs. (3

Figure 11.7
Hillary W.'s Teaching Book Page on Manatees

the page (see Figure 11.7). Making these teaching books provided a terrific follow-up to the earlier nonfiction feature books and page designs.

Later that week, after they had completed the teaching books, Jacqueline gave the kids plenty of time to share their information with one another. Sharing their specialties built community. The kids came to see each other as specialists in a particular area. Some specialties were expected. Some were a complete surprise. Everyone learned new information on fresh topics and built background for nonfiction features as well. Because the kids included information they deemed important, their classmates learned essential content. When kids do the teaching, their peers take note.

Using a Digital Tool to Record and Sort Important Versus Interesting Information

Purpose: **Using a digital mind-mapping tool to sort and share thinking about important versus interesting information in an article**

Resources: **Nonfiction book or article and devices with access to a mind-mapping or organizing app or website, such as Padlet or Popplet**

Responses: **Sorting information on a digital mind-mapping tool and sharing with a wider audience**

Audience: **Intermediate and middle**

In this lesson the use of a digital tool provides students with the flexibility to revise and refine their thinking as they read. It also allows for easy sharing of the work with their chosen audience, in this case a group of classmates.

Fifth-grade teacher Amber Cordell uses an app that students have on their tablets called Popplet to augment her lesson on teaching students to sort important versus interesting information in a text. This tool enables students to create bubbles with images and typed or written text. They can also color code, draw, connect bubbles, reorganize, and easily add or delete items.

Amber revisits a picture book she has used with students before, *Pink Is for Blobfish* by Jess Keating. She wants to be sure that the text is familiar so that students can focus on the thinking piece of the lesson and working with the technology. She reminds students of their lessons on determining importance by asking them to review the class anchor charts on their reading wall and then rereads a selection of the book with the class, modeling how she gathers her ideas on the Popplet, making a new bubble for each piece of text that she identifies as important or interesting. She shows students how they might set up two columns or use color coding to distinguish between the two.

As she continues modeling and engaging the students with turn and talks, she also demonstrates how she might change her thinking as she reads on: "At first I thought this line was important. But now that I've read a bit more, I see that it's just an interesting detail. I'm going to quickly move it over here." Amber reads a few more pages, this time asking students to create alongside her on their own devices. She pauses while reading to allow them to stop and type, and engages them through turn and talks as they debate about which elements are truly important to understanding the text and which sentences are interesting details. Before releasing students to work independently, she has a few of them share their thinking and their format with the class.

Students then apply this strategy in their own nonfiction books. They work with partners, reading, discussing, and making adjustments as they go. (See Figure 11.8.) When they are close to finished, Amber asks students to review the text by

Figure 11.8
Students Sort What's Important and What's Interesting Using a Digital Tool

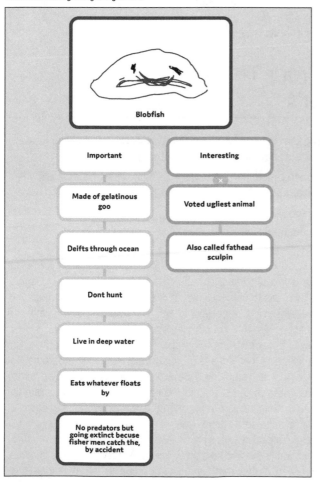

skimming and scanning to confirm that they have pulled out the most important information and interesting details. Students do this and then discuss their chart using sentence stems like "I know this is important because" or "This must be an interesting detail because."

Students then take a screenshot and share their work with the teacher before gathering in small groups to talk through their work of the day. In these small groups, students explain what they determined was important from the text, and why, justifying their thinking.

Amber quickly scans her inbox as students are talking, taking names of students she wants to pull to a small group for more instruction or clarification. She ends the lesson by gathering students at the carpet and asking a few of them to share their work with the class.

Mira used color coding on her Poppet to help her organize her thinking; can you tell us more about that, Mira? Shawn, I see that you have two webs instead of columns. Can you talk more about how you chose to set this up and why? How does that help you understand the text better?

I've asked Violet to share her process with you a little bit. She did quite a bit of reorganizing as she worked today. Violet, can you talk about that and maybe share how using this tool today helped you?

Because Amber's students have used a digital tool, they can easily add this work to their digital portfolio, post it on their blog and write more about their thinking, e-mail it to a parent with an explanation about the strategy and the work they did in class, or add it to an app where they can record their voice and use the chart to retell what they learned from the text.

Distinguishing Your Thinking from the Author's

Purpose: **Understanding that there may be a difference between what the reader thinks is most important and the writer's big ideas**

Resources: **Articles from magazines like *Time for Kids, Scholastic News, National Geographic Explorer*; websites; nonfiction trade books; and so on**

Response: **Response notebooks**

Audience: **Intermediate and middle**

Teachers often report that their kids have trouble picking out the most important information when they read. And test scores are frequently depressed in the "find the main idea" category. One of the primary reasons that kids have trouble picking out the most important information is that in a sense they are asking themselves, "Important to whom?" In other words, what the reader thinks is most important is not necessarily the author's main idea.

Readers frequently find a detail to be more important than the big idea in the article. For instance, let's say a reader reads an article that focuses primarily on antismoking programs that are effective at stemming the tide against teen smoking. As the student reads, she comes across a factual detail saying that over 400,000 people die of smoking each year. If that student's mom is a smoker, that detail surfaces as more important to her than the main idea of the success of antismoking programs. The main idea often depends on who the main reader is!

We teach our kids to make a distinction between what they think is most important to remember and what the writer most wants them to take away from the article. We have to model this, because they frequently choose what they think is most important as the main idea even when it is not. So whenever we ask kids to pick out the main idea, we ask them first to write down something they learned that they think is important to remember. Then we ask them to draw a line under that response and write down what they think the author most wanted them to learn and remember. Sometimes they jot down the same response. Other times, their responses are quite different. We have found that kids are much better at picking out the main idea if they first consider what they think is most important and then think about what the author most wanted them to get out of the article.

We want our kids to know that nothing matters more than their thinking when they read, and giving them an opportunity to consider what they think is most important serves that goal. But we also want them to recognize that nonfiction writers have something in mind that they are trying to convey to the reader and that it is the reader's responsibility to pick up on that as well.

One caveat: we can't forget to let kids know that when they are taking a standardized test, the only answer that counts is the one that reflects the author's main idea. So we remind them to choose the answer that expresses what they think the author most wants them to take away from the reading. And the good news is that we have found that our kids do even better on these tests once they understand how to distinguish between their notion of what's most important and the writer's big ideas.

Distinguishing Between an Opinion and an Informed Opinion

Purpose: **Discerning the difference between an opinion and an informed opinion**

Resource: **"Lend Me a Paw," an article on the Navy Marine Mammal Program (National Geographic Learning)**

Response: **Three-column think sheet headed Opinions, Questions/Thoughts, and Informed Opinions**

Audience: **Intermediate and middle**

We live in the information age. Every day we are blasted with info from all directions, not all of it accurate. Misinformation abounds. It's easy to have an opinion on just about anything. We want our kids to understand that their thinking and opinions matter, but also that many issues and ideas are multifaceted and complex. Often what we think on first blush may not be wholly correct. So we teach the difference between a run-of-the-mill opinion and an informed opinion, one that requires us to read, think about, and study the issue before deciding on our opinion. The entire world would work more effectively if we all educated ourselves about information before having a dyed-in-the-wool opinion about it.

Steph begins this lesson by explaining the difference between an opinion and an informed opinion. She explains that opinions carry more weight if there is evidence to back them up and that the more evidence there is, the more informed that opinion is. She adds that thoughtful people reach informed opinions after much reading and study, and she tells the kids that that is what education is all about.

Next, she thinks aloud about a personal example of something she has an opinion about: that baseball players are better athletes than football players. Her brother disagrees. Although she has this opinion, the truth is, she doesn't really have enough information to argue this point. It is simply her opinion and not a very informed one. She concedes that her brother is both more knowledgeable about and more interested in sports than she is and that his opinion is probably more informed than hers.

She asks the kids to turn and talk about any opinions they might have about books, sports, movies, types of pets—something they connect with and can think of relatively quickly. The conversation explodes. They have lots of different opinions and love to talk about them and share them. Many admit that their opinions are really just their beliefs and probably not all that informed.

Steph begins to think aloud with an article on the Navy Marine Mammal Program. The article describes a program in the US Navy that uses marine mammals to participate in military operations. She explains that some people think this is a good idea (Pro) and others think this is a bad idea (Con). She reads the first two pages of the article to build a little background knowledge for kids, having them turn and talk at various stopping points. Then she hands out a think sheet with the headings Opinions, Questions/Thoughts, and Informed Opinions and asks them to jot down their opinion in the first column using *Pro, Con,* or *NEI* (not enough information) and to add their thoughts, questions, and reasons for their choice in the middle column. No surprise—a majority of kids, animal lovers that they are, jot *Pro*, several jot *Con*, and one jots *NEI*. Steph then jots *NEI* on her form, saying that she doesn't have enough information to make an informed opinion yet. But she explains that they are going to get to read a few more pages to get more information, which might give them a more informed opinion.

Steph has the kids pair off and read the next two pages of the article, one that states the Pro side and the other that states the Con side. As they read, she moves around the room conferring with them. She hears that some kids are even more committed to their original idea, others are changing their thinking, and some now feel like they need more information. At the end of the work time, they come back and share how their thinking changed or how they added to it. Several have gone from Pro to Con; more are now NEI. All agree that their opinion is a bit more informed than when they first jotted it down.

The discussion and reading has really fired kids up about the topic. Steph asks them if they would like to do more research to get an even more informed opinion, and they all climb aboard, so she follows this lesson the next day by sharing a variety of articles on using animals in the military to do various types of work, some quite dangerous. She chooses articles that take no side on the issues, as well as those that do express an opinion, making sure to have an equal number of each. As kids read and research, they become more informed. Some are more committed to their original stance. Some have reversed their opinion, and some still want more information, which we welcome. We have found this lesson to be quite effective and teach it across the curriculum when we come upon issues and problems that are likely to have two sides to them. (See Figure 11.9.)

Figure 11.9
A Student Works Through Her Thinking
to Come to a More Informed Opinion

Opinions	Questions/Thoughts	Informed Opinions
•I think that I don't have enough information to either be on the pro or con side. I think that the Marine made a good plan of sending the mammal's under water with their traits. (need information) special • Pro	•What other animal can help people? • How can the marine best prevent animals from getting hurt? • How can we ensure that mammals don't get hurt? • Why do they make mammals do what they don't want to do? • Why does the Navy treat the animals badly?	•The Marines ensure that the mammals can not get hurt. (pro) •Sea mines are designe to detonated by large ships not marine animals. (pro) •Marine animals are well cared for. (pro) • The dolphins don't have a proper habitat. (con) •Animals are tooken away from their family. (con) •When dolphins are captured it could be violent. (con) •They are held captive (con) I am a NI NEI Not enough info

Creating Listicles by Analyzing Nonfiction Text

Purpose:　**Analyzing information, picking out what's most important, and using it to write a listicle**

Resources:　**A variety of listicles as models plus a listicle written by the teacher about the big ideas and themes in the picture book *Nelson Mandela* by Kadir Nelson**

Response:　**Original listicles**

Audience:　**Primary, intermediate, and middle**

A listicle is a short form of writing that uses a list as its thematic structure. The word *listicle* is adapted from the word *article*. Listicles are a relatively new genre. They didn't exist as such when we wrote the previous edition of this book. The form is quite common now. We are likely to see listicles on websites, in magazine articles, and so forth. Lists are everywhere: the ten best songs of 2017, the twenty-five best beaches in the world, the most popular dogs. We also see listicles that describe the most important aspects of a topic.

Kids at any grade level can write listicles, ranging from kindergartners who might draw five of their favorite pets to third graders who jot six sentences about a topic to middle schoolers who investigate a big idea and break it down into its most salient pieces. We can teach listicle writing that requires us to analyze information and come up with the most important ideas. With our students, we have found listicles to be a quick and useful way for them to pick out the most important information on a topic from a piece they have read and share it with others.

Steph brings in several listicles she finds on the Internet to expose kids to the genre: the five most important things to know about the Indian festival of Diwali, ten superfoods you should eat every day. Then she models one with a book she loves. She talks about the big ideas in the book and then explains that her listicle is going to break down the text into the most important ones. She uses the picture book *Nelson Mandela* by Kadir Nelson. As she reads it out loud, she jots down what she believes to be the most important ideas. She explains that she has already read the book, and she begins her listicle with a short synthesis of it, and then while reading, she breaks each big idea down into important themes that might have led Nelson Mandela to be such a courageous leader.

Steph begins as follows: "This is my synthesis of what the book was mainly about."

Nelson Mandela was a South African politician and activist who fought the government-approved institution of apartheid, which denied black Africans the rights and human dignities that all people should enjoy. He spent his life fighting these laws, and when apartheid was overturned he became the first democratically elected black head of state in South Africa.

"Now I am going to create a listicle, or a list, of what I think were the most important ideas in the book by analyzing the text, noting what the author writes, and listing the ideas."

- *As a young boy, Nelson Mandela was the only one in his family who was selected to go to school. Only the smartest kids were chosen for school. It was obvious that young Nelson was very smart.*

- *When he was only nine, Nelson's father died and he was sent to live with a powerful chief who made sure he received a fine education.*

- *Nelson became a lawyer and fought for equal rights for all oppressed people in South Africa, the racist government that denied rights to black Africans.*

- *People from all corners of the nation listened to him, loved him, and followed him. The government feared that he was gaining power so they captured him and put him in jail.*

- *He remained in jail for twenty-seven and a half years, but he became a symbol of the horrors of apartheid, and during his time in jail, many people fought for his freedom and the freedom of others. South Africa changed slowly and eventually apartheid was rejected, in many parts because of the courage of Nelson Mandela.*

- *Nelson was let out of prison an old man, but the people elected him to be the president of the country because he had shown himself to be a courageous, determined leader who was loved by so many. As president, he worked hard to bring all people together.*

Kids can create listicles of all sorts. This idea of a listicle about the big ideas in literature gives a little more weight to listicle writing than simply jotting down favorite songs. But kids will come across listicles of all kinds, which makes it useful for them to know what listicles are and what to expect from them when reading online as well as when learning to write them to sift out the most important information.

Using FQR Think Sheets
to Understand Information

Purpose: **Determining importance, asking questions, and responding to historical fiction**

Resources: **Picture books relating to the Civil War**
Follow the Drinking Gourd by Jeanette Winter
Nettie's Trip South by Ann Turner
Sweet Clara and the Freedom Quilt by Deborah Hopkinson

Response: **Three-column note form headed Facts/Questions/Responses (FQR)**

Audience: **Intermediate and middle**

When it comes to note-taking scaffolds, the three-column think sheet headed Facts/Questions/
Responses has stood the test of time. It's helpful for science texts, when kids have to pull out
important information from a huge array of facts. Jotting down questions and responses about
the information makes it much more comprehensible and memorable—and the response column
in particular provides a window into kids' thinking that informs our teaching. Questions that arise
throughout reading provide opportunities to both clarify information and spark further investigation. Teachers we have worked with are thrilled that, for once, all the new information kids are
learning, as well as their questions and responses, is in one place!

While historical fiction works with the FQR note-taking scaffold, we explain to kids that the
"facts" that they record are just that—information rather than the story narrative. In this Civil War
unit, fifth graders read several different picture books to build their background knowledge about
the time period.

To begin, we show kids how we stop and put important information into our own words. We
usually begin by recording information in the Facts column and then work across the page, jotting down questions and responses about those facts. Once students understand how to gather
facts, ask questions, and respond with their own thoughts, they read in pairs or independently. At
the end of the lesson, students are eager to share their own personal responses based on facts
they gathered and the questions they asked. The following three-column FQR form illustrates
their in-depth reading of a historical fiction picture book; nonfiction articles and even textbook
chapters work as well. Kids record the title and author at the top of their scaffold.

Several students read the historical fiction picture book *Nettie's Trip South*, stopping after
each page or so to discuss their ideas and note information and questions. In the story, a young
girl visiting from the North observes slaves being sold on the auction block. Students pull out the
information about slavery from the narrative events in the story and complete FQR charts. This
sample of one student's Facts/Questions/Responses form illustrates how kids focused on the
important ideas in each book and developed a deeper understanding of larger historical issues.

Title: *Nettie's Trip South*
Author: Ann Turner

Facts	Questions	Response
Slaves weren't allowed to learn.	Who is Addie?	I think Nettie is writing to her friend Addie.
I can't believe the Constitution could say that slaves were 3/5 of a person.*	Who is writing the letter?	She didn't expect to see what she saw.
(*How could I check this?)	Why were slaves considered to be only 3/5 of a person?	It makes me angry that slaves were sold away from families who were in tears because they were split apart and sold.
	Were the husband and wife split apart?	You can tell Nettie had a mind of her own.

This student connected information they had previously learned during a study of the Constitution to the information they encountered in this picture book. She commented, "I thought the Constitution was written to protect people. Didn't the Bill of Rights give people rights like freedom of religion and freedom of speech?" Her background information, accurate to a point, did not include the knowledge that slaves were not protected by the Constitution in the years before the Civil War. Like Nettie, the young girl in the story, this student was outraged at the slave auction and went online to find out the answers to her question: "Why were slaves considered to be only 3/5 of a person?" Rather than merely summarizing the events of each story, the FQR form encouraged students to investigate and find answers to lingering questions.

For more information on creating FQRs with history topics, see our video series *Strategic Thinking: Reading and Responding, Grades 4–8* (2004). (See FQR think sheets in the assessment section at the end of the chapter.)

Digital Note Taking with Primary Kids

Purpose: **Kids record their learning, questions, and reactions.**
Resources: **Padlet and Google Docs with nonfiction text**
Response: **Note-taking scaffold titled I Learned/I Wonder/Wow!**
Audience: **Primary**

Instructional coach Jen Burton and second-grade teacher Ms. Pride engaged students in a mini inquiry into plants and seeds. For primary children, we use a more developmentally appropriate form of the Facts/Questions/Responses note-taking scaffold. It's headed I Learned/I Wonder/Wow!

As kids read, listen, or view, they jot down what they learned in the first column. Often once kids meet new information, they have a question or a reaction. They place their questions in the second column and their reactions, or as they like to say, their Wows, in the third column. Wows are made up of amazing facts, new learnings, and personal reactions that strike kids. As we introduce this scaffold, we demonstrate how kids can think across the page, but we are not rigid about deliberating whether a fact goes in the I Learned or the Wow! column. The idea is to engage kids in their reading and have them process the information so they remember it.

In this lesson, kids respond digitally on Google Docs and Padlet, where the teachers have created the I Learned/I Wonder/Wow! think sheet. (See Figure 11.10.) What's really cool about these apps is that when the teacher projects the scaffold, kids can see what everyone is thinking in real time—a great opportunity for them to collaborate and share their learning. (See another example in the assessment section at the end of the chapter.)

Figure 11.10
An I Learned/I Wonder/Wow! Think Sheet in Google Docs

	I learned: (L)	I Wonder..?	Wow! (!)	
	A	**B**	**C**	**D**
1	**I learned: (L)**	**I Wonder..?**	**Wow! (!)**	
2	Some plants don't grow from a seed	What arere seed leaves?	This book reminds me of when we planted plants.	
3	I learned that potatoes don't have "eyes"	I wonder if there's no seed in the plant, does something else drop the seed?	I am planing a plant today	
4	I don't know what is velvet	I wonder if the runner is a root?	I seen potato eyes	
5	Spores Looks. Like seeds	Is the runner a stem?	I have that plant	
6	Spores can be green	What is in a seed?	I did not know that	
7	Spores are hard to find	I don't think that potato have really ((eyes))	Me too	
8	Spores can be different shapes	I wonder what are leaf buds? How do they start a new plant?	Spores look like green beans	
9		What are potato eyes	Spores look like little spikes	
10		I wonder if potatoes have eyes?	What are spoers	
11			WHAT ARE APPL TREES THAT ARE GOLDEN	
12				

Reading for Details

Throughout this chapter we emphasize reading to answer questions and reading for important information. We tend to downplay reading for details, perhaps because we spent so much time doing it in school ourselves. But authentic reading experiences remind us that there are many reasons to read, often for the big ideas and also for the details. Close reading of text of any sort is frequently central to understanding as Steph discovered one day at the dog kennel.

Upon heading out of town, she left written directions to bathe and groom her beloved ball of fur, a keeshond named Indiana Jones. Upon her return, the kennel keeper retrieved a dog Steph was convinced was not in any way hers. The dog he presented to her was shaved down almost to the skin. As the dog leapt at her in great glee, it dawned on her that this bald-as-a-ping-pong-ball dog was in fact hers. We ignore details at our peril!

Seriously, we see the value in all kinds of reading. Reading is about purpose, and there is a time and place for every type of reading, reading for details as well as reading for the big picture.

Teaching with the End in Mind: Assessing What We've Taught

Determining Importance

Based on the lessons in this chapter, we look for evidence that

1. *Students gain important information from text and visual features.* We look for evidence that students are paying attention to text and visual features when they read and incorporating them when they write nonfiction.
2. *Students sift and sort the important information from the details and merge their thinking with it.* We look for evidence that students acquire information and decide what's important to remember. They also think more deeply about the information by asking questions and responding.
3. *Students learn to make a distinction between what they think is most important and what the author most wants them to take away from the reading.* We look for evidence that students can sort out their own thinking from the important ideas in the text and the author's perspective.
4. *Students use text evidence to form opinions and understand big ideas and issues.* We look for evidence that students tie their opinions and ideas to the text and change them in light of evidence.

Suggestions for Differentiation

Text coding offers many opportunities for differentiation. Kids leave tracks of their thinking with a variety of codes that will remind them of what they want to remember. Question marks, exclamation points, asterisks, and stars can all be indications of what's important and what kids think about it. Highlighting and underlining alone are not enough. We need to see our kids' thinking, and they need to express it to remember why they highlighted in the first place. So we teach kids to jot a quick note or sketch a picture next to important information to better learn, understand, and remember it. We also teach kids to bracket paragraphs and sections and paraphrase what they learned. When all of us, and especially English language learners, put information into our own words, we are much more likely to understand what we are reading. So we focus on supporting kids to put information into their words and to shape it into their own thought.

Determining Importance Assessment Commentary

Facts/Questions/Responses (FQR) think sheets from the lesson "Using FQR Think Sheets to Understand Information"

Facts Rebecca

- Walruses spend most time in water
- they rest and give birth on the ice
- ~30 below in Arctic
- North Polar reg. is Arctic Ocean and surrounding land
- a treeless plain where soil remains frozen all year
- spends all spring, summer, and fall eating and storing up fat. Then it hibernates and lives off the fat
- it grows longer front claws to dig tunnels to hibernate in.
- walruses have 6 in. of body fat to keep out the

Questions

- why don't the babies freeze?
- how could animals live in such a harsh place
- warm blooded or cold blooded?
- what's tundra?
- what does the temperature drop down too
- how does their fur change from grayish brown to white?
- how do they get all of this information if it's way too cold

Response 4th grade

- this is so cold I can't even imagine it being this cold
- probably warm because cold blooded would freeze
- their body fat helps them keep warm

Kids read informational text and applied the FQR strategy to science topics independently.

◄ Rebecca did a nice job recording factual information. Her questions are focused on details and help to clarify unfamiliar vocabulary. She hasn't used the response column as effectively. We would want to help her get the idea that exploring her thinking in this column will make a difference in her understanding.

▶ Kyle records facts that represent the important information in an article on saving the Everglades. You can see how he asks authentic questions, such as, "Are we really the smartest mammals on earth?" He keeps trying to think of solutions for the problem posed by the article in the response column. This is a terrific example of how we are hoping our kids will use FQR think sheets to work out thinking and better understand the information.

Facts Kyle

- Settlers thought the everglades was a worthless swamp.
- Everglades is not worthless but unique.
- Many species in everglades all need eachother and a steady supply of water.
- Humans messed up because they took away animals homes to make homes for themself.
- Everglades were now only half their former size. ove
- 68 endangered or threatened species.
- 1 of top ten most endangered parks.
- Bush has a plan to restore everglades w/ 8 billion dollars, biggest environmental plan ever.

Questions

- why is it called a river of grass?
- Is the number of species going down after this.
- what was the size of the everglades?
- Are we really the smartest mamals on earth?
- how can they fix it?
- why does it Matter?
- where will he get the money?
- when will this start?
- How long has the water been gone from the Everglades?
- How many species lived there?

Response

- Maybe the everglades are this river of grass.
- probably settlers saw everglades as an obstacle.
- There's some type of problem with the water supply.
- There are many more endangered species which is a real drag.
- we need more water
- we should help the animals.
- Maybe taxes
- named the river of grass because it is a river flowing into a grassy field.
- Make a zoo for the animals.
- Instead of blowing everything away just reconstruct.

Note taking on Padlet with the form I Learned/I Wonder/Wow! from the lesson "Digital Note Taking with Primary Kids"

▸ Jen Burton and second-grade teacher Mrs. Komosa used Padlet, an alternative to the Google Docs FQR or paper FQR, to share their new learning, questions, and Wow! facts. Padlet is a digital bulletin board where students can add digital sticky notes with their thinking and move them around, and everyone in the class can see the thinking of other students simultaneously in real time. The teacher can see what kids are thinking and writing as they work and respond accordingly. These second graders commented on information they were learning about weather and natural disasters.

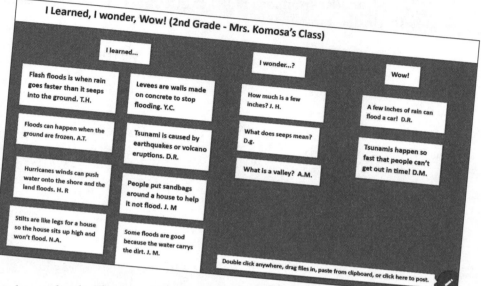

Independent observation and response to viewing bird behavior with the bird cam from the lesson "Recording Important Information Through Real-Time Observations"

◂ Maddie uses a think sheet with separate columns for new learning, observations, and questions. The very fact that she came up with her own categories shows her engagement and enthusiasm for the topic. Real-time observations like these hone kids' scientific thinking. They learn how scientists go about observing and thinking about information. As she views a number of birds, she notes what she learns through observation and asks questions about what she doesn't understand.

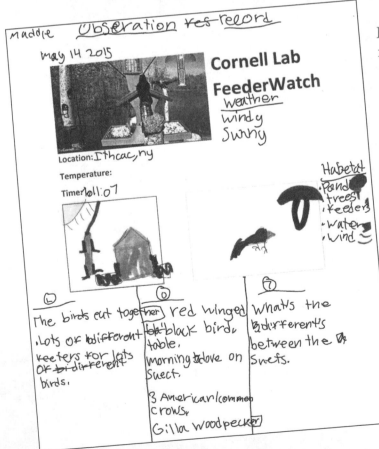

Chapter 12

Summarizing and Synthesizing Information: The Evolution of Thought

Among Steph's fondest childhood memories are the summer afternoons spent in the great room of her grandparents' log house on a lake in northern Wisconsin. The musty smell of worn Oriental carpets, the shiny pretzel log walls, the Scott Joplin tunes on the player piano, and the continuous whir of the ceiling fan filled her senses as she whiled away those lazy days, in tandem with her grandmother, working jigsaw puzzles of every size and shape. A card table in the far corner of the room housed all the action. One week a Bavarian castle, the next a nineteenth-century painting of the Grand Canyon. As the years went by, a portrait of Captain Hook, a can of Coca-Cola, and a pepperoni pizza materialized on that card table. A battalion of two, grandmother and granddaughter attacked the puzzles together and were delighted as entire pictures slowly emerged from the hundreds of scattered cardboard pieces.

When we summarize information during reading, we pull out the most important information and put it in our own words to remember it. Each bit of information we encounter adds a piece to the construction of meaning. Our thinking evolves as we add information from the text. Synthesizing is a process akin to working a jigsaw puzzle. In the same way that we manipulate hundreds of puzzle pieces to form a new picture, students must arrange multiple fragments of information until they see a new pattern emerge (McKenzie 1996). Sometimes when we synthesize, we add to our store of knowledge and reinforce what we already know. Other times, we merge new information with existing knowledge to understand a new perspective, a new line of thinking, or even an original idea. Our thinking may evolve slowly over time, as Steph's jigsaw puzzles did, or we may have a flash of insight based on startling, new information.

How Background Knowledge Impacts Synthesizing

We begin by teaching our students to take stock of meaning while they read, summarizing the information to add to their store of knowledge. To do this we encourage readers to stop every so often and think about what they have read. Steph and Alverro, the incredulous boy reading about giraffes whom we met in the second chapter, agreed that Alverro would view the end of each page as a red light to stop and think about what he had read. In this way, he would construct meaning before powering through the text. Stopping and actively thinking about the information helps readers stay on track with the text and monitor their understanding. Sometimes the goal of reading is to sift and pare down meaning to get the gist. Other times we pull the details together to draw conclusions, consider implications, or even take action.

Background knowledge makes a difference. Several years ago, Steph had an experience that led her to understand how much prior knowledge is a determining factor as we synthesize information. She read an article in the *Washington Post* called "More Questions than Answers," which focused on the effectiveness of polygraph testing (Eggen and Vedantam 2006). Although she had known that polygraphs were by no means perfect, she did believe that they were reasonably reliable and had even thought a person was likely guilty if they failed a polygraph test. The *Post* article reported a study that found if polygraphs were administered to 10,000 people, ten of whom were spies, 1,600 innocent people would fail the test and two of the spies would pass. The article concluded that one of the main reasons law enforcement continues to use polygraphs is that so many perpetrators actually confess while undergoing a polygraph test. This was stunning new information for Steph which led her to change her thinking and come to an entirely new understanding of polygraph testing. She recounted the article and her astonishment to her friend Lydia at lunch. Lydia was terribly interested in the article, but not at all surprised by the information. Her husband was in law enforcement, and she had known the limitations of polygraph testing for years. As she read the article, her thinking did not change, but the article confirmed, reinforced, and enhanced what she already knew.

Both Steph and Lydia synthesized the information. Steph's lack of background about polygraph testing led her to a whole new perspective on the topic. Lydia added to her accurate and substantial knowledge base. If we know a lot about something and we read more about that topic, we add that information to our store of knowledge and come to understand the topic more completely. If we know little about a topic and then read further on that topic, our thinking is likely to evolve and change because of all the new information we have gained. And we may have a flash of insight as Steph did.

So how does this type of insight come about in reading? When readers synthesize, they use a variety of strategies to build and enhance understanding. They summarize the information, listen to their inner voice, and merge their thinking so that the information makes sense and is meaningful to them. They connect the new to the known, they ask questions, they pick out the most important information—all of these strategies intersect to allow us to synthesize information and actively use it.

Genre makes a difference too. In fiction, we might gain insight into the characters by observing their actions and piecing together their motives. In a mystery, we gather clues, ask questions, and draw inferences to solve it. Nonfiction text often conveys information that leads readers to a particular point of view. Readers' thinking may change as they ingest new information gleaned from the text. An article on rain forest deforestation might point a finger at governmental forestry policies. A synthesis could involve forming an opinion about the shortsightedness of the government in question. The new information combined with readers' thinking can lead to new insight.

The following strategy lessons support an evolving notion of synthesizing. We realize that "Summarizing and Synthesizing" is the last chapter in Part II. But in truth, we have been asking kids to summarize and synthesize throughout this book. We teach summarizing—getting the facts, ordering events, paraphrasing, and picking out what's important—as one aspect of synthesizing information. When kids are able to understand information on the page and can organize their thinking around it, they are more prepared to synthesize the information. So as we teach kids a repertoire of reading and thinking strategies, there is no reason to wait until the end of the year to bring up summarizing and synthesizing. In this chapter, we share lessons that we have found help our kids to do both. But we wager you'll find, as we did, that kids have been summarizing and synthesizing all along.

Strategy Lessons: Summarizing and Synthesizing Information

Making Synthesizing Concrete

Purpose: **Using baking to make the abstract synthesizing strategy more concrete**
Resources: **Ingredients for making a cake**
Response: **Class discussion**
Audience: **Primary**

Kindergarten teacher David Harris thinks carefully about how to make abstract comprehension strategies concrete for kids. Aware that synthesizing requires combining a number of parts to form a new whole, David uses baking to demonstrate synthesizing for little kids. He tells his young scholars that reading is about taking in a lot of different facts, thinking about them, putting them together, and learning something new.

David decided to use baking a cake to demonstrate the notion of synthesizing. Together with the kids, he measured out the different ingredients and set them on a table in front of the class. The kids counted seven ingredients in all. Together they poured each ingredient into the bowl and blended it with a spatula. David left what remained of the separate ingredients in the bags and bowls that held them. When they finished mixing the batter, David pointed out that these seven separate ingredients were now blended into one thick, gloppy mixture ready for the oven. They slid it in, waited an hour, and out popped a golden cake.

"What do we have here?" David asked them.

"A cake," they said in unison, their eyes wide.

"That's right," David told them as he pointed to the leftover ingredients still in the boxes and bowls. "All of these different parts mixed together became a whole new thing, that delicious cake you baked. Guess what: when you read and listen to a story, there are lots of different parts and characters, but in the end, all of those parts come together to make up the whole story, kind of like this cake."

David didn't expect his kindergartners to talk about "synthesizing," but he would remind them to think about all of the ingredients that came together to create the cake when he next read aloud to them. He hoped this experience would help them think about the different parts of the story and how they fit together to make a whole story. Kids love to bake. This rather offbeat and fun way of making synthesizing concrete fired them up and scaffolded their understanding of the nature of story.

Some other activities for making synthesizing concrete include making orange juice, doing jigsaw puzzles, constructing with blocks, and building with Legos. All are activities that involve putting together assorted parts to make a new whole, which is what synthesizing is all about.

Retelling to Summarize Information

Purpose: **Providing a basic framework to help students begin to summarize and synthesize information through a brief retelling of a story**

Resources: **Assorted picture books, including *For Every Child a Better World*, by L. Gikow**

Responses: **Recording brief summaries on sticky notes or charts, or through discussion; one-word lists of a synthesis**

Audience: **Primary**

When teacher Debbie Miller introduces summarizing to her first graders, she provides them with a basic framework for thinking and talking about summarizing. She tells her students that when readers summarize, they do the following:

- Remember to tell what is important
- Tell it in a way that makes sense
- Try not to tell too much

Debbie models this with a variety of well-loved picture books. After she finishes reading a story, she shows her students how she restates it in her own words, following the above guidelines. Sometimes she records her thinking on a chart, sometimes on a sticky note. At other times she merely talks about her summary. But she always keeps it brief, salient, and to the point.

Young kids in particular have trouble with brevity when they attempt summarizing. We've all heard a retelling of *Star Wars* that lasted longer than the movie itself. But as Debbie models extensively, kids begin to get the hang of it.

Several weeks into the teaching of this strategy, Kent shared his summary of the book *For Every Child a Better World* (Gikow). During sharing time, he took out a piece of paper and began to read: "Every child needs food, but sometimes there isn't any. Every child needs clean water, but sometimes they can't find it. Every child needs a home, but some don't have one." When he finished reading, Debbie commented on his good thinking and asked him about his writing. Kent explained that after he read, he thought about what was important and how it would make sense, and then he made some notes to help him remember. His notes, translated from his temporary spelling, follow:

food
clean water
home
clean air
medicine
school

Kent went on to explain that when he finished reading, he went back through the book and thought about the most important information and then wrote only a word to help him remember. "Then when you tell somebody, you can just look at your paper and put in all the rest of the words that are in your head." Kent's note taking helped all of the kids in the class who tried to summarize information the next day. In fact, what Kent was really doing by merging his thinking with the information was moving toward a synthesis of the piece. He discerned what was important, and he kept his notes short enough to help him remember the information, a valuable skill for kids as they move on through school and life (Harvey et al. 1996).

Creating Field Guides in Science

Purpose: **Creating a field guide using mentor texts; summarizing science information**

Resources: **An assortment of field guides on different topics, in this case, birds**

Response: **Determining essential information based on reading field guides and creating one**

Audience: **Primary and intermediate**

It's never too early to teach young children about the many types of nonfiction that explain and bring to life the natural world. Kids read a variety of field guides, such as the Peterson series of field guides to various animals and plants, coming to understand how these guides help nature observers identify and learn about different species. With their succinct information, clear purpose, and extensive visuals, field guides are a perfect genre for kids to learn from and to create themselves to share their new learning.

Second-grade teacher Brad Buhrow flooded the room with bird field guides in preparation for a unit on birds. Kids eagerly grabbed the ones available and raced outside to learn about the birds in their neighborhood—their markings, specific behaviors, habitat and nest information, and even their songs and calls. When these junior ornithologists were ready to write their own

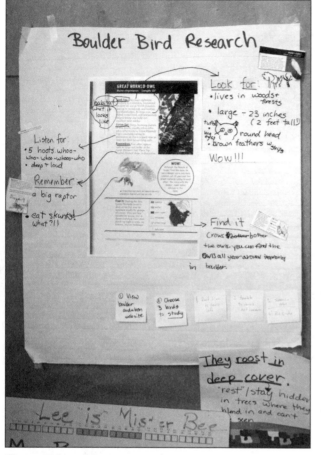

Figure 12.1
Class Notes About the Format of Field Guides

field guide pages, they discussed which of the formats were most helpful for them in identifying birds and designed their pages accordingly. (See Figure 12.1.) A template for creating their own field guides helped kids think about the information they needed to include. (See Figure 12.2.)

Brad reviewed the purposes of field guides before the kids went off to write their own. He shared that bird field guides describe birds so that we can figure out which ones we are seeing in the wild. He posed a few questions for kids to discuss regarding the purposes of field guides, including the following:

- Why do people use field guides?
- Why do bird specialists write field guides?
- What's in a field guide?

The kids brainstormed what goes into a field guide:

- A specific and clear description of a bird's physical characteristics—its wings, beak, feet, colored body markings, and feathers
- An explanation of where we might see the bird—its habitat (trees, ponds, grasses, mountains, plains, streams, and so on)
- A description of what the bird sounds like
- A description of any unusual characteristics, such as colorings and markings, shape of tail, and so on.

Next, Brad and the kids jotted down steps for creating a field guide for birds:

Making a Field Guide

1. Choose a bird.
2. Design your field guide page—think about where you will want to put photographs of the bird that match the information in your template.
3. Create your headings.
4. Read and write information. Under each heading, write the information that helps your reader identify the bird by its song (Listen for) or what it looks like (Find it). Add some amazing facts (Wow!) or information that the reader would want to remember (Remember), such as the bird's habitat or type of nest.

Kids put all of their paper pages together to create a whole-class field guide, which they shared with their families and other classrooms. Students and their families were able to use these on nature hikes and field trips. They also created digital field guides using Wixie, a publishing platform for kids to share information. Creating these field guides, both print and digital, provided a great way for kids to discover new information and share their learning authentically.

Figure 12.2
Template for Making Field Guides

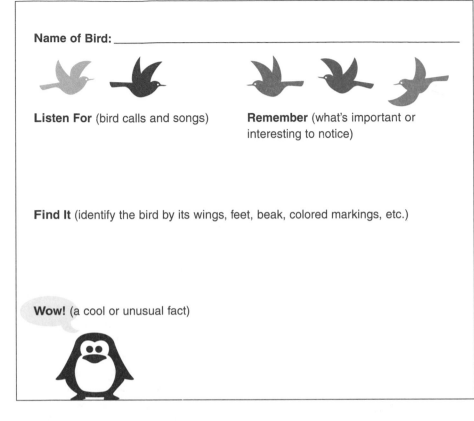

Name of Bird: _____

Listen For (bird calls and songs)   **Remember** (what's important or interesting to notice)

Find It (identify the bird by its wings, feet, beak, colored markings, etc.)

Wow! (a cool or unusual fact)

Synthesizing: How Reading Changes Thinking

Purpose: **Noticing how our thinking evolves and changes as we read**

Resource: **"Freedom Readers," an article by Fran Downey in *National Geographic Explorer***

Response: **Keeping track of changed thinking in reading logs**

Audience: **Intermediate and middle**

To make synthesizing understandable for our kids, we talk with them about how reading changes and adds to thinking. The main purpose of reading is to add to our knowledge base, think about new information, and integrate it. Sometimes the new information adds to and reinforces what we already know. Other times, new information changes us in certain ways—gives us a different perspective, a new angle on our thinking, some further insight. Whichever the case, we are synthesizing the information as we go. We need to ask kids every day to think about how their reading and learning is adding to and/or changing their thinking.

   One of the simplest yet most important considerations we can suggest to our kids is simply to notice their thinking before and after they have read or heard something. Mary Pfau found an article in *National Geographic Explorer* titled "Freedom Readers," which reported that, by law, slaves were not allowed to read, discussed the reasons why, and provided portraits of slaves who learned to read in spite of this law. This article led with the question "What does reading mean to you?" So before thinking through the article together, Mary asked her fourth graders to consider this question and jot down a response in their notebooks. The kids wrote down some terrific responses regarding what reading meant to them. Mary transferred them to a chart as follows:

- *Reading teaches you new information.*
- *Reading lets you picture stuff in your minds.*
- *The movie gets going and you can't stop.*
- *Reading is a pastime that cures boredom.*
- *You play someone else's voice in your mind.*
- *Reading takes you on an adventure.*
- *Excitement—Reading puts you on the edge of your seat.*
- *Reading takes you places you have never been.*
- *The truth is there are a lot of things I'd rather do than read, but then I get interested and I can't stop.*

After the class shared their responses, Mary read and thought through the article with the class. As she read about the struggle certain slaves endured just to learn to read, the kids' thinking began to evolve. Before reading the article no one had mentioned that reading was power or that reading meant freedom. Their own personal experience hadn't prepared them to think in this way. But as Mary read and guided a turn-and-talk discussion about the article, the powerful role that reading played in the lives of slaves began to impact the kids' thinking about the role of reading in everyday life. By the time they finished, they had a new take on reading and a new insight on the power of reading to inspire freedom and independence in a democratic society.

When she finished the interactive read-aloud, Mary simply asked the kids to open their notebooks again, draw a line under their first answer, and answer the question "Now what does reading mean to you?" Most of their answers reflected some additions to or changes in thinking after having read about the topic. We ask kids to reflect on how their thinking changes after they have read something. Additionally, we try to remember to ask them to consider this before and after a unit of study. We might ask, "What does immigration mean to you?" Then after they investigate the topic of immigration, we would ask, "Now what does immigration mean to you?" This gives us information about what students have learned and how their thinking has changed, but even more importantly, it gives our kids a clear understanding of the power of learning to add to and change thinking. Nothing gives us a better idea of how our kids' thinking changes as they learn. Lessons such as this one encourage them to regularly reflect on how new information impacts thinking. (See the assessment section of this chapter for examples of students' work related to this lesson.)

Synthesizing Media with Text

Purpose: **Using a graphic organizer to synthesize information from a media clip and a related text**

Resources: **Article and video "What Is Parkour?" from the Wonderopolis website (http://wonderopolis.org/wonder/what-is-parkour)**

Responses: **Student graphic organizers that include What I think I already know, what I learned from the text, what I learned from the video**

Audience: **Intermediate and middle**

Fourth-grade teacher Emily Sanders knows that in today's media-heavy world, readers are frequently called upon to synthesize information from video and print. She prepares students for this by using high-interest articles and videos to engage students and teach them to synthesize. For this lesson, she uses a high-interest topic and one that most students do not have significant background knowledge on: parkour. Parkour is an activity usually carried out in urban areas and features people athletically running, jumping, climbing, and swinging through, over, and around obstacles that are already in place in the surrounding environment: fences, walls, stairs, and so on. Emily chooses Wonderopolis, a site that shares videos with a question of the day; this day's question asks, "What is Parkour?" She begins her lesson by asking students to identify what they think they already know about parkour. This encourages students to acknowledge that not everything in their background knowledge may be correct and to be aware of new learning that might challenge their preconceived notions. Students jot their prior knowledge at the top of their graphic organizer.

What I think I already know:	
New Learning from the Video:	*New Learning from the Text:*

Emily plays the video for students, modeling how she stops and pauses it to jot down some of her thinking. Students also take this time to jot their own thinking on their organizers, working alongside Emily and referring to her model when needed. As the video continues, Emily lets kids' ideas take a front seat as they jot and confer with classmates.

As students work, she coaches partnerships as needed or listens in and jots some observation notes of her own. She might pop into a partnership and ask students to talk more about an important point, compare the article with the video, revisit the text, rewatch part of the video, or look for inconsistencies between the two.

Once partners have finished with the article, Emily gathers students back at the carpet. She asks a few pairs to share with the group—what they noticed, what they learned, and what lingering questions they have. She then demonstrates synthesizing all of her new learning from the day into a quick summary response on the back of the page. Students follow suit by writing their own summary responses to synthesize, summarize, and cement their new learning from the day's work.

This lesson serves as a starting point for helping students learn how to synthesize media and text. As they become more adept at this skill, we present them with increasingly complex informational video and texts that require more active thinking practices to determine important elements and synthesize them with new learning. We might also pair text and videos that share multiple perspectives on an issue or that have conflicting information to engage students' critical thinking and analysis skills. Our most advanced students can work to synthesize text and video sets that we build around topics of study—engaging with multiple texts, images, and media over the course of a few days. (See the example of student work in the assessment section at the end of this chapter.)

Reading for the Gist

Purpose: **Taking notes and using a variety of strategies to synthesize**
Resource: **The picture book *An Angel for Solomon Singer*, by Cynthia Rylant**
Responses: **Lists of notes and strategies; one-page written response**
Audience: **Intermediate and middle**

Near the end of a two-year loop through fourth and fifth grade, the kids in Glenda Clearwater's class had become increasingly adept at reading strategically, having practiced strategies over the course of two years. They understood that reading was about constructing meaning, and they read for that purpose. Glenda knew that writing while reading can show the reader's evolution of thought. Although her students had been coding the text and writing in margins while they read independently, they hadn't done much note taking while she read aloud. This was more of a challenge.

Glenda decided to up the ante and have them take notes as she read. She chose to read them Cynthia Rylant's picture book *An Angel for Solomon Singer*, the story of a sad, lonely old man who lives in a New York boardinghouse and laments his station in life. Things change when he wanders into a twenty-four-hour café and sees a friendly waiter with a smiling face.

Glenda began by having her students list the comprehension strategies they'd studied, and reiterated that these strategies could help them make sense of the text. She asked them to write down their thinking as well as story events as they took notes. She believed that notes of their questions, predictions, important ideas, and visual images would be of more use to them than mere content notes as they tried to synthesize the material. She knew that this book was difficult to understand and required questioning, visualizing, and inferential thinking to gain meaning.

As Glenda read *An Angel for Solomon Singer* out loud, she stopped and took notes in her own journal periodically and then shared her writing with the kids. Some of the students wrote practically nonstop throughout the read-aloud. Others needed a few moments to collect their thoughts and record their thinking. So Glenda paused intermittently to allow them to jot down some notes and complete their thoughts. When they finished, their notes revealed that they had visualized, asked questions, made connections, inferred, and synthesized while Glenda read.

Jessica's notes, which follow here, include examples of her flexible use of multiple strategies, a requirement when readers synthesize:

> He doesn't like where he lives.
> I think all of his wishes will come true.
> His life isn't that great.
> The café has made him happy.
> He is poor.
> I think the waiter is an angel.
> He is lonely / I've been lonely before.
> He wants to go back home.
> He likes to dream.
> He really likes to go to the Westway Café.
> He's starting to like New York better now.
> The Westway Café brightened up his life and made him feel like New York was his home.
> Why is he in New York City if he loves Indiana so much?
> How come he is so poor?

When Jessica wrote that she thought the waiter was an angel, she was inferring. When she mentioned that she'd been lonely before, she was making a connection. When she commented that the Westway Café made New York feel like home, she was synthesizing.

Claire drew a barn on her notes, which showed she was visualizing. She labeled the barn and wrote notes, predictions, and questions (see Figure 12.3).

When Glenda's students finished their note taking, they wrote responses in their journals based on their notes, their memories of the story, and their thinking. These notes and responses show how thinking evolves as kids read. As they derive more information from the text, they begin to synthesize it into the bigger picture. Claire's response follows:

Figure 12.3
Claire's Response to *An Angel for Solomon Singer*

> I think Mr. Singer has a horrible place to live. He hates everything in New York until he wanders into the Westway Café, "where dreams come true." This is a wonderful book about feelings, dreams, and angels. When our teacher was reading, it made me visualize. I had a picture of a perfect home for Solomon, in Illinois where I used to live. It had a balcony, bouncy grass, everlasting fields of corn and wheat. At night, he could lie down and stare at the stars in the sky. He would have three cats, two dogs, five fish, ten hamsters, etc. They would be free to run all over and Mr. Singer wouldn't be lonely. The sun would shine all day long. But New York isn't that bad, now that he found the Westway Café, especially when the angel watches over him.

In her response, Claire shows how she activates multiple strategies to understand the story. Ultimately, she reads for the gist of the story, how the Westway Café changes Solomon Singer's life. When readers synthesize, they get the gist.

Writing a Short Summary

Purpose: **Distinguishing between a summary and the reader's thinking**

Resource: ***The Librarian of Basra: A True Story from Iraq,* by Jeanette Winter**

Responses: **Two-column think sheet headed What the Piece Is About/What It Makes Me Think About**

Audience: **Intermediate and Middle**

For this lesson, Steph chose to read *The Librarian of Basra* by Jeanette Winter and use one of her favorite think sheets, a two-column form titled What the Piece Is About/What It Makes Me Think About. With the kids gathered in front of her, Steph read the book aloud. After she finished reading, she handed out the think sheet folded on the center line so that only the right column titled What It Makes Me Think About was showing and asked kids to write what the story made them think about. She reminded them that nothing is more important than the reader's thinking. She always emphasizes this by having her students record their thoughts first and then do the task at hand. While the kids wrote their thoughts, she wrote hers on the same think sheet.

After kids finished writing down their thinking, they read what they wrote to a partner. When they were done, Steph invited them to share their thinking with the class, and she shared her own. The right side of Steph's think sheet follows:

> This story reminds me that one person can truly make a difference. Alia, elderly and relatively powerless, risked her life to preserve the history and culture of Iraq by saving the books from the ravages of a war. It makes me think about Oscar Schindler, who saved so many Jews from the Nazis. What is it that makes some people risk their lives for others or for a cause? Passion maybe? I wonder for what I would risk my life other than my family.

Steph then asked the kids to unfold their two-column form and focus on the first column, What the Piece Is About. She explained that this is the summary part, not so much the reader's thinking about it. After they had a chance to turn and talk about what the story was about, she asked them to consider three things when trying to write a summary, things very similar to the ones Debbie Miller, in an earlier lesson, asked her kids to consider when retelling orally.

1. Pick out the most important ideas.
2. Keep it brief.
3. Say it in your own words in a way that makes sense.

Steph then asked the kids to turn and talk about what they thought were some of the most important ideas in the story and then share them with the class. As they shared, she recorded their ideas on a chart.

Important Ideas

Librarian saved the books
She was passionate.
She loved books.
War
Teamwork—her friends helped
Loyalty
Risked her life
30,000 books
Iraq

After completing the chart, they talked about each one and decided whether it was important enough to include in the summary with an eye toward keeping it brief. They agreed that most of the ideas were important but some details could be combined into one idea, such as the fact that she was passionate and loved books, or that they really didn't have to include the specific number 30,000 but needed to include that she saved most of the books in the library. Finally, together they wrote the following in the first column of the think sheet:

At the beginning of the war in Iraq, a brave, passionate librarian risked her life to save many books with the help of loyal friends.

Summaries don't have to be only one sentence. Two or three work. At the conclusion of the lesson, Steph thanked them and reminded them that although it is important to be able to summarize the story as they did, the most important thinking is always the reader's thinking!

A thoughtful example of a completed think sheet is shown in Figure 12.4. (See an example of a short summary in the assessment section at the end of the chapter.)

Figure 12.4
A Student's Think Sheet Distinguishing Between a Summary and a Personal Response

What the piece is about...	What it makes me think about...
An amazing libarian who loved books saved alot of them so they wouldn't be destroyed by the War in Iraq.	Would I risk my life for some books proably not IS she going to build a new library? She has a lot of guts to stay there with her books. I would proably be on my way to Egypt or Turkey. Why would she go out middle of a war to ask someone to help her move her books? I would feel like crying If I didn't not leave I would be in my house trying to calm myself down and saying it's okay not worried about some books. How did she feel after the war? She should definatly be honored and she should have her name like mohmad

Synthesizing Big Ideas and Common Themes Across Several Texts

Purpose: **Summarizing and synthesizing themes across texts in a series of lessons**

Resources: **Picture books on a world issue—in this case refugees who are fleeing conflicts or difficult conditions. Texts: "Garana's Story," an article from *National Geographic Explorer* by Kent Page; *A Thirst for Home* by Christine Ieronimo; and *Four Feet, Two Sandals* and *My Name Is Sangoel* by Karen Lynn Williams and Khadra Mohammed**

Responses: **Sticky notes and class chart**

Audience: **Intermediate and middle**

Kids are curious about the big wide world out there. Sometimes we shy away from tackling difficult international or domestic issues because they are complex and can be distressing. But kids often know what is going on—and they want to know more. They see photos or stories on the news about wars, conflicts, and other world problems and issues and often bring these concerns into the classroom.

Erin Livingston and Gerardo Dillehy began the year by reading picture books that focused on developing empathy and compassion in their third-grade students. As they worked to build caring and respectful communities in their classrooms, seeking out ways to bring issues from the larger world to the kids' attention made sense. As Erin and Gerardo discussed ideas about empathy and compassion close to home, one child mentioned how sad she was to see pictures on the evening news about children in Syria, describing a news report about a refugee camp in this war-torn country. While reticent to get into a study of war and conflict in the Middle East, Erin, Gerardo, and librarian Melissa Oviatt were able to find a list of books that provided a variety of texts on refugees appropriate for third graders' interests and sensibilities. Creating a text set, with picture books, nonfiction articles, and even videos on the theme of refugees introduced kids to the issues. An article about Garana, a young girl who had fled her native country of Afghanistan for a refugee camp in Pakistan, provided the kids with background about refugee camps, reasons why refugees had to flee their countries, and what life was like for refugee kids on a day-to-day basis.

Based on the many questions kids had about Garana's life, the class focused on these essential questions as they delved into additional texts and resources about refugees:

- Why do people have to leave their homes and go to another place or country?
- How do they feel when they have to leave their home and perhaps their families?
- What kinds of experiences and feelings do refugees around the world have in common?

While there weren't easy answers to important questions and issues, the teachers began reading picture books, which had different perspectives on the issues raised by the kids' questions. The teachers created a chart for each picture book to record the big ideas, asking, "What is important to remember?" As kids listened to and jotted their questions and inferences about the picture book *A Thirst for Home* (Ieronimo) on sticky notes, they realized that the title had multiple meanings. During the first few pages of the book, the young girl Alemitu and her mother experience hunger and drought as they walk miles each day to collect water. This is the reason Alemitu's mother takes her to an orphanage. This shocked kids and left them wondering why she had to go and why her mom couldn't come with her to live in the orphanage. As the story unfolds and Alemitu is adopted by a family in what appears to be the United States, students' interpretation of the title is more fully realized: Alemitu remembers her mother and her original home but realizes her mother's sacrifice as she experiences a new life.

With the book *Four Feet, Two Sandals* (Williams), the kids had a lot to say about the theme of friendship. While they were at first puzzled why the two girls in a refugee camp shared one pair of sandals between them, they came to understand that the sandals symbolized the girls' friendship and their willingness to share what little they had. Kids understood that despite hardship, friendship can flourish and that it can also continue "even when you are not in the same place."

As the teachers read the books, they led guided discussions that prompted kids to surface big ideas from the text. The teachers recorded these big ideas on an anchor chart as kids jotted their thinking on sticky notes. The kids' sticky notes represented evidence that supported the big ideas on the chart.

After several days of investigating three different books on similar themes, the kids illustrated and wrote about the themes in all three of the books. (See Figure 12.5.) Kids had many lingering questions about refugees that these picture books encouraged, so the group returned to the essential question—"What kinds of experiences and feelings do refugees around the world have in common?" Kids discussed common themes across texts, such as memory and remembrance, seeking a better life even though it meant leaving one's home and family, and valuing traditions, family, and friendship.

Figure 12.5
A Student's Work Expresses Themes in Three Books

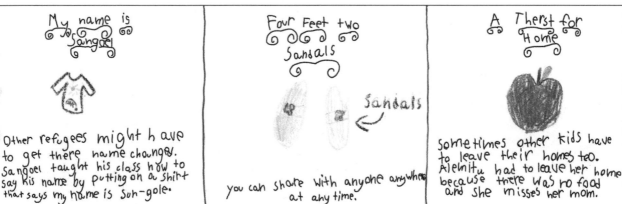

Video Summaries

Purpose: **Summarizing learning in different medium**

Resources: **Online articles, for this lesson "The 3-D Zebra Crossings That Are Making India's Roads Safer for Pedestrians" by Meera Dolasia, and a device with a camera**

Responses: **Bulleted lists of essential information from a text and individual student recordings**

Audience: **Intermediate and middle**

Technology has changed the way we gather information from our students. While some students are able to clearly articulate their thinking in writing, sharing details in a well-organized manner, not all of them reveal the depth and breadth of their thought process in written form. This is where teaching students to create video responses can amplify how we connect with kids and those responses can act as powerful formative assessments.

In this lesson, we help students create a summary response using some quick notes and a video recording. This work will support students in their written summaries later on.

Fifth-grade teacher Marcus Rodriguez models how to synthesize the important points of a text. He uses an article from a favorite class website for news, DOGOnews.

When everyone is gathered together on the carpet, Marcus poses a question to engage them in today's topic: "Have you ever tried to cross the street when a car is coming and it doesn't stop?"

The students respond in an animated manner, naturally turning to their neighbor and sharing their story. In the city where they live, it is commonplace for cars to neglect to stop for pedestrians even if they are in the crosswalk. Marcus knows that students will be engaged in this topic because he's carefully selected a text that speaks to their experiences. Then Marcus explains:

> *Today we're going to work on using our verbal skills to summarize an article about this topic. Instead of jotting down a summary after reading, we're going to try and create a short list of words and phrases. We will use this list to help us record a quick video to share with one another.*

Marcus then projects the article for the entire class to see and begins to read aloud. He stops after each paragraph and gives kids a chance to talk about and process the information:

> *Turn and talk about your thinking.*
> *What seems like important information here?*

They read the article again and Marcus asks students to give a thumbs-up anytime they hear something they think should go on a bulleted list of important information. He writes these points on an anchor chart for all to see. Students turn and talk about which points should be included in the summary and why. They debate the importance of each item and pare down the list to the most essential parts.

This conversation is an effective support for students who often include too little or too much information in their summaries.

Chart of Summarized Information

Zebra crossings at crosswalks aren't effective at helping cars to stop for pedestrians.

Research shows 3 out of 4 drivers did not stop.

Only 5% stopped when they saw someone trying to cross.

A mother-daughter team of artists decided to use an optical illusion to fix the problems.

Now the stripes appear to be 3-D and they are working!

Marcus guides the kids as they talk about what they would say in a summary video using their notes. Marcus reviews the steps needed to make the video and demonstrates how he speaks loudly and clearly, including the information the class has just discussed. He reviews his video to do a quick check and makes sure he's within the time limit, then posts the video to the class learning management system for feedback. Students observe and note what Marcus does to apply it to their own videos. Using the chart for support, students then rehearse their summaries with partners, using the language of summarizing:

The gist of this article is . . .
What happens is . . . then . . . and finally . . .
Some important points you should know are . . . as well as . . .
The problem is . . . It is resolved by . . .
Something we can do about this issue is . . .

Once students have worked through the rehearsal, they break off to record their own video summaries. In one-to-one environments students can all record at the same time. Otherwise, we have students rotate through a recording booth (station) during the workshop. The teacher confers with kids and follows up with those who need more support. As a follow-up to this lesson, Marcus has students watch the video newscast that accompanies the article and synthesize the information from the article with the information from the video.

Trying to Understand: Seeking Answers to Questions That Have None

Purpose: **Synthesizing information by attempting to answer difficult questions**
Resource: ***The Triumphant Spirit: Portraits and Stories of Holocaust Survivors, Their Messages of Hope and Compassion,* by Nick Del Calzo**
Responses: **Sticky notes with questions**
Audience: **Middle**

The genre of narrative nonfiction personalizes the human experience for readers in ways other genres simply can't. Personal tales of triumph and tragedy become indelibly etched in our brains when we read them. Sometimes these experiences are horrific and unthinkable. The Holocaust, above all else, reflects the worst, most grotesque aspects of human nature. Teachers understandably shy away from topics that are almost beyond comprehension, feeling ill-equipped to deal with such horrendous information and at a loss to explain reasons for this behavior when children ask how such a thing could happen. We believe, however, that children deserve to know about what has really happened in the past. Furthermore, there are clear connections between historical events such as the Holocaust and situations of intolerance and genocide in many parts of the world today. In some ways, not to deal with these tragic events is to prevent children from learning about the strength of the human spirit and the triumph of survival.

Seventh-grade teacher Carla Mosher understands that it is easier not to think about unthinkable acts. And she knows that if we don't think about them, we will forget them. Carla wants her students to leave her class with an understanding of, and a personal commitment to, the warning "Never Again." To do this, she and her students build background knowledge about these times by reading a wide range of literature, including novels, picture books, poetry, editorials, essays, and feature articles. Their inquiry culminates with each student entering a local writing contest named in honor of Anne Frank. Carla's commitment to the vow of "Never Again," along with a message of compassion and hope, is central to their exploration.

Carla subscribes to the *Denver Post*'s Newspaper in Education Program. As a subscriber, she receives occasional special student supplements published by the *Post*. One such supplement included multiple copies of a student edition of *The Triumphant Spirit: Portraits and Stories of Holocaust Survivors, Their Messages of Hope and Compassion*. This excerpt is from a book by the same name created by Nick Del Calzo. The *Denver Post* excerpt includes

MARCUS

I wonder how he survived the Holocaust. It's Amazing how he Survived that camp. It would Be hard to tell the story. I would cry to see people die.

I wonder how Harry Glaser can go three days without Food or water. I know in 3 hours I'm hungry right away and I'm a little guy.

I wonder how Harry Glaser. Would feel Not ever to see your family. I would cry every single Night I cant amagine how he would feel Just thinking about it. It's sad

I wonder how hard that gas chamber would affect His Life. I Bet he has alot oF nightmares about the Holocaust And his parent's dieing.

I wonder how Harry Glaser would feel about Collecting dead bodies and Seing them dead. I'd thow up And then he was ordeard to do that, they would have to shoot me I would not Do it

I wonder how you Can shoot some one with a machine gun and killed 25,000 Prisoners I cant Imagine Seeing bodies Scatterd all over the place,

Figure 12.6
Marcus's Questions About *The Triumphant Spirit*

fourteen inspirational portraits of Holocaust survivors. To preserve this treasure, Carla cut up each copy and laminated every page. In that way, there were more than enough to go around.

Carla asked her students to think about the title as they read these portraits. She recognized that the text would be shocking and disturbing, and she wanted her students to keep the notion of the triumphant spirit of survival in mind. She gave them sticky notes and encouraged them to record their thinking as they read, reminding them to use the strategies they had practiced to help comprehend text.

Carla was not surprised that most of her students were recording questions as they read. A student named Marcus was reading the story of Harry Glaser, who at age twenty-two arrived at Auschwitz from his native Romania. His tragic story tells the horrors of becoming separated from his family and never seeing them again, of being forced to drag dead bodies to mass graves at Auschwitz and Bergen-Belsen, and of triumphant survival and eventual liberation by the British in 1945. A photograph taken by the British liberators accompanies the story and shows Mr. Glaser holding a newspaper photograph of mass graves.

When Carla stopped to confer with Marcus, his sticky notes were jammed with questions, beginning with "What is in that photograph he's holding?" As Carla began to help him look at the horrifying photo and work through it with him, he told her that he had thought those might have been bodies, but he couldn't believe it. Each sticky note he wrote began with "I wonder" and included his own reaction (see Figure 12.6). Most of what he read was inconceivable to him. Carla realized that his questions were so prolific because he was trying desperately to make sense of this tragedy. He just couldn't comprehend it. These questions seemed to have no answers.

As the students shared their disbeliefs, most were overwhelmed with questions. It soon became clear to Carla that the discussion spawned by these questions helped the class construct meaning. Their questions led them to synthesize their thoughts and feelings. These questions nudged their thinking and gave them insight into personal feelings that they had not explored before. The more the students shared their questions and talked about these portraits, the more they knew about the Holocaust, and the more they came to realize that some things can't be explained and some questions can never be answered.

What they did come to understand, however, was the spirit of triumph that tied these survivors to one another and the sense of hope and compassion that is still with them today. Their stories live on. They bravely speak out about the unspeakable horror they endured to ensure that people will not forget. Carla's students read the survivors' personal stories, and remember never to forget. This was their synthesis.

Teaching with the End in Mind: Assessing What We've Taught

Summarizing and Synthesizing

Based on the lessons in this chapter, we look for evidence that

1. *Students summarize information by retelling.* We look for evidence that students can summarize by picking out the most important information, keeping it brief, and saying it in their own words.

2. *Students become aware of when they add to their knowledge base and revise their thinking as they read.* We look for evidence that students are learning new information, adding to their background knowledge, and changing their thinking.

3. *Students synthesize information through writing.* We look for evidence that students pick out the most important information and merge their thinking with it to come up with responses that are both personal and factual.

4. *Students use a variety of ways to synthesize information and share their learning.* They share information through writing, drawing, speaking, creating video, and so on. We look for evidence that students use authentic questions, inferences, and interpretations to synthesize information and share it with others through a variety of projects and products.

Suggestions for Differentiation

When kids actively use their knowledge, they create many different ways to synthesize and share it. All of our kids—English language learners, developing readers, students with special needs—have opportunities to share in a wide variety of contexts. Giving them choices about how to organize and present their new learning fosters engagement. Kids love to create a variety of posters, projects, videos, podcasts, PowerPoints, books, models, mobiles, murals, and so on to demonstrate learning and understanding.

Summarizing and Synthesizing Assessment Commentary

Responses from the lesson "Synthesizing: How Reading Changes Thinking," where the teacher asks what the reader thinks about a topic both before and after reading an article

> I like reading because you can go (Before) places without leaving your chair.
> I'm glad that I'm able to read.
> I can't imagine life without books.
>
> after
>
> Reading is POWER

◀ This student had some good thoughts about the meaning of reading before reading "Freedom Readers," an article by Fran Downey about slaves not being able to read. She even said she couldn't imagine life without books. After reading the article, however, she realized that reading also meant power, something she hadn't thought of before. She understands something about reading that she didn't know before, which is what education is all about.

▶ This student has a marvelous way of expressing what reading means to him. But his brain comes alive with the entire new world of thinking after reading the article. He recognizes that reading also gives us power and independence and that there is nothing more important than the power of knowledge. He now seems to understand that reading is one way to achieve that knowledge. Again, we see how reading the article added to and enriched his already terrific notions about reading.

> It's as if your (B) world disapears and the world of the book unravels before your eyes.
> It means a way to (A) get power and a way to get indipendance. How you get indipendance is with the power of knowlage, knowlage is mightyer than any thing!!!

▶ In this response, we don't see much change in thinking after reading the article. As a matter of fact, there is little evidence that the student thought much about the article or understood the assignment. We would meet with this student and reread the article with her to help her understand how reading can add to and change thinking.

> Reading means a lot Before to me. I like readin because you can picture stuff in your mind
>
> After
> Helps you learn a lot more tha you knew before you read a book, novel, articl or even a textbook. I helps me pass th time away, and you don't want to stop doing it. I'm really thankful for reading because it is a gift.

Using a think sheet to synthesize new learning from both text and video from the lesson "Synthesizing Media with Text"

▾ Ally responds on a think sheet that scaffolds her to synthesize information on the topic of parkour. She knew a bit about it before viewing a video and reading text related to it. You can see in the new learning columns that she added a great deal to her background knowledge and then synthesized all of the new information into a brief summary that shows deeper understanding of the topic. She jotted new information, asked questions, and concluded with some of the big ideas she learned from reading and viewing, such as that parkour was not only good for physical health but good for mental health as well.

Topic: Parkour

What I already think I know   parkour is obstacles and doing tricks that are difficult to do i.e.
Flips, handstands etc. It is like gymnastics but with objects everyday objects
Stunts

Name: Ally   16

New learning from the video
- City setting
- Jump across spaces
- Dangerous
- Flips on small areas
- Athletic
- Train
- Making use of normal things
- Jump to and over things
- Gymnastics moves
- Train, skate park, stairs
- Course
- Coordinate (set-up path)
- Scary
- Group of people
- Cartwheels
- Jump high and far to, across, over, and off things
- Flips off of objects + ground
- Talented, brave people

New learning from the text
- Parkour chase scene in action movie
- Stunt doubles
- Non competitive
- traceur/ces
- Vaulting, rolling, running, climbing, jumping on over +
- around things
- City streets
- Eastern martial arts (beginning) ninjitsu
- 20's french military training
- 80's Yamakas: (1st parkour group)
- le parcours training, known as parcours du combattant
- Art/sport getting over obstacles
- Discipline, training very careful (risky is discouraged)
- Where do they practice?
- Free running a.k.a. parkour, now different
- artistic / efficient
- Parkour self improvement (physical + mental) freedom from society's thinking and constraints

Synthesize to put together

I thought that parkour was just tricks and stunts that were dangerous. Now I know that traceurs + traceuses train and work hard to get good at the art form. Parkour has deep roots in martial arts as well as training in the French army. Parkour is not only for physical health but for mental health too. traceurs and traceuces are free from society's usual thinking and are healthy and fit.

A summary of new learning from the lesson "Writing a Short Summary"

▾ This second grader summarized her knowledge about John Muir as her class studied environmentalists who have made a difference. As young kids learn to summarize, they write what they are learning in their own words, keep it short, and share what most intrigued them.

John Muir

This is a true story of John Muir.

I learned that John Muir walked 1,000 miles. Jon John Muir walked all the from wascanson all the way to the gulf of Mexico. John carried a notebook and wrote and drew what he saw. John studied nature—forests plants, animals even the stars and snowflak He wrote to people to get people to stop cutting down trees! John starte loved Yosemite. John started the Sierra Club to save nature.

Part III

Comprehension Across *the* Curriculum

Content Literacy: Reading, Writing, and Researching in Science and Social Studies

Content matters! Big time. We agree with David Perkins when he says, "Knowledge does not just sit there, it functions richly in people's lives to help them understand and deal with the world" (1992). The time has come to teach social studies and science in a way that reflects the rich, textured, intriguing nature of these disciplines. For years, we have said kids are passionate about the world. High time to immerse students in compelling content topics so that they think critically and actively use their knowledge. To give content the attention it deserves, we have created these two new chapters where we show how we integrate comprehension and content instruction across the curriculum and throughout the year.

Since the previous edition of this book, we have become even more convinced of the need to lay down a foundation of thinking across the curriculum. And research backs this up. As we have said before, Cervetti suggests that knowledge building is the new frontier in literacy instruction

235

(2011). So teaching comprehension strategies in science, social studies, and all matters of content is imperative. We teach comprehension throughout the day in every discipline and integrate science and social studies topics with literacy instruction. Content area specialists, whether they teach history, science, or geography, all need to be teachers of reading. No one knows better how to teach kids to read and think about science than a science teacher. History teachers are the best prepared to teach kids the ins and outs of reading primary sources. Content area teachers, however, may not realize this since they studied the content and did not necessarily study how to teach kids to read and understand it. But it's really true that those who read and study history and/or science have the most expertise in how to teach it. This section will support all teachers to merge content teaching with comprehension instruction.

Reading, writing, and thinking across disciplines promote literacy in the broadest sense of the term. P. David Pearson suggests that "science is about how the natural world works and social studies is about how people live in the world. We'd all be better off if schools taught reading as a tool to support learning those big ideas found in science and social studies instruction. This transforms reading instruction from its current role as a curricular 'bully' in our schools into a role it is better suited to play—being a curricular 'buddy'" (2006a).

Content Literacy Principles

To be a curricular "buddy," we need to ensure that kids are reading, writing and researching across the disciplines. This is essential if our students are to meet 21st century standards. We believe the following content literacy principles are most likely to result in a classroom full of engaged, active learners with teachers who have a deep understanding of pedagogy, content, and their students. These principles support kids not only to learn and understand the content but also to become curious and excited about it, nudging them to continue studying and learning.

Content Literacy Principles

- Use comprehension strategies flexibly to turn information into knowledge and actively use it
- Live a life full of wonder and curiosity
- Grasp the big ideas and essential questions they encounter as they read and research
- Read with an inquisitive mind and a skeptical stance
- Interact with text, media, resources, artifacts, teachers, and each other
- View nonfiction as compelling and accessible
- Merge thinking with new learning
- Make thinking audible and visible
- Bathe content learning in rich talk and discussion
- Build interest and intrigue with visuals, videos, artifacts, and interviews as well as text
- Engage in collaborative inquiry and action

For kids to learn to do these things, teachers must design lessons that teach them how. Teachers who emphasize content literacy craft learning environments and experiences to make content active, exciting, and challenging.

Current Trends in Science and Social Studies Instruction

Much to our chagrin, since the previous edition of this book, time spent on social studies and science in school has continued to decline. A report issued by the Center on Educational Policy found that five years into No Child Left Behind (NCLB), 44 percent of school districts reported decreased time for social studies and science instruction as well as art, music, and, of course, recess. Social studies has fared the very worst. Thirty-six percent of schools decreased the time allocated to social studies (McMurrer 2008). That equals a net loss of four weeks of social studies instruction per year. According to *Atlantic* writer Jen Kalaidis (2013), only one-third of Americans can name all three branches of government and only 23 percent know that the First Amendment supports freedom of religion. Clearly more time on social studies is crucial. In a democracy, we don't think history and civics should be optional!

If you doubt that this lack of history and civics is a problem, consider this. In the 2016 presidential election, 46.5 percent of eligible voters did not exercise their right to vote. That clocks in at over one hundred million people who didn't believe their vote made a whit of difference. Recent studies by the Center on Education Policy found that from 2002 to 2007, classroom time devoted to civics decreased by 33 percent nationally (McMurrer 2008). We think there is a cause-and-effect relationship here. When you don't take civics, you don't learn the importance of living in a participatory democracy and the power of expressing your voice through voting.

Unfortunately, according to one survey, "Students in the US, at all grade levels, found social studies to be one of the least interesting, most irrelevant subjects in the school curriculum" (Loewen 2007). We believe that part of the reason kids feel this way is related to how it's been taught for time immemorial. Too often, a slog through the gargantuan textbook ends up being the default curriculum. Students experience what Diane Ravitch calls "boring, abbreviated pap in the history text book that reduces stirring events, colorful personalities and riveting controversies to . . . a few leaden paragraphs" (2010). We're with Robert Bain, who says that history is all about "enduring human dramas and dilemmas, fascinating mysteries, and an amazing cast of historical characters involved in events that exemplify the best and worst of human experiences" (2007).

In recent years, science education has fared better than social studies. One reason is that since 2007 students are required to be tested in science at least once during grades three to five, six to nine, and ten to twelve by federal mandate. We all know that what gets tested gets taught. We have also seen a flurry of interest in science-related curriculum due to increased funding for STEM initiatives. The Next Generation Science Standards (NGSS Lead States 2013) developed by the states to prepare students for both college and careers have generated much attention.

However, as of this writing, this increased attention to science has not led to the most optimal environment for science teaching and learning. In fact, we see a number of states passing legislation that questions evolution and climate change, as well as other issues, in what is commonly agreed upon as settled science. In March of 2017, the EPA director, Scott Pruitt, strongly rejected the established science of climate change and suggested that human activity was not a primary contributing factor. Scientists around the globe were stunned and outraged (Mooney and Dennis 2017). The head of the American Association for the Advancement of Science said in an interview that "if evidence becomes optional, if ideological assertions or beliefs are just as good as scientifically vetted evidence, then [people's] quality of life suffers . . . There's a level of concern [among scientists] unlike anything I've seen" (Holt 2017).

As Rush Holt says, beliefs and uninformed opinions should not drive policy, or science curriculum for that matter. What is really needed in terms of science policy and education is to emphasize evidence-based learning, critical thinking, and serious scientific analysis.

The strategies we emphasize in this book foster the critical reading and analytic skills needed to learn and understand the evidence that science presents. "Situating reading comprehension instruction in science is good for both reading and science—reading deepens science investigations and supports better conceptual understanding in science when combined with firsthand investigations, and science puts reading to work in authentic and knowledge enriching ways" (Cervetti 2011).

Maxine Greene views the promise of literacy as extending across many subject areas and disciplines:

> *We owe young people the open doors and expanded possibilities that only literacy can provide. Teaching for literacy conceives of learning not as behavior but as action—of process, of restlessness, of quest. To encounter the arts and other subjects in a mood of discovery and mindfulness and rational passion is to have experiences that exclude inertness. Literacy empowers people, it is a beginning, a becoming—not an end in itself.* (1982)

Active Learning in the Researcher's Workshop

Content classrooms that make a difference spur curiosity and spark exploration. Magazines, Big Books, websites, aquariums, maps, and charts fill these rooms. One child sketches a molting crayfish in the classroom terrarium. A small group of fourth graders check out images of their homes on Google Earth and compute how far they walk to school every day. Middle school students engage in a gallery walk of images and photos to build background as they begin a unit on the Civil War. Whether it's literacy block, science, or social studies, kids are reading, writing, drawing, talking, creating, listening, and investigating. They observe, discuss, debate, inquire, and generate new questions about their learning. Active literacy in all content areas is the means to deeper understanding and diverse, flexible thinking.

To build intrigue, knowledge, and understanding, students read, learn about, and interact with the questions, controversies, discoveries, and drama that are the real stuff of content learning. This kind of deep dive often leads kids to care about and act on what they are learning. But how does this happen in our classrooms? We continue to be big fans of reading and writing workshop. Why not researcher's workshop? In researcher's workshop, the teacher and kids follow workshop rituals and routines, including teacher-led mini-lessons;

practice through reading, writing, talking, viewing, and drawing; and time built in for conferring and sharing. To immerse kids in the vast ocean of content, we use a four-phase inquiry framework for researcher's workshop. In Chapter 14 we share this framework and examples of ways we use it for research and exploration, including three units of study for different grade levels.

Thinking About Content

Ron Ritchhart (2002) suggests that we cultivate student thinking by encouraging attitudes of curiosity, mindfulness, and inquiry. These ideas resonate with our goals for content literacy. Ritchhart and his colleagues at Harvard's Project Zero suggest that teachers look for signs that thinking is happening in classrooms. They ask the following questions:

- Are students explaining things to one another?
- Are students offering creative ideas?
- Are students (and teachers) using the language of thinking?
- Are students debating interpretations?

We agree with these and add some of our own questions to the mix:

- Are kids wondering and asking questions?
- Are they synthesizing as they read text?
- Are they connecting the new to the known?
- Are they using text evidence to draw conclusions and infer themes?

We keep all of these questions in mind as we work with our students. When we design instruction in the content areas, we focus on comprehension and understanding. As teachers, we take stock of what happens in our classrooms, and use the following hallmarks to guide our planning and instruction to sustain a culture of thinking across the curriculum and support content literacy (adapted from Ritchhart 2002).

Hallmarks for Creating an Environment for Thoughtful Content Literacy Instruction

The learning opportunities we create

- focus on comprehension, meaning making, and understanding rather than memorization;
- connect us with real-world, real-life issues;
- center on content-related big ideas, essential questions, and key concepts;
- engage students' interest and enthusiasm;
- encourage student choice and independent thinking;
- provide time for thinking to take place; and
- set expectations that push students toward higher levels of thinking.

When we demonstrate our thinking, we

- illustrate what good thinking looks like;
- focus on topics and ideas worth thinking about;
- reveal our curiosity, interests, and passions; and
- explicitly show how we understand what we read through questioning, drawing inferences, synthesizing information and ideas, and so forth.

We support attitudes and interactions that

- emphasize a common language for talking about thinking and learning;
- encourage and respect different viewpoints and perspectives;
- ensure that students experience positive ways of thinking about and engaging with content;
- spark thoughtful discussion and debate; and
- support students' enthusiasm for discovery and their readiness to investigate what's new or unusual.

Student artifacts and work products

- are authentic in nature;
- are the result of thoughtful work and send the message that thinking matters;
- make thinking visible;
- involve sharing knowledge and teaching others; and
- illustrate the process of thinking and learning.

Materials/texts/literature that students read

- encourage a variety of perspectives, opinions, and interpretations;
- require students to solve or discover problems;
- provoke discussion and raise significant issues; and
- focus on content-related themes, issues, and/or essential questions.

To learn more about classroom environments that teach for understanding, enhance engagement through content learning, and create cultures of thinking, we suggest you pick up a copy of Ron Ritchhart's *Creating Cultures of Thinking* (2015).

Practices for Reading to Learn in Social Studies and Science

We teach kids to think about and actively use the knowledge they are learning as they read. To merge comprehension and content instruction, we engage kids in real-world reading and focused content reading. Real-world reading is the kind of reading we usually do outside of school, such as newspapers, magazines, websites, nonfiction books, and historical fiction. Focused content reading is the reading we do in school that is directly related to our curriculum. But we believe in bringing the real world into the classroom in social studies, history, and science instruction, so these practices work with a wide variety of texts and sources.

We have many options for gathering resources and exploring information. We remain big fans of school librarians with whom we search and scrounge for all kinds of resources: realia, picture books, nonfiction trade books, videos, maps, magazine articles, websites, documents, and even textbooks. It's never been easier to go online and find several relevant articles within thirty seconds. We make sure kids have as many hands-on experiences as we can find and the field trip budget will allow. We advocate a multigenre, multilevel, multimedia, multicultural curriculum that gives access to all of our students, not just the at-benchmark readers. Most important of all is that kids have ongoing opportunities to express their thoughts, questions, and ideas about what they are reading and experiencing.

Many of the practices suggested here are described in detail in the previous pages of this book. We use the lessons in the strategy chapters again and again to teach science and social studies. We show how interactive read-alouds with picture books can launch a study of the civil rights era, dangerous avalanches, or quirky animals. In Chapter 11, we describe a variety of note-taking strategies that are useful for a range of informational text in any discipline, and in Chapter 12, we share ways to pull together larger concepts and themes so that kids come away with important ideas rather than disconnected facts. In the following section, we suggest practices that you might easily adapt to your own content area units.

Literacy Practices for Social Studies and History

These literacy practices link reading comprehension instruction with what we view as best practices in history and social studies teaching. When we design history and social studies instruction, we teach students to do the following:

- Ask and investigate authentic questions about other people, places, and times
- Read, view, and interpret a variety of sources—primary and secondary sources, images, artifacts, historical fiction, and so on
- Research and understand multiple perspectives and interpretations
- Actively use reading, writing, discussion, and artistic expression to acquire and share knowledge
- Merge thinking with information and ideas to glimpse "ways of thinking" in the discipline
- Speak, write, and advocate to express opinions, take a stand, and act

Some of the instructional techniques that support these practices are discussed here.

Interactive Read-Alouds with Picture Books
We use interactive read-alouds (see Chapter 6) with picture books to immerse kids in narratives about historic people and events. Listening to picture books

creates a common experience for the whole class and provides an imaginative entry point into times and places that are far away and long ago. Through narratives, kids are introduced to big ideas and themes or thought-provoking questions. With young children, especially, we often use props and artifacts to make story events and characters come alive. Kids of all ages are eager to act out important events or take on the roles of historic characters. As kids engage in all manner of responses, they talk, write, and sketch their way to understanding.

Observe Artifacts and Analyze Primary Sources

To read and think like historians, kids react and respond to photographs, images, journals, diaries, and other documents. They explore and interpret artifacts and historical realia. (See Figure 13.1.) Constructing meaning from a wide array of historical sources requires students to combine their background knowledge with text clues to draw inferences about historical people and times. They leave tracks of their thinking, showing how the evidence they gather from sources leads to conclusions or to further exploration. Kids learn firsthand what it means to be a historian and practice historical interpretation.

Figure 13.1
Students Examine Native American Artifacts

Book Club Discussions with Historical Fiction Picture Books or Nonfiction Trade Books

There's no better way to build kids' background knowledge than to read historical fiction picture books that zero in on authentic information and engage their interest. Historical fiction gives kids a sense of the drama, emotions, and excitement of history. Well-written nonfiction trade books, such as biographies, also work well with book club discussions. Historical fiction and nonfiction trade books provide opportunities for kids to learn about dilemmas, issues, and ideas that are missing from most textbooks.

To get started with the book clubs, students meet in small groups and read and talk about a variety of picture books that present different perspectives on a topic. They can use a variety of think sheets to ask questions about and merge their thinking with the historical information they glean from the text. After kids read and talk about several books in their small groups, the class comes together to discuss important themes and lingering questions. As the topic study continues, kids often investigate those lingering questions arising from book club discussions.

Create Concept Maps, Posters, and Other Visual Representations of Events, People, and Ideas

In social studies and history, it's tempting to try to "fill kids up" with information—dates, events, people, and more. We know these details are important, and so we ask kids to do this work themselves by teaching them to organize and share all the important information they are learning. Kids organize and visually represent concepts and information in a way that makes sense to them. For instance, concept maps show how historic details support a larger idea or demonstrate the causes and effects of historical events. A biographical poster of a famous person, for example, illustrates many facets of that person's life and accomplishments. (See Figure 13.2.) Illustrations, diagrams, and other features provide ways for kids to blend artistic and written expression as they share important information with others.

Figure 13.2
A Student's Biographical Map of Emily Dickinson

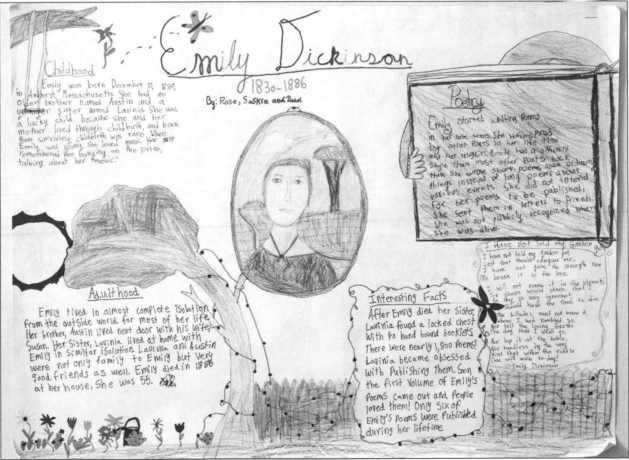

Stop, Think, and React to Videos and Various Media

Historical reenactments of events get kids engaged in a topic by showing the drama, problems, and dilemmas of history. Videos from cultures far and wide provide a sense of being there that books can't match. To discourage kids from watching videos on autopilot, we frequently pause the video and ask them to stop, think, and react to what they see and observe. We provide a variety of scaffolds to guide their thinking—forms headed Observations/Questions and Comments or Notes/My Thinking—and ask kids to turn and talk about their reactions to the video before recording their thoughts. Kids learn more when they talk and write about what they are viewing.

Create Maps of Countries or Cultures: Merge Thinking with New Information

Kids create large wall maps of a region, country, or continent so they can share their new learning in ways that are visible and concrete. They gather information, paraphrase it in a sentence or short paragraph, and then illustrate what they have learned about people, places, physical features, natural resources, and cultural traditions. Kids love using their imaginations to create three-dimensional forests, pop-up mountains, or pebble-spewing volcanoes in appropriate places on the map. They incorporate a variety of nonfiction features such as close-ups, captions, labels, and diagrams and create a key to help viewers navigate and learn from the map. As a giant visual, the map captures children's thinking and learning over time. (See Figures 13.3 and 13.4.)

Figure 13.3 Key for Map of Japan

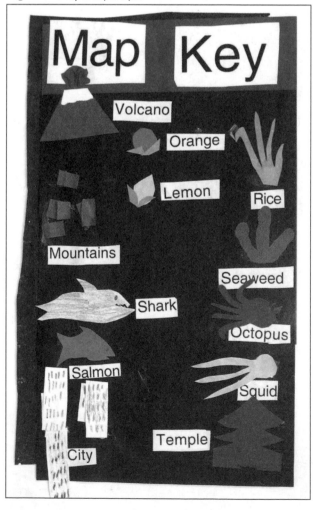

Figure 13.4 Map for a Study of Japan

Co-construct a Time Line of Historical Events, People, and Places to Support Historical Thinking

Providing children with a context for understanding events in history is a challenge. To make the journey back in time as concrete as possible, we create time lines that serve as reference points. We examine images and text about cultural aspects of the time period we're studying. When we move on to another period of history, the time line is there to build on and refer to—an ongoing representation of how our learning grows and changes. As kids learn more information about specific events and people, they add to the time line with their own illustrations and descriptions of events. Then they teach their classmates about their individual contributions.

According to Levstik and Barton, children's learning is enhanced when they "associate visual images of history with time periods and dates" (2001). We teach kids to read for the gist, summarize information, and illustrate their learning through drawing and sketching. Since kids gravitate to interesting, unusual, or quirky details about people and events, we teach them to incorporate what's interesting without losing sight of what's important.

Create Journals, Personal Narratives, and Simulations to Understand Historical Perspective

Historical fiction diaries and journals contain riveting information about the lives of people and events of the times. When we focus on a time period, we teach students that people living in those times had many different perspectives—and that those different points of view are important to understanding history. Kids gather into literature circles that focus on narratives and journals of people living in the time period under study. After reading and gathering information about historical events and personal perspectives, kids write a journal entry from the point of view of a historical person—real or fictional. They weave information and personal reactions into their writing, as one child did by writing from the perspective of a young woman on the *Mayflower* (Figure 13.5). Once kids have put themselves in the shoes of those from other time periods, we often have them recreate historical events through dramatic interpretations, such as arrival at Ellis Island.

Figure 13.5
Colonial Journal Entry from the Perspective of a Young Woman on the *Mayflower*

October, 1620

I got this journal from my own dear great, great grandmother in England. She wanted to come on this voyage, but we lost her before we left. Her heart was strong, but her body was not strong enough to deal with all the sickness and filth of this voyage of the Mayflower. I miss her.

But I live on for all the blessings in life. I had an extremely beautiful baby boy today. I named him Oceanus because he was born aboard this ship sailing in the ocean.

This is not what I would call a luxurious or a healthy place to have a baby, but at least God has provided me a place out of the cold gale. There are cracks and leaks on this ship. The sailors laugh at us and say that we were stupid to come on this voyage and expect to survive.

As I look down at my tattered and filthy clothing, I long to wash and mend and be ladylike again.   I bid you a worried but hopeful goodbye,

M. Hopkins

Explore Current Events and Issues

Because we are news fanatics, it's a no-brainer for us to share with kids our passion for reading the newspaper, keeping up on current events via magazines or the Internet, and thinking about issues that affect our lives. We are just trying to do our part to create a nation of skeptics and informed citizens! As we read a variety of news stories, essays, and editorials with our students, we show them how we distinguish the authors' ideas and perspectives from our own. We demonstrate how we weigh arguments and evidence, helping kids articulate how to merge their thinking with the information to form an opinion. Kids learn how to discern writing that tugs at their emotions and to identify ways that writers use information to persuade us. They learn to read closely and with a critical eye, becoming aware of how language and writing can influence thinking.

Literacy Practices for Science

The real world is rich, fascinating, and compelling. Science, more than many areas, requires a careful, thoughtful approach to reading. Science literacy practices include the following:

- Learning through observation; recording and reflecting on these experiences
- Gaining accurate information from a variety of texts, visuals, and realia
- Constructing meaning with vocabulary, concepts, and information by drawing, writing, and
creating to make learning visible
- Investigating questions that invite discovery and add to learning
- Investigating how natural phenomena impact society—environmental, medical, health issues, and so forth—to develop informed opinions

Scientific Observation and Documentation: Science Journals, Field Notebooks, and Wonder Books

Careful observation and descriptive writing introduce children to scientific habits and ways of thinking. Kids keep track of their own learning via science journals, Wonder Books, and self-authored books that teach others what they have learned. (See the lesson in Chapter 11, "Determining What's Important When Writing Information.") If there's one thing we want kids to do in science, it's to keep those questions coming! Wonder Books provide a way for them to capture, wonder about, and reflect on experiences and observations. They are a record of new learning and evolving thinking. We view science writing as more than "just the facts," and encourage kids' natural curiosity and personal reactions. Careful observation and descriptive writing introduce children to scientific habits and ways of thinking. (See the lessons in Chapter 12 on field notes to capture observations and record thinking.)

Visual Analysis and Interpretation: Learning and Teaching from Graphics, Video Streaming, and Other Features

We all know the saying *A picture is worth a thousand words*. More than in any other content area, information in science is conveyed through riveting video images and compelling graphics, as well as engaging text. In this digital and visual age, kids are bombarded with images and features bursting with information—videos, infographics, diagrams, maps, flowcharts, graphs, sidebars, photographs; the list is endless. When reading science content, we need to teach kids to view closely if they are to interpret and analyze visual information. Science is infinitely more enticing for kids when they are engaged in a multimodal experience: following action on webcams, vicariously experiencing exotic locales as they interview scientists in far-flung places, and going on

Figure 13.6
Science Poster on the Life Cycle of the
Butterfly, Incorporating Nonfiction
Features

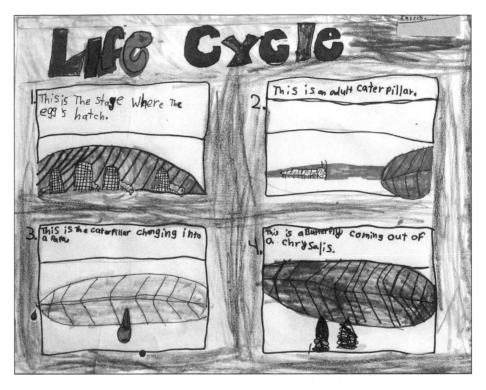

Figure 13.7
Science Infographic on Solar Energy

virtual field trips with apps that make visiting science museums almost as exciting as being there. As kids learn from these visual and interactive representations of information, we pose questions that encourage them to think more deeply about what they are seeing and learning. And they ask numerous questions of their own. When it comes time to present information, kids create movies, digital books, infographics, and the like to teach others about what they have learned. (See Figures 13.6 and 13.7.)

Learning Vocabulary and Concepts Through Picture Dictionaries and Content Word Walls

When introducing kids to new vocabulary and building background, we make sure they understand the language and vocabulary essential to an understanding of the topic. Kids love illustrating and writing up short definitions of words. They write definitions of the vocabulary and illustrate the concepts they are learning, posting them to create a concept word wall for a particular topic. When kids illustrate and write about concepts in their own words, they are much more likely to remember the information.

Note-Taking Strategies for Merging Thinking with Science Information

Sorting out details, relationships, and important ideas in information-laden science texts can be a challenge. Note-taking scaffolds such as the Facts/Questions/Responses or Topic/Details/Response forms support students to organize the facts they are learning in the face of TMI—Too Much Information. Information and ideas in science articles are often organized around cause-and-effect relationships or a problem-solution format. Giving kids a heads-up about these different text structures and designing note-taking scaffolds that reflect these structures make it easier for them to paraphrase, take notes on, and remember the information. Adapting note taking to the ways information is organized in science textbooks, especially, can be particularly helpful, as these are famous repositories of TMI! See Chapter 11 for ideas on determining importance.

Creating Representations: Posters, Projects, Murals, and Museum Exhibits

Kids love working big! As they learn information, there's nothing like sharing what they've learned on large paper. (See Figure 13.8.) Young children can create murals of all their learning about a topic—often kids work together to illustrate their thinking and learning and write captions to share it. Other kids comment on sticky notes about what they've learned from the work, so that everyone's a learner and everyone's a teacher.

Figure 13.8
Iguana Poster Synthesizing Information

If kids love making big posters to share learning, creating artifacts and museum exhibits are even better. Fifth graders studying dangerous weather created a "wall of storms" outside their classroom. (See Figure 13.9.) To make 3-D models of each of these dangerous weather events, kids investigated how different storms formed and labeled different parts, such as the eye of the hurricane or the giant cumulonimbus clouds that spawn tornadoes. Primary kids studying animal adaptations and bats, in particular, created bat caves and sanctuaries out of Legos. Labeling and describing these creations demonstrates that kids genuinely understand the scientific phenomena under study. They create exhibits similar to those in natural science museums in their classrooms.

Figure 13.9
Kids Created a 3-D Wall of Storms
Outside Their Classroom

Summarizing and Synthesizing Learning on a Mind Map

Mind maps of all sorts give kids opportunities to share their learning in visually interesting ways. As kids create mind maps, they synthesize their learning—imagining new possibilities for thinking about and organizing it. Mind maps are a genre unto themselves (Buzan and Buzan 2005). One way to start a mind map is to put the topic in the center of a big piece of paper. Kids draw giant arms branching off in different directions, with each branch containing illustrations and information about different aspects of the topic. Mind maps are ultimately collaborative efforts, as kids work together to represent their learning and thinking. (See the photo of a mind map on page 235.)

Reading Picture Books About Scientists to Learn How They Think and Investigate

What better way to combine science and literacy than to read all about scientists and how they think about, study, and investigate topics they are passionate about. Heisey and Kucan (2010) suggest a text set of books that show scientists at work: John James Audubon observing and recording bird behavior, Snowflake Bentley capturing the mysteries of snowflakes, and Jane Goodall devoting her life to the study of chimpanzees, deepening our knowledge of primate behavior. If we hope to get kids motivated to think and act like scientists themselves, they need examples of people such as these and an understanding of how they thought about scientific content and issues. Most important is that kids are often amazed at these stories and how these people followed their passions with a strong sense of purpose. (See Figure 13.10)

Figure 13.10
Kids Research Jane Goodall's Scientific Contributions to the Study of Chimpanzee Behavior

Several series of books, especially the Scientists in the Field series, focus on adventures in science, including paleontologists digging for bird dinosaurs, entomologists studying honeybees, microbiologists sharing hidden worlds, and biologists swimming with sharks, among others. Kids read about what scientists do every day, how they investigate important questions and finally share their knowledge with the wider world.

Exploring Issues, Questions, and Problems in Science

When kids are reading nonfiction, particularly in science, we can scaffold their critical reading by teaching them the framework called Definition, Consequence, and Action Questions. First we ask readers to ask a definition question, such as "What is this?" or "What is happening?" Once they have answered the definition question from information in the text, we share with them the idea of the consequence question. Teachers ask us frequently how we get kids to go deeper into a science issue or problem. The consequence question explores the reasons that something might happen, and why thinking about it matters. It may be answered in the text, but it often requires analysis and inferential thinking to come to a fuller understanding. Once they have addressed the consequence question, kids may care enough to do some additional research and act on their knowledge. And, bonus! This framework works equally well with social studies topics.

Definition, Consequence, and Action Questions Framework

Definition Question	*Consequence Question*	*Action Question*
What is the problem?	What are the consequences?	What are some ways to tackle the issue?
What's the issue?	What effects does it have?	What needs to happen to solve the problem?
What is happening?	Why does it matter?	What can I do about it?
What is it?	What difference does it make?	What can I do to help?
What is going on?	Why should I care?	How can I get involved?

• • •

Content literacy gives kids the tools to learn information, ideas, and ways of thinking in a variety of disciplines. When kids ask important and thoughtful questions, evaluate information and evidence, observe and wonder about nature, and read, write, and talk about current events and issues, they eagerly explore their world. In the next chapter, we show how teachers use a four-part inquiry framework and incorporate these content practices into social studies and science units, enabling kids to build their knowledge in these disciplines and use comprehension strategies to design and carry out research and investigations.

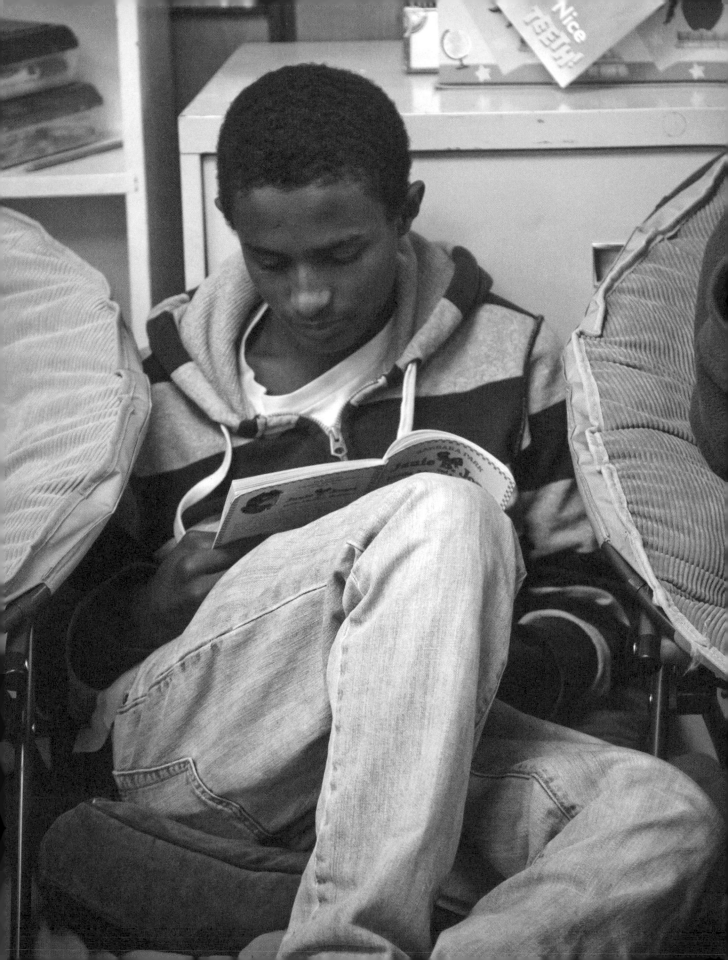

Chapter 14

Researcher's Workshop: Inquiry Across the Curriculum

Inquiry is about empowering students to find out: to investigate authentic questions they have posed for themselves or that have been inspired by the curriculum. Both matter. Inquiry-based learning is not always about a project at the end. There may be one, but the emphasis is on the journey, not merely the final destination. Inquiry is, above all, about living in a way in which questions matter. It's a way of life. Curiosity is at the core of inquiry-based teaching and learning.

We distinguish between an inquiry approach to content and the more common coverage approach (Harvey and Daniels 2015). One defining distinction between inquiry and coverage is that an inquiry approach is child centered, whereas a coverage approach tends to be more teacher focused. In inquiry-based learning, we pay attention to kids' questions as well as the larger curricular questions.

Inquiry Framework

The units of study in this chapter follow a four-part inquiry framework: Immerse, Investigate, Coalesce, Take Public (Harvey and Daniels 2015). Comprehension informs the foundation of this framework and is embedded in each phase of the inquiry process. As presented in Figure 14.1, we share the framework and emphasize the comprehension strategies that teachers teach and kids use to read, research, and understand content. Sometimes in these inquiries, the content is derived from the curricular standards and grade-level expectations. Other times these investigations stem from kids' interests and desire to know more. And often, it is a combination of both.

Essential Questions and Enduring Understandings

Our inquiry approach is tied to Wiggins and McTighe's notion of essential questions and enduring understandings that are grounded in the concepts, ideas, and issues in various disciplines (Wiggins and McTighe 2005). We have adapted these ideas in our inquiry framework with one important addition. In our version, comprehension is at the core of each phase of the inquiry framework. You'll notice in the framework that comprehension is front and center in terms of the teacher's instruction and how kids go about learning. We strongly believe that comprehension strategies create a pathway to long-lasting learning across the curriculum.

The essential questions may emerge from the kinds of questions asked by scientists and historians as well as from the curricular content. Wiggins and McTighe describe essential questions this way:

> *Essential questions:*
> - *Spur genuine and relevant inquiry into the big ideas in core content*
> - *Provoke deep thought, lively discussions and new understandings*
> - *Spark meaningful connections with prior learning and personal experiences*
> - *Naturally reoccur, creating opportunities for transfer to other situations and subjects.* (2005)

Implicit here is the idea of enduring understandings representing the learning that results from in-depth study and investigation of content topics. Enduring understandings go beyond the fascinating details and amazing facts that kids gravitate toward and remember so easily. The disparate facts by themselves are not enough. Enduring understandings endure! They are the important ideas we want students to be able to use long after they have forgotten the isolated facts. Enduring understandings have lasting value beyond the classroom.

Through essential questions and the related enduring understandings, kids organize and think about information and integrate it into large concepts and ideas that are critical to building knowledge. These large concepts transfer to other domains. For instance, if kids are studying habitats and adaptations, one essential, overarching question would be "How are animals adapted to life

Phase	Teachers	Kids
Immerse		
Invite curiosity.	Flood the room with topic-related resources.	Explore, experience, and learn about the topic.
Build background knowledge and intrigue.	Develop essential questions and connect topics to kids' interests and experiences as well as to standards.	Connect the new to the known.
	Encourage kids' questions, responses, and reactions.	Wonder, react, and think to engage in the topic.
Investigate		
Develop questions.	Model how to ask questions.	Keep notebooks with questions and new learning.
Search for information.	Model annotation and how to organize information.	Annotate and keep track of new learning.
Discover answers.	Model how to read, listen, and view with a question in mind.	Read, talk, listen, and view a wide variety of text and online sources to learn information.
Coalesce		
Intensify research.	Model how to read for the gist and synthesize information.	Engage in deeper reading and research.
Synthesize information.	Confer about the research process and pull together findings.	Reflect on and monitor findings.
Build knowledge.	Demonstrate multiple ways to evaluate and organize information.	Organize information and determine accuracy of sources.
Take Public		
Share learning.	Co-construct expectations for final projects.	Co-construct expectations for final projects.
Demonstrate understanding.	Share a wide range of options for going public.	Demonstrate learning and understanding in many ways.
	Assess, and evaluate projects.	Reflect on new knowledge and the research process.
Take action.	Share possibilities for taking action.	Take action through writing, speaking, drawing, creating, making, and so on. Advocate for a position or a cause.

Figure 14.1
The Four-Part Inquiry Framework
(Adapted from *Comprehension and Collaboration*, Harvey and Daniels (2015.))

in their habitat?" This essential question around habitats and species is transferable. When studying the rain forest, a specific, related question might be "How are toucans adapted to living in the rain forest?" or, when studying the desert, "How are rattlesnakes adapted to living in the desert?" This approach to inquiry builds both content and concept knowledge. In curricular study, it is the teacher's responsibility to link kids' specific questions and learning to the essential questions and enduring understandings.

Classroom Inquiries

In this chapter, we share three inquiry units that have comprehension at their foundation. All of the units take place in a researcher's workshop as described in Chapter 13 and follow the inquiry framework described in this chapter. Jen Burton, Amy Rimko, and Lindsey Hurst designed a kindergarten mini-inquiry focused on learning about community helpers. Second-grade teacher Brad Buhrow created a paleontology unit that explores how scientists learn about dinosaurs and fossils. Fifth-grade teacher Karen Halverson concludes the chapter with a social studies inquiry on voting and the power of voice, particularly timely in light of the 2016 presidential election.

Investigating Community Workers: An Inquiry with Young Children

Inquiries can be short and sweet. Mini-inquiries are very useful to introduce kids to the research process. It's never too early to teach young children to inquire and do research. Through the process of wondering, learning, and sharing they discover new knowledge and realize that their questions matter. In this mini-inquiry, instructional coach Jennifer Burton joined kindergarten teachers Amy Rimko and Lindsey Hurst early in the year for an inquiry unit into community workers. They knew that these brand-new kindergartners would be doing lots of viewing and listening to learn new information. They also decided that in order to teach kids the inquiry process, they would need to model their own inquiry on a specific community worker. In this way, the kids could see the entire process unfold.

Immerse
They began by immersing students in nonfiction text rich with text features such as colorful photographs, labels, and captions that would allow for multiple entry points for students to gather information. Short video snippets allowed kids to view community workers in action. The possibilities were exciting! After reading aloud books about community workers such as *Helpers in My Community* by Bobbie Kalman, students chose one career that they would be interested in learning more about. They watched short videos of people at work in the community. Some kids talked to relatives who were firefighters, dentists, or construction workers.

To continue with the study, kids shared what they already knew and the new knowledge they were building through their class conversations, their exposure to these resources, and the interactive read-alouds.

Investigate

Jennifer and the teachers launched their own inquiry to model and scaffold the process of inquiry for the students. The teachers began their own inquiry into chefs and cooking. They asked questions that came to mind about what chefs wore, what tools they used, and what chefs did. They shared their questions below as anchor questions, which the kids would use as they investigated their own community worker.

1. What clothes do they wear?
2. What tools do they use?
3. What do they do?

As Amy, Jennifer, and Lindsey read aloud about chefs, they modeled how they noticed that most chefs wore white coats, but sometimes they wore funky pants. This made them wonder: "Do all chefs wear funky pants?" They recorded what they noticed along with this new question on their chef chart paper, drawing a picture of a chef with some wild pants and a circle around the pants with a big question mark next to them. It's kindergarten—this should be fun!

As the teachers moved into guided practice to involve the kids in their inquiry, some students noticed that some of the spoons chefs used didn't quite look like spoons. The students wondered, "Is that a spoon?" The teachers recorded this on a chart and kept the question in mind as they continued reading the rest of the book, looking closely at the different utensils that chefs use. This led to more reading and discovering that chefs use many different kinds of tools. The teachers wanted students to realize that not all questions are answered by reading one book and that readers may need to seek out other resources to find answers to their questions.

Now it was time for students to go off to do their own research in their inquiry groups. Students gathered around chart paper with books sprawled around and markers galore, invitations to dig in. As kids began to look at pictures, notice, and read (if they could), they began to draw, write, and talk. There was magic in the air. Jennifer and the teachers were able to confer with inquiry groups, using the anchor questions to help guide student thinking.

As Jennifer conferred with one student in the firefighter group, she noticed that the student had colored blue over some red and asked the student to tell her more about this. The student explained that firefighters spray water on the fire, saying, "That's what firefighters do. It says so right here, so the water is blue!"

Coalesce and Take Public

As students continued to find information, discuss it, and draw their learning to answer questions, the teachers noticed they were inferring from clues in the pictures or words in the text. As they researched, the kids learned a lot of new information and were able to evaluate what was important about these helpers. Seeing what kindergartners can accomplish at the beginning of the year is a great reminder for us to trust our students and give them time and space to do this important work.

Learning from Scientists: Exploring Paleontology, Dinosaurs, and Fossils

Second-grade teacher Brad Buhrow integrates science and literacy in a researcher's workshop model. His classroom day consists of four workshops: reading workshop, writing workshop, researcher's workshop, and math workshop. Rather than trying to squeeze five subjects into a day, Brad integrates science and social studies into one researcher's workshop or spends a few weeks on science content and the next few weeks on social studies content. Because kids are reading and writing all day, every day, reading, writing, and sometimes math are incorporated into researcher's workshop, too.

Within the researcher's workshop framework, comprehension practices are the foundation for whole-class instruction and support students as they move into research on their own. Once kids have internalized practices like observing, viewing, and synthesizing information, they use these as tools for independent investigation.

In a curricular inquiry on prehistoric life, children explored artifacts, visuals, online sources, and many different texts both inside and outside the classroom to understand what paleontologists do. Kids learned from museum exhibits as well as from a practicing paleontologist who came into the classroom and created centers for kids to explore. As we describe the unit and the kids' enthusiasm for the topic, Brad's own words give us insight into why he created this unit and how the instruction unfolded.

Brad began the unit of study by creating several essential questions that encompassed district science standards and focused on enduring understandings. Essential questions launched the study but also provided a structure within which kids asked their own questions as the unit progressed. Brad's goal was to make this unit as authentic as possible, so the kids could experience the ways real scientists go about their research.

Here are the enduring understandings and essential questions (Wiggins and McTighe 2005) that launched this unit:

Enduring Understandings

- Scientists make contributions that make a difference: they help us understand nature and our world more deeply by discovering new knowledge and sharing it with the rest of us.
- When we learn about and understand the history of the earth and prehistoric life, we more fully understand the planet we live on.

Essential Questions

- What can we learn about the history of the earth from fossils and prehistoric finds?
- How do scientists learn about the history of the earth? How do they study and think about life long ago?
- What do paleontologists do? What methods do they use to study prehistoric life? What contributions did Mary Anning and others make to the science of paleontology?

Brad: When we study how scientists learn and explore their passions, kids get a sense of how someone pursues questions, explores the natural world, and dedicates a life to find out more. We learn from the example of real people and what they did. We study scientists and what they did to follow their questions and discover answers. We learn what drove them to seek out new information and understand how curiosity shaped their lives. We come to grasp how their discoveries changed our thinking about the world.

The kids in Brad's room took field trips to a local museum at the university and met with a university paleontologist who brought specimens and models to the classroom. Real experiences matter. Since the previous edition of this book, we can't help but notice a downturn in the number of field trips. Whether for financial reasons or, worse, testing priorities, this demise is a shame. Brad understood, as did his principal, the power of getting out of the classroom and experiencing what you are studying in the real world rather than merely vicariously. We urge you to find creative ways to keep field trips on the front burner. Kids benefit immensely.

We describe how the unit unfolded using the inquiry framework.

Immerse

It doesn't take much to tap into kids' intrigue with this topic—from the get-go the classroom is alive with spirited discussions about life in the time of dinosaurs. Kids share their personal connections to museum visits, to conversations with relatives, to their plastic dinosaur collections. They pore over a recent article about ancient artifacts unearthed right in their own town. They sort, investigate, and label fossils. They read about and view scientists at work all over the world. Brad creates an environment where kids experience what it is to be a scientist.

During the immersion phase, Brad ascertains what students know and what they wonder, and honors that. Kids share the information they already have at their fingertips, and in this way, they all build or add to their knowledge. Kids are excited because they realize they are going to have a go at becoming paleontologists themselves. The following are some of the lessons that Brad teaches in each phase of the inquiry.

Ascertain and activate background knowledge. On a large chart, Brad records kids' prior knowledge, asking, "What do we think we know about fossils?" As kids investigate fossils and other artifacts, they record their inferences and questions on the same class chart. Reading a variety of informational texts addresses basic questions about fossils: What are fossils? Where are they found? What do they tell us about ancient life?

Build knowledge through observation. Kids use a selection of books to identify fossils and record their hands-on experience in their notebooks. They jot down questions and inferences and illustrate what they are observing about fossil specimens. They are beginning to get a sense of how scientists observe closely and sketch and record the information (see Figure 14.2).

Figure 14.2
Brad's Students Examine Fossils

Investigate

Interactive read-alouds. Building on the work of Heisey and Kucan (2010), Brad launches the prehistoric life unit by studying a paleontologist. He chooses the scientist Mary Anning, who was one of the first woman paleontologists. He addresses the essential question "What does a paleontologist do?" by reading about her life and discoveries in an interactive read-aloud. (See Chapter 6, page 78, on interactive read-alouds.)

Brad: As we read about Mary Anning, we learned that research is not always easy or rewarding. Researchers sometimes feel discouraged or experience hardships working under difficult conditions. Paleontologist Mary Anning worked for years uncovering sea fossils on the crumbling sea cliffs of England. She took many risks because she wanted to understand ancient life, and she helped launch the science of paleontology.

The interactive read-aloud about Mary Anning gets kids wondering about her passion for dinosaurs and prehistoric life. When planning the read-aloud,

Brad doesn't just wing it. Rather, he reads through the text, deciding ahead of time which big ideas he wants to focus on and where he will pause to think aloud about them. Here are some of his questions:

- What is Mary curious about as a scientist?
- How does she study fossils and dinosaurs?
- What are some of the challenges Mary faces as she follows her passion?

He stops and ponders these questions himself, modeling his thinking, and then guides the kids through a group conversation. When Brad asks, "What did you notice that Mary does as a scientist?" the kids are full of ideas. They chime in, sharing that she asks lots of questions, records her thinking with notes and sketches, shares what she learned, and takes risks. Bravery and courage surface as themes in the story.

Reading to ask and answer questions. With the question "What was the earth like millions of years ago?" guiding their reading, kids focus on finding some answers. Kids read different sources that relate to this question. One small group observes an illustration of rock layers and notices the traces of fossils in them; they respond in their journals. The double-entry scaffold titled New Information and My Thinking is open-ended enough so that kids can determine the information they think is important—and share all the information they have found that answers this question.

Note-taking strategies for building knowledge. Comprehension practices like taking notes to summarize information support kids as they begin to ask and answer their own questions and pursue their own research interests. Kids are well versed in several kinds of note-taking routines. One routine they have internalized is recording thinking with field notes. Field notes, Brad suggests, encourage scientific study and thinking as kids do the following:

- Record new learning with sketches, illustrations, and even photographs as well as writing
- Record information while reading, as well as their own questions, inferences, and connections
- Organize learning according to questions, concepts, and big ideas
- Use field notes as a source for synthesizing information on posters, in self-published books, on Wixie pages, and so forth
- Experience success because the process is easily differentiated and individualized

Brad: How do I teach recording in field notes? First, we create a two-column chart on big paper. As I do this, the kids record this same template in their notebooks. We label the columns—New Information in the left column, My Thinking in the right. We use compelling text, videos, or artifacts and real-time observations to model how to read, think, and take notes. The bridge for kids who need a bit more support is the group chart; we continue this together until I'm confident kids have the process down and can succeed independently. (See Figure 14.3.)

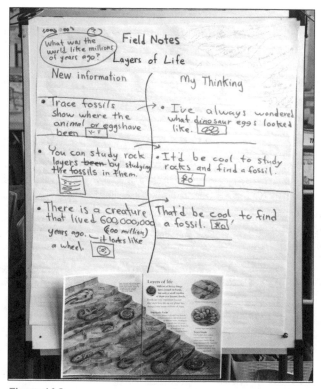

Figure 14.3
Brad's Chart on Field Notes

Moving into independent research. Once we have introduced learning routines for asking and reading to answer questions and taking notes, kids use these tools again and again. Kids acquire knowledge this way—well-practiced routines ensure success as they plunge into independent research. When kids are engaged in and curious about the topic under study, it doesn't take long for them to come up with their own questions. Then they're eager to find some answers.

Brad: At our school, the library is the beating heart of the school. The librarian and I plan together and coteach various lessons. Kids know where things are; they know they can go there and search for whatever they need. They understand that reading is a big part of studying something, and their library is an extension of the classroom, a place they go to read and study.

After a trip to the library where they get help accessing some appropriate online sources, they are off and running on their prehistoric rock research. They read and view several sources, and then they collaborate to write and illustrate their new learning on a poster.

Coalesce and Take Public

Create posters. In the tradition of scientific conferences, where scientists present information in a poster session, kids create posters, stand by them, and present the information in their own poster session.

Brad: We create a poster together as a shared experience. The kids offer information to write about and illustrate using text and graphic features. Kids consider features they think might work best with their own poster. They create the posters to present them in an authentic poster session just like practicing scientists do. Authenticity is key here. We always try to create sharing opportunities that occur outside of school in the real world. I'm careful to explain why I've included a close-up, a diagram, or a map on my poster, which prompts kids to think about features they might incorporate.

As kids create their posters, Brad reminds them to think about their audience: "What surprising information would be really interesting to your friends or families? What amazing information are you most eager to share?" Conferring with kids helps them see the possibilities and plan out what they want to write and draw before they have committed pen to paper. This prevents frustration later on and helps kids narrow down their vision to something they can realistically create. See Figure 14.4.

Figure 14.4
A Student's Poster About Mary Anning

With his kids, Brad co-constructs a chart with conversation starters for sharing as follows:

Language for Sharing Posters

I am studying _____. I was really interested in it because _____.
Here's what I thought was most fascinating: _____. I added this feature to show _____.
I drew _____ to represent _____.

During the poster-session share, half of the kids present their posters and the other half learn from and respond to the kids who are sharing. Then they switch. Armed with sticky notes, pencils, and clipboards, they respond with comments, questions, and connections. Brad has taught everyone respectful and thoughtful ways to share work and respond. Kids have opportunities to share their posters with other classrooms as well as with their parents.

Making and creating research labs. Brad and the kids create a scientific research lab in the classroom to replicate what real scientists do. The university paleontologist brings models of prehistoric tools from many different eras and models of skulls of early people. Kids are ready with their field notes and magnifying glasses. In small groups, they measure, view closely, record observations in their field notes, and, of course, ask lots of questions, just like real scientists. See Figure 14.5.

Figure 14.5 A Student Measures a Bone in the Class Research Lab

Kids as curators. Just as in museums, Brad and the kids curate an exhibit in their classroom. Kids, teachers, and others in the community bring in fossils, ancient arrowheads, and other early human tools. The students organize the specimens, write labels and captions, and display them so others can learn about them. Brad posts photographs of the kids creating the museum on Seesaw, which is an invitation to parents and families to stop by the classroom.

In Brad's paleontology unit, kids learn how scientists study, learn, and think. Most importantly, they've taken on the role of scientists themselves—doing research and taking their new learning public. They have learned a great deal about prehistoric times and the paleontologists who study those times, but most importantly, they have learned through their own experiences that there are myriad ways to investigate and better understand the world.

Voice and Vote: From Inquiry to Action

Our lives begin to end the day we become silent about things that matter.
—Martin Luther King Jr.

Hiking in the hills above my Boulder, Colorado home, I pondered the upcoming school year. Usually in the fifth grade, our social studies focused on colonial times and the American Revolution, but this was an election year, and I wanted to weave these current events into the historical study of our country. At the same time, across our country, social justice issues seemed to be heated and illuminated more than they had been in decades. I wondered how to bring an awareness of issues into a classroom of ten- and eleven-year-olds. What was the common thread among these pieces? Voice, vote, rights, freedom. These words were arising again and again.

Essential questions surface:

In what ways do people express their voices?
How is a vote an expression of voice?
Who has or has not had the right to vote? Why?
In what ways have people expressed voice for the right to vote?
How has the expression of voice affected change?

A big idea emerges: throughout the history of our country, people have expressed their voices in pursuit of freedom, rights, and equality.

• • •

It is August. I return to my classroom to create our learning space for the year. I write "Your voice matters" in large white chalk pen on the board in the back of my room. Surrounding this message I sketch rough, chalk-drawn images of some who have expressed their voices in powerful ways: Malala Yousafzai, Marian Anderson, Elizabeth Cady Stanton, Clara Lemlich, Trombone Shorty, and Langston Hughes. Along the sides of the chalkboard are several quotes on voice. Malala's words are among them:

I speak not for myself but for those without voice . . . those who have fought for their rights . . . their right to live in peace, their right to be treated with dignity, their right to equality of opportunity, their right to be educated. (Yousafzai 2013)

These voices will speak as mentors, guiding our historical studies, encouraging our questions, and uncovering the voices and messages within ourselves that most fervently desire expression.

Immerse

October. Trees stand in radiant red, orange, and yellow while fifth graders turn and talk, discussing the question "In what ways do people express voice?" More obvious ways tumble forward first: speeches, e-mails, newspapers, music, poetry, books. From here, we move this enthusiasm into small-group work. Kids read, talk about, and explore picture books about artists, dancers, musicians, poets, and activists. Their mission is to learn more about individuals who have expressed their voices in various ways to effect change and to wonder why people are willing to speak out and what risks they are willing to take.

Four questions guide our inquiry:

How is voice expressed?
What is the message?
Why did he or she speak out?
How did it effect change?

I model my thinking and interaction with text by reading aloud the picture book *Malala, A Brave Girl from Pakistan/Iqbal, A Brave Boy from Pakistan* by Jeanette Winter. As I read, I record our thinking and responses to the guiding questions on paper and project them with the document camera. When we finish the story and our discussion, small groups of students choose from a variety of a picture books and take a large piece of butcher paper to record the questions and their responses to their own books.

Circulating among groups reading aloud and discussing, I notice their engagement with the stories of these individuals' lives ("I can't imagine biking that far with one leg!"), their struggle to articulate the deeper messages of action and expression ("Well, he made a new kind of music that people liked, but is there a message he is trying to express?"), their insight into why people have taken risks to speak out ("Wow. Those workers were treated so unfairly! That just seems so wrong"), and their wonder at the change effected by such courage and determination ("I didn't realize black people weren't allowed to do so many things. Marian must have been nervous singing to such a large audience at this time!")

As groups are wrapping up their work, I direct them to gather back at the rug. Each group presents their learning. We are beginning to understand the importance of voice, the myriad of ways one can express it, and how this can effect change in one's life, community, and even country. Later that day, in a writing workshop, students freewrite to begin to bring these ideas into their personal, everyday lives: Write about a time when you used your voice in a powerful way. How did that feel? What change did it effect?

The next day, wanting to expand students' background knowledge and to give them a deeper sense of the power words have to affect others, I pass out the article "The Power of Speech" (Manos 2013). Beginning with my copy of the article on the document camera, I model reading while annotating the gist and my thinking. We work together to understand different purposes for speeches and various reasons they can powerfully affect others, call for change, and bring people together. Kids turn and talk and jot throughout.

They collect quotes for homework that evening, record them in their journals, and eagerly share those that inspire them the following day. They think about all they have learned from the picture books about the many ways people express themselves. They think back to articles they have shared about the Dakota Access Pipeline and the Standing Rock Sioux Reservation, among others. Kids get fired up. The room bursts with enthusiasm as they discuss expressions of voice they read about—signs, banners, body painting, clothing, marches, bodies as blockade, work strikes, hunger strikes, film, social media. This is relevant, and they want to be a part of it.

Investigate

An election year offers a unique energy and perspective to the exploration of voice. Our essential questions invite into our conversations not only current voices urging the American people to vote, but also historical voices of the American people who have not had that right. We wonder: "How is a vote an expression of voice? Why is it important? At this time, who votes? Who does not? Why? Historically, who has voted? Who has not? Why?" This inquiry leads us to seek understanding of how our government and electoral system work; the agreements, documents, and individuals who founded our country; the perspectives and experiences of diverse groups of people; what it means to have equal rights; and the role voice plays throughout.

At the rug, we begin by discussing the questions "How is vote an expression of voice?" and "Why is it important?" We talk about ways we might make decisions through voting, such as whether our class has extra reading or recess time. Our conversation expands to consider voting for local issues, for members of Congress as well as for president. "What happens if people don't vote? Why might people not vote? How might this change things?" To help us consider these questions from a more informed position, we view and annotate an infographic that shows the breakdown of various groups of people and whether or not they voted in the 2008 election.

One statistic that stands out in everyone's mind is the fact that voter turnout increases with age. "Wow! The eighteen- to twenty-four-year-olds have the lowest voter turnout!" "Why might that be so?" I ask. We turn our attention to pages in our *Scholastic Election Magazine*. Grabbing our attention is a percentage breakdown of the most common reasons why people don't vote. Students eagerly argue against most of these reasons, based on the idea that voting is a right, an opportunity, a responsibility. Propelled by wonder and enthusiasm, students unload their questions, concerns, and convictions by freewriting in their writer's notebooks. Students share their most potent lines. I share several videos that highlight the importance of voting. Kids follow up by responding to these questions in their notebooks: "What is your message to voters? What would you most like to say?" Through their writing, students highlight essential words and potent phrases, distilling and clarifying the essence of their message.

With these messages in mind, we consider the mash-up of word and art as a vehicle for expression. We consider the election and the importance of the vote. We consider all the reasons Americans have for not voting. And we create, designing drafts of artistic word messages for signs that we will stake on the front lawn of our school. Signs that we hope will encourage all passersby to get out and vote! Fifth graders may be too young to vote, but they are not too young to have a voice and share it.

Yet, this investigation has only begun. While students have a sprinkling of information suggesting everyone has not always had the right to vote, they have no idea how immense and hard fought the battle for the vote has been in American history. Through this lens, it is my intention for students to gain a deeper understanding of the risks taken and the courage and determination required by some groups of people to win the right to vote. At the same time, I expect this lens will challenge our thinking in a way that opens the floodgates of our questioning minds.

While reading, annotating, and discussing articles that highlight events in America's voting history, students touch upon the inequalities that have existed between groups of people. To help organize and keep track of important events, individuals, and amendments, students each create a labeled and illustrated time line that becomes a working document for new information throughout our learning. To deepen our inquiry, we focus on two primary voting rights movements: women's suffrage and the voting rights marches of 1965.

As the inquiry continues, kids read picture books on women's suffrage and the African American struggle for voting rights. They watch the movie *Selma* and learn about the voting rights march of 1965. They read numerous articles on these events and issues and explore information online. Students are shocked and amazed at the systematic denial of a basic right many have taken for granted. These resources allow students to witness the truth of the injustices throughout history as well as the absolute determination of African Americans, women, and others who supported them to stand up for justice and equality regardless of the personal risks involved. They learn about and understand the courage, hope, and determination shown by these people throughout our history as a nation.

Questions burn heavily in the hearts and minds of these students. We list them on an anchor chart and post them at the front of the room so we can come back to them again and again.

Why has there been separation between groups of people?
Why has there been superiority of one group over another?
Who has had the power? Who has not? Why?
What was it like when our country began?
Has our country included all voices? Is it fair?
What is a democracy? Do we really have one?
WE THE PEOPLE—who is that, really?

To bring this learning more fully into our bodies, we step into drama. Students are put into groups of five to seven. Each group draws a slip of paper with either *women's suffrage* or *Selma* written on it, determining the focus for their drama. The task: to create a tableau that shows people expressing their voices to effect change during that time in history. Students have time to plan and create what they will do and say. While the audience closes their eyes, one group moves into their tableau, a sort of frozen scene, at the front of the room. When they are ready, the audience opens their eyes to view and understand what might be happening. I gently unfreeze the scene by tapping on each tableau member's shoulder, one at a time. In turn, each speaks from the point of view of his or her person in history. After each person has spoken, the group relaxes back into fifth graders. This is a powerful way to help students grasp another's perspective and to deepen their understanding.

After viewing all tableaux, students turn to their journals to synthesize their learning. I ask two questions to stimulate their writing: "What lingers in your mind from the women's suffrage movement?" "What stands out for you from the Selma to Montgomery marches?" Students must create an illustration or symbolic drawing to represent their answers to these questions. Leaving space at the bottom of the page for a paragraph of text, students write a more in-depth response referring to our essential questions: How was voice expressed? What change did it effect? What lingers most in your mind?

Coalesce and Take Public

The importance of voice and vote is expanding in the hearts of these fifth graders. With enthusiasm and conviction, students pound the stakes holding their voting messages into the ground. They know that voting is a right and that people have fought and even died to have this right. They know that not everyone exercises this precious right to vote. They want to make a difference, to speak out, to encourage everyone to appreciate and to use their voting rights. As the last sign is staked firmly into the ground, we hope. We hope the wind or mischievous neighbors won't take away the signs overnight. We hope passersby will be impacted by our messages. And then, we think of the youngest population of voters, only six blocks away on the University of Colorado campus—and an idea is born. Still humming with the energy of the marches of 1965, we decide to march. We will take our signs and march onto the CU campus, encouraging these young voters to take action. Since fifth graders cannot vote, they will use their voices to speak out to others, to get out the vote.

The excitement is contagious! Parents eagerly volunteer, Colorado Public Radio promptly commits their team, students double-staple their signs and nervously consider possible interview questions. The morning of our march, we gather to discuss how we want to express our message. What will that look like? What will that sound like? We reflect on recent presidential debate clips that we had analyzed for passive, assertive, and aggressive behavior. We consider how each of those behaviors had affected us as an audience and how the behaviors had affected the speakers' messages. Together, we agree that we want to be assertive, but not aggressive. That we want to shout out our messages of encouragement, but do not want to turn listeners away with any negativity. We also consider how our verbal silence could amplify the message of our artistic-word pieces. With beating hearts, excitement in our legs and lungs, and our signs held high, we set out the door of our classroom.

"V–O–T–E, Vote!" students chant as we march onto campus. College students turn, watch, listen, smile. Some shout out, "I voted!" which elicits cheers from the fifth-grade marchers. Past dorms and classrooms, we march, chant, and shout our message that all voices matter; vote, it's your right! As we lounge on the quad for a snack break, college students wander over to encourage these young marchers: "Did you make these signs yourselves? They look great! Keep marching. What you are doing is cool—important." In between bites of apples and sandwiches, students offer their insights to Colorado Public Radio reporter Jenny Brundin. They eagerly express their thinking. They want to be heard! Hours later, after a final march through campus, we take the public bus rather than walk home. Exhausted from the day's mission, students rest quietly, still holding their signs, while curious passengers smile and take phone videos of the weary messengers. As we step off the bus and back into our classroom, it feels as if we have been on a long journey, a journey that has changed us. Together, we have felt the passionate spark of conviction and allowed it to move us into real-world action. Days later the story airs on Colorado Public Radio. Then, NPR decides to air the story the day before the election! These students' voices are heard by an audience far greater than anything we had ever imagined. E-mails roll in about the positive, uplifting impact of their message and at least one story of a nonvoter whose mind was changed and decided to vote.

Through the lens of history, students have considered multiple perspectives; analyzed primary sources; read, annotated, and discussed informational texts; cultivated critical thinking skills; and asked questions through it all. As I reflect on our learning, two things linger most powerfully: the questions and the real-world action. Asking questions seems absolutely essential in our work as educators. The word *educate* originates from the Latin word *ducere*, meaning "to lead." Rather than being fountains of knowledge, we lead our students to knowledge, through our thoughtfully constructed questions and their authentically rising questions. To think outside the box, to question the way things are and the way things have been, to critically look at information, to wonder how things can change, to ponder one's own choices and actions in the world—these are essential tools we have the responsibility to teach our students how to effectively use for the rest of their lives. How are we preparing them to lead? Along with the questioning mind, how are we preparing them to contribute? Marching with signs on a university campus is a relatively small action, but its relevance and impact was great. And the students experienced that directly. Maybe this taste of real-word action has planted a seed that will grow into greater action in the world for some students. I overheard a few boys discussing, "Next election, we will be freshmen in high school, but the election after that—we get to vote!" At the very least, I am quite confident that this real-world action has created twenty-seven American citizens who will absolutely vote the moment they have that opportunity.

What a perfect place from which to launch the road to revolution, the American Revolution of 1776, that is.

Biblioholics both of us, we confess that we have been worried since the previous edition of this book that print books might appear on the endangered species list. So we never would have dreamed this, but right now the hottest thing in Brooklyn, Boston, and Berkeley are coffee shop–bookstores that make you check your laptops and phones at the door. Not a Wi-Fi connection in sight. Conversation and reading in print seems to be on the upswing. Hugh Geiger, owner of The Thinking Cup coffee shop in Boston, says that business is booming since they shut down Wi-Fi. "We wanted to avoid an 'internet café' scene but instead encourage conversation and just some old fashioned newspaper and book reading" (Ribons 2014). And people are flocking to his shop.

In 2016, figures from the Association of American Publishers found that sales of e-books declined substantially compared with print sales. This phenomenon is referred to as "digital fatigue." When asked, 59 percent of people said they prefer print books to e-books (Milliot 2016). So print books are coming back. Hooray!

But the truth is, books, no matter the format—print or digital—are nothing without readers. When we interact with a compelling piece of text, it engages our whole being. Reading is about so much more than grades, quizzes, and test scores. Distinguished author and Newbery Award winner Katherine Paterson says, "It is not enough to simply teach children to read; we have to give them something worth reading. Something that will stretch their imaginations—something that will help them make sense of their own lives and encourage them to reach out toward people whose lives are quite different from their own" (1995).

When teachers flood their rooms with great text, teach kids to read for understanding, and give kids plenty of time to read and think, their classrooms explode with learning. Kids can't wait to share their excitement, talk about burning questions, express opinions, and even take action based on their reading and learning. This is why we educators must care so passionately about helping children become real readers who eat, drink, breathe, and live books. Reading changes everything, from the way we view our world to the way we view ourselves. We read not because we are teachers or students but because we are human beings.

Abercrombie, Barbara. 1990. *Charlie Anderson*. New York: McElderry Books.

Baillie, Allan. 1994. *Rebel*. New York: Ticknor and Fields.

Ballard, Robert. 1988. *Exploring the Titanic*. New York: Scholastic.

Bell, Cece. 2014. *El Deafo*. New York: Abrams.

Berne, Jennifer. 2016. *On a Beam of Light: A Story of Albert Einstein*. San Francisco: Chronicle Books.

Borden, Louise. 2005. *The Journey That Saved Curious George: The True Wartime Escape of Margret and H. A. Rey*. Boston: Houghton Mifflin.

Borden, Louise, and Mary Kay Kroeger. 2001. *Fly High! The Story of Bessie Coleman*. New York: McElderry.

Brown, Margaret Wise. 1992. *The Sailor Dog*. Racine, WI: Western.

Bunting, Eve. 2001. *Gleam and Glow*. San Diego: Harcourt.

Burgess, Matthew. 2015. *Enormous Smallness: A Story of E. E. Cummings*. Brooklyn, NY: Enchanted Lion.

Burnett, Frances Hodgson. 1938. *The Secret Garden*. New York: Lippincott.

Carlson, Lori Marie. 1998. *Sol a Sol*. New York: Henry Holt.

Chall, Marsha Wilson. 1992. *Up North at the Cabin*. New York: Lothrop, Lee and Shepard.

Condra, Estelle. 1994. *See the Ocean*. Nashville, TN: Ideal.

Cowley, Joy. 2006. *Red-Eyed Tree Frog*. New York: Scholastic.

Cruise, Robin. 2006. *Little Mama Forgets*. New York: Farrar, Straus and Giroux.

Crutchfield, James A. 1993. *It Happened in Colorado*. Helena, MT: Falcon.

Davies, Nicola. 2004. *Bat Loves the Night*. Cambridge, MA: Candlewick.

———. 2005. *Surprising Sharks*. Cambridge, MA: Candlewick.

Day, Alexandra. 1985. *Good Dog, Carl*. New York: Scholastic.

Del Calzo, Nick. 1997. *The Triumphant Spirit: Portraits and Stories of Holocaust Survivors, Their Messages of Hope and Compassion*. *Denver Post* Newspaper in Education Program.

Dolasia, Meera. 2016. "The 3-D Zebra Crossings That Are Making India's Roads Safer for Pedestrians." DOGOnews June 2. https://www.dogonews.com/2016/6/2/the-3-d-zebra-crossings-that-are-making-indias-roads-safer-for-pedestrians.

Downey, Fran. 2006. "Freedom Readers." *National Geographic Explorer*, January/February.

Franklin, Stuart. 2000. "Celebrations of Earth." *National Geographic Magazine*.

Freeman, Don. 1976. *Corduroy*. New York: Puffin.

Gikow, L. 1993. *For Every Child a Better World*. Wave, WI: Golden.

Golenbock, Peter. 1990. *Teammates*. San Diego: Harcourt Brace Jovanovich.

Hakim, Joy. 1995. A History of US series. New York: Oxford University.

———. 2004. The Story of Science series. New York: Smithsonian.

Henkes, Kevin. 1987. *Sheila Rae the Brave*. New York: Mulberry.

———. 1990. *Julius, the Baby of the World*. New York: Mulberry.

———. 1991. *Chrysanthemum*. New York: Mulberry.

———. 1993. *Owen*. New York: Greenwillow.

———. 2015. *Waiting*. New York: Greenwillow.

Hoose, Phillip. 2001. *We Were There, Too! Young People in U.S. History*. New York: Farrar, Straus and Giroux.

Hopkinson, Deborah. 1993. *Sweet Clara and the Freedom Quilt*. New York: Knopf.

Ieronimo, Christine. 2014. *A Thirst for Home: A Story of Water Across the World*. New York: Walker.

Jones, Charlotte Foltz. 1991. *Mistakes That Worked*. New York: Doubleday.

Kalman, Bobbie. 2011. *Helpers in My Community*. New York: Crabtree.

Keating, Jess. 2016. *Pink Is for Blobfish: Discovering the World's Perfectly Pink Animals*. New York: Knopf Books for Young Readers.

Kramer, Stephen. 1992. *Avalanche*. Minneapolis, MN: Carolrhoda.

Leedy, Loreen. 2011. *The Shocking Truth About Energy*. New York: Holiday House.

MacLachlan, Patricia. 1985. *Sarah, Plain and Tall*. New York: Harper and Row.

Manos, John. 2013. "The Power of Speech." In *Ladders Reading/Language Arts 5: Speak Out*. Washington, DC: National Geographic School.

McCully, Emily Arnold. 1992. *Mirette on the High Wire*. New York: Putnam.

Mindset Works. 2014. "You Can Grow Your Intelligence: New Research Shows the Brain Can Be Developed Like a Muscle." Mindset Works. https://www.mindsetworks.com/websitemedia/youcangrowyourintelligence.pdf.

Mosel, Arlene. 2007. *Tikki Tikki Tembo*. New York: Square Fish.

National Geographic Learning. 2012. "Lend Me a Paw." *Ladders Reading/Language Arts 4*. Washington, DC: National Geographic School.

Nelson, Kadir. 2013. *Nelson Mandela*. New York: Katherine Tegen Books.

New York Times. 2016. "What's Going On in This Picture?" *New York Times*. https://static01.nyt.com/images/2016/02/11/learning/VTS02-22-16LN/VTS02-22-16LN-superJumbo.jpg.

Newsela. 2015. "Breathe and Give It All You've Got: How Mindful Athletes Raise Their Game." Newsela. https://newsela.com/articles/mindful-athlete/id/10528/.

Page, Kent. 2002. "Garana's Story." *National Geographic Explorer*. September 1.

Parr, Todd. 2009. *The Peace Book*. Boston: Little, Brown Books for Young Readers.

Pascoe, Elaine. 1996. *Seeds and Seedlings*. San Diego: Blackbirch.

Polacco, Patricia. 2012. *The Art of Miss Chew*. New York: G.P. Putnam's Sons Books for Young Readers.

Pollan, Michael. 2009. *The Omnivore's Dilemma: The Secrets Behind What You Eat*. Young Readers Edition. New York: Dial Books.

Raven, Margot Theis. 2002. *Mercedes and the Chocolate Pilot*. Chelsea, MI: Sleeping Bear.

Rowling, J. K. 1999. *Harry Potter and the Sorcerer's Stone*. New York: Scholastic.

———. 2000. *Harry Potter and the Chamber of Secrets*. New York: Scholastic.

Rusch, Elizabeth. 2015. *Electrical Wizard: How Nikola Tesla Lit Up the World*. Cambridge, MA: Candlewick.

Rylant, Cynthia. 1996. *An Angel for Solomon Singer*. New York: Scholastic.

———. 1996. *Henry and Mudge First Book*. New York: Simon Spotlight.

Seuss, Dr. 1954. *If I Ran the Zoo*. New York: Random House.

———. 1991. *The 500 Hats of Bartholomew Cubbins*. New York: Random House.

Sewell, Anna. 1941. *Black Beauty*. New York: Dodd, Mead.

Sidman, Joyce. 2011. *Swirl by Swirl: Spirals in Nature*. Boston: HMH Books for Young Readers.

Sif, Birgitta. 2012. *Oliver*. Cambridge, MA: Candlewick.

Smithsonian. TweenTribune. www.tweentribune.com.

Steig, William. 1971. *Amos and Boris*. New York: Farrar, Straus and Giroux.

Sutcliffe, Jane. 2016. *Will's Words: How William Shakespeare Changed the Way You Talk*. Watertown, MA: Charlesbridge.

The Kid Should See This. 2017. "Toothpaste—Ingredients with George Zaidan." http://thekidshouldseethis.com/post/toothpaste-ingredients-with-george-zaidan.

Time for Kids. 2002. "Could You Survive a Week Without TV?" *Time for Kids* 7 (22). April 12.

Toupin, Laurie Ann. 2002. "What's the Fuss About Frogs?" *Odyssey*. May.

Turner, Ann. 1987. *Nettie's Trip South*. New York: Aladdin.

———. 1997. *Red Flower Goes West*. New York: Hyperion.

———. 2011. "Street Painting." In *Reading Poetry in the Middle Grades: 20 Poems and Activities That Meet the Common Core Standards and Cultivate a Passion for Poetry*, ed. Paul B. Janeczko. Portsmouth, NH: Heinemann.

Viorst, Judith. 1971. *The Tenth Good Thing About Barney*. New York: Aladdin.

Ward, Geoffrey, Ken Burns, with Jim O'Connor. 1994. *Shadow Ball: The History of the Negro Leagues*. Baseball, the American Epic series. New York: Knopf.

Ward, Geoffrey, Ken Burns, with Robert Walker. 1994. *Who Invented the Game?* Baseball, the American Epic series. New York: Knopf.

White, E. B. 1952. *Charlotte's Web*. New York: Harper and Row.

Williams, Karen Lynn. 2009. *My Name Is Sangoel*. Grand Rapids, MI: Eerdmans Books for Young Readers.

———. 2016. *Four Feet, Two Sandals*. Grand Rapids, MI: Eerdmans.

Winter, Jeanette. 1988. *Follow the Drinking Gourd*. New York: Trumpet.

———. 2005. *The Librarian of Basra: A True Story from Iraq*. San Diego: Harcourt Brace.

———. 2011. *The Watcher: Jane Goodall's Life with Chimps*. New York: Schwartz and Wade.

———. 2014. *Malala, a Brave Girl from Pakistan/Iqbal, a Brave Boy from Pakistan: Two Stories of Bravery*. San Diego: Beach Lane Books.

Wonderopolis. 2017. "What Is Parkour?" *Wonderopolis*. National Center for Families Learning. http://www.wonderopolis.org/wonder/what-is-parkour.

Woodson, Jacqueline. 2012. *Each Kindness*. New York: Nancy Paulsen Books.

Yolen, Jane. 1992. *Encounter*. San Diego: Harcourt Brace.

Yousafzai, Malala. 2013. "Malala's Speech." United Nations. http://www.un.org/News/dh/infocus/malala_speech.pdf.

Yurkovic, Diana Short. 1998. *Meet Me at the Water Hole*. Denver, CO: Shortland.

Allington, Richard. 1994. "The Schools We Have. The Schools We Need." *The Reading Teacher* 48 (1): 14–29.

———. 2011. *What Really Matters for Struggling Readers*. 3rd ed. Boston: Pearson.

Allington, Richard, and Rachael E. Gabriel. 2012. "Every Child, Every Day." *Educational Leadership* 69:12.

Anderson, Richard C., Rand J. Spiro, and Mark C. Anderson. 1978. "Schemata as Scaffolding for the Representation of Information in Connected Discourse. *American Educational Research Journal* 15 (3): 433–440.

Bain, Robert B. 2007. "They Thought the World Was Flat? Applying the Principles of How People Learn in Teaching High School History." In *How Students Learn: History in the Classroom*, ed. M. Suzanne Donovan and John Bransford. Washington DC: National Academies Press.

Beane, James A. 2005. *A Reason to Teach: Creating Classrooms of Dignity and Hope*. Portsmouth, NH: Heinemann.

Bentley, W. A., and W. J. Humphreys. 1962. *Snow Crystals*. New York: Turtle Books.

Block, Cathy Collins, and Michael Pressley, eds. 2002. *Comprehension Instruction: Research-Based Best Practices*. New York: Guilford.

Block, Cathy Collins, Joni L. Schaller, Joseph A. Joy, and Paolo Gaine. 2002. "Process-Based Comprehension Instruction: Perspectives of Four Reading Educators." In *Comprehension Instruction: Research-Based Best Practices*, ed. Cathy Collins Block and Michael Pressley. New York: Guilford.

Britton, James. 1970. *Language and Learning*. Harmondsworth, UK: Penguin.

———. 1983. "Writing and the Story World." In *Explorations in the Development of Writing: Theory, Research, and Practice*, ed. B. Kroll and G. Wells. New York: John Wiley.

Brown, A. L. and J. D. Day. 1983. "Macrorules for Summarizing Texts: The Development of Expertise." *Journal of Verbal Learning and Verbal Behavior* 22:1–4.

Buhrow, Brad, and Anne Upczak Garcia. 2006. *Ladybugs, Tornadoes, and Swirling Galaxies: English Language Learners Discover Their World Through Inquiry*. Portland, ME: Stenhouse.

Burkey, Mary. 2013. *Audiobooks for Youth: A Practical Guide to Sound Literature*. Chicago, IL: ALA.

———. 2016. "New Research Shows Audiobooks Have Powerful Impact on Literacy Development." Booklist Reader. April 28. http://www.booklistreader.com/2016/04/28/audiobooks/new-research-shows-audiobooks-have-powerful-impact-on-literacy-development/.

Burns, Ken. 2017. BrainyQuote.com. https://www.brainyquote.com/quotes/quotes/k/kenburns263381.html.

Buzan, Tony, and Barry Buzan. 2005. *The Mind Map Book: How to Use Radiant Thinking to Maximize Your Brain's Untapped Potential*. New York: Plume.

Cervetti, Gina. 2011. "Comprehension in Science." In *Comprehension Going Forward*, ed. Harvey "Smokey" Daniels. Portsmouth, NH: Heinemann.

Cervetti, Gina, Carollyn Jaynes, and Elfieda Hiebert. 2009. "Increasing Opportunities to Acquire Knowledge Through Reading." In *Reading More, Reading Better*, ed. Elfrieda Hiebert. New York: Guilford.

Cervetti, Gina, and Elfrieda Hiebert. 2015. "Knowledge Literacy and the Common Core." *Language Arts* 92 (4): 256–269.

Cervetti, Gina N., P. David Pearson, Jacqueline Barber, Elfrieda H. Hiebert, and Marco A. Bravo. 2007. "Integrating Science and Literacy: The Research We Have, the Research We Need." In *Shaping Literacy Achievement*, ed. Michael Pressley, Alison K. Billman, Kristen H. Perry, Kelly E. Reffitt, and Julia Moorehead Reynolds. New York: Guilford.

Chen, Chih-Ming, and Fang-Ya Chen. 2014. "Enhancing Digital Reading Performance with a Collaborative Reading Annotation System." *Computers and Education* 77:67–81. http://www.sciencedirect.com/science/article/pii/s0360131514000955.

Coiro, Julie. 2011. "Predicting Reading Comprehension on the Internet: Contributions of Offline Reading Skills, Online Reading Skills, and Prior Knowledge. *Journal of Literacy Research* 43 (4): 352–392.

Coiro, Julie, and David W. Moore. 2012. "New Literacies and Adolescent Learners: An Interview with Julie Coiro." *Journal of Adolescent and Adult Literacy* 55 (6): 551–553.

Costa, Arthur, 2008. "The Thought-Filled Curriculum." *Educational Leadership* 65 (5): 20–24.

Cullinan, Bernice E. 1981. *Literature and the Child*. San Diego: Harcourt Brace.

Cunningham, Anne, and Keith Stanovich. 2003. "What Principals Need to Know About Reading." *Principal* 83 (2): 34–39.

Daniels, Harvey, and Nancy Steineke. 2011. *Texts and Lessons for Content Area Reading*. Portsmouth, NH: Heinemann.

———. 2013. *Texts and Lessons for Teaching Literature*. Portsmouth, NH: Heinemann.

Daniels, Harvey, and Steven Zemelman. 2014. *Subjects Matter: Exceeding Standards Through Powerful Content Area Reading*. 2nd ed. Portsmouth, NH: Heinemann.

Daniels, Harvey "Smokey," ed. 2011. *Comprehension Going Forward: Where We Are and What's Next*. Portsmouth, NH: Heinemann.

Dartmouth, Mary Flanagan, and Geoff Kaufman. 2016. "High-Low Split: Divergent Cognitive Construal Levels Triggered by Digital and Non-Digital Platforms." Proceedings of the 2016 CHI Conference on Human Factors in Computing Systems. Santa Clara, CA, May 7–12.

Davey, Beth. 1983. "Think Aloud: Modeling the Cognitive Processes of Reading Comprehension." *Journal of Reading* 27:44–47.

Doerr, Anthony. 2014. *All the Light We Cannot See*. New York: Scribner.

Dole, Jan. 1997. Public Education and Business Coalition Reading Comprehension Workshop. Denver, CO. April.

Duke, Nell. 2014. *Inside Information: Developing Powerful Readers and Writers of Informational Text Through Project-Based Instruction.* New York: Scholastic.

Duke, Nell K., P. David Pearson, Stephanie L. Strachan, and Alison K. Billman. 2011. "Essential Elements of Fostering and Teaching Reading Comprehension." In *What Research Has to Say About Reading Instruction.* 4th ed. Newark, DE: International Reading Association.

Durkin, Dolores. 1979. "What Classroom Observations Reveal About Reading Instruction." *Reading Research Quarterly* 14:481–533.

Dyson, Alan. 1999. "Inclusion and Inclusions: Theories and Discourses in Inclusive Education." In *World Yearbook of Education 1999: Inclusion*, eds. Harry Daniels and Philip Garner. London: Kogan Page.

Eggen, Dan, and Shankar Vedantam. 2006. "More Questions than Answers." *Washington Post*, May 1.

Esquibel, Curtis L. 1999. "Frigid Weather Teases State." *Denver Post*, March 13.

Everett, Chad. "Windows and Mirrors: Why We Need Diverse Books." Scholastic Book Fairs blog. http://www.scholastic.com/bookfairs/readerleader/windows-and-mirrors-why-we-need-diverse-books.

Feynman, Richard. 1985. *"Surely You're Joking, Mr. Feynman!"* New York: Bantam.

———. 1988. *What Do You Care What Other People Think? Further Adventures of a Curious Character.* New York: Bantam.

Fielding, Linda, and P. David Pearson. 1994. "Reading Comprehension: What Works?" *Educational Leadership* 51 (5): 62–67.

Flynn, Kylie, Bryan Matlen, Sara Atienza, and Steven Schneider. 2016. "An Effective Tool in the Fight for Better Literacy." Tales2Go. WestEd. https://www.tales2go.com/research-study/.

Gallagher, Kelly. 2009. *Readicide: How Schools Are Killing Reading and What You Can Do About It.* Portland, ME: Stenhouse.

Gardner, Howard. 1991. *The Unschooled Mind: How Children Think and How Schools Should Teach.* New York: Basic Books.

Gavelek, J. R., and T. E. Raphael. 1985. "Metacognition, Instruction, and the Role of Questioning." In *Metacognition, Cognition, and Human Performance*, ed. D. L. Forrest-Pressley, G. E. MacKinnon, and T. Gary Waller. New York: Academic Press.

Gilbar, Steve. 1990. *The Reader's Quotation Book.* New York: Barnes and Noble.

Graves, Donald. 1991. *Build a Literate Classroom.* Portsmouth, NH: Heinemann.

Greene, Maxine. 1982. "Literacy for What?" *Visible Language* 16 (5):326–329.

Guthrie, J.T. 2003. "Concept Oriented Reading Instruction." In *Rethinking Reading Comprehension*, ed. C. E. Snow and A. P. Sweet. New York: Guilford.

Guthrie, J. T., and N. M. Humenick. 2004. Motivating Students to Read: Evidence for Classroom Practices That Increase Reading Motivation and Achievement. In *The Voice of Evidence in Reading Research*, ed. P. McCardle and V. Chhabra. Baltimore: Brookes.

Hansen, Jane. 1981. "The Effects of Inference Training and Practice on Young Children's Reading Comprehension." *Reading Research Quarterly* 16:391–417.

Harrer, Heinrich. 1997. *Seven Years in Tibet.* New York: Putnam.

Harvard College Library. 2007. "Interrogating Texts: 6 Reading Habits to Develop in Your First Year at Harvard." Harvard University. http://hc/.harvard.edu/research/guides/lamont_handouts/interrogatingtexts.html.

Harvard Project Zero. 2017. "See Think Wonder." Visible Thinking. visiblethinkingpz.org/VisibleThinking_html_files/03_ThinkingRoutines/03c_Core_routines/SeeThinkWonder/SeeThinkWonder_Routine.html.

Harvey, Stephanie. 1998. *Nonfiction Matters: Reading, Writing, and Research in Grades 3–8*. Portland, ME: Stenhouse.

Harvey, Stephanie, and Harvey "Smokey" Daniels. 2015. *Comprehension and Collaboration: Inquiry Circles for Curiosity, Engagement, and Understanding*. Rev. ed. Portsmouth, NH: Heinemann.

Harvey, Stephanie, and Anne Goudvis. 2002. *Think Nonfiction! Modeling Reading and Research* (video). Portland, ME: Stenhouse.

———. 2004. *Strategic Thinking: Reading and Responding, Grades 4–8* (video). Portland, ME: Stenhouse.

———. 2005a. *Read, Write, and Talk: A Practice to Enhance Comprehension* (video). Portland, ME: Stenhouse.

———. 2005b. *Reading the World: Content Comprehension with Linguistically Diverse Learners* (video). Portland, ME: Stenhouse.

———. 2007. *Strategies That Work: Teaching Comprehension for Understanding and Engagement*. Portland, ME: Stenhouse.

———. 2013. "Comprehension at the Core." *Reading Teacher* 66 (6): 432–439.

———. 2016. *Content Literacy: Lessons and Texts from Comprehension Across the Curriculum*. Portsmouth, NH: Heinemann.

———. 2016. *The Comprehension Toolkit: Language and Lessons for Active Literacy*. 2nd ed. Portsmouth, NH: Heinemann.

Harvey, Stephanie, Anne Goudvis, Katie Muhtaris, and Kristin Ziemke. 2013. *Connecting Comprehension and Technology: Adapt and Extend Toolkit Practices*. Portsmouth, NH: Heinemann.

Harvey, Stephanie, Sheila McAuliffe, Laura Benson, Wendy Cameron, Sue Kempton, Pat Lusche, Debbie Miller, Joan Schroeder, and Julie Weaver. 1996. "Teacher Researchers Study the Process of Synthesizing in Six Primary Classrooms." *Language Arts* 73: 8.

Harwayne, Shelley. 1992. *Lasting Impressions: Weaving Literature into the Writing Workshop*. Portsmouth, NH: Heinemann.

Heisey, N., and L. Kucan. 2010. "Introducing Science Concepts to Primary Students Through Read-Aloud: Interactions and Multiple Texts Make a Difference." *Reading Teacher* 63 (8): 666–676.

Hemingway, Ernest. 1952. *The Old Man and the Sea*. New York: Charles Scribner's Sons.

Hiebert, Elfrieda. 2012. *The Common Core State Standards and Text Complexity*. Santa Cruz, CA: Text Project and University of California Santa Cruz.

Hiebert, Elfrieda H., and Leigh Ann Martin. 2015. "Changes in the Texts of Reading Instruction During the Past 50 Years." In *Research-Based Practices for Teaching Common Core Literacy*, ed. P. David Pearson and Elfrieda H. Hiebert. New York: Teachers College Press.

Holt, Rush. 2017. Interview in "The Scientific Community Is Facing and Existential Crisis." *New Republic*. February 27. https://newrepublic.com/article/140889/scientific-community-facing-existential-crisis.

Howard, Jeff. 1992. "Getting Smart: The Social Construction of Intelligence." *Network Newsnotes* 6 (1):1.

Johnston, Peter. 2004. *Choice Words: How Our Language Affects Children's Learning*. Portland, ME: Stenhouse.

———. 2011. *Opening Minds: Using Language to Change Lives*. Portland, ME: Stenhouse.

Kalaidis, Jen. 2013. "Bring Back Social Studies: The Amount of Time Public-School Kids Spend Learning About Government and Civics Is Shrinking." *The Atlantic*. September 23. https://www.theatlantic.com/education/archive/2013/09/bring-back-social-studies/279891/.

Kasten, G. Randy. 2015. "Critical Thinking: A Necessary Skill in the Age of Spin." George Lucas Education Foundation. Edutopia. May 7. https://www.edutopia.org/blog/critical-thinking-necessary-skill-g-randy-kasten.

Keating, Kevin. 1998. "This Is Cruising." *Hemispheres Magazine*. March.

Keene, Ellin. 2008. *To Understand: New Horizons in Reading Comprehension*. Portsmouth, NH: Heinemann.

Kelley, David, and Tom Kelley. 2013. "How to Gain Creative Confidence at Work." *Forbes*. October 15. http://www.forbes.com/sites/danschawbel/2013/10/15/david-and-tom-kelley-how-to-gain-creative-confidence-at-work/#6b9888eab1bd.

Konnikova. 2014. "Being a Better Online Reader." *The New Yorker*, July 16. http://www.newyorker.com/science/maria-konnikova/being-a-better-online-reader.

Krashen, Stephen. 2001. "The Lexile Framework: The Controversy Continues." *California School Library Association Journal* 25 (1): 21–24.

Levstik, Linda, and Keith G. Barton. 2001. *Doing History: Investigating with Children in Elementary and Middle Schools*. Mahwah, NJ: Lawrence Erlbaum.

Loewen, James W. 2007. *Lies My Teacher Told Me: Everything Your American History Text Book Got Wrong*. New York: Simon and Schuster

Lynton, Michael. 2000. Keynote address at the Mid-Atlantic Venture Fair, Philadelphia. Oct. 25.

McKenzie, Jamie. 1996. "Making Web Meaning." *Educational Leadership* 54 (3): 30–32.

McMurrer, Jennifer. 2008. *Instructional Time in Elementary Schools: A Closer Look at Changes for Specific Subjects*. Washington, DC: Center on Education Policy. http://www.cep-dc.org/displayDocument.cfm?DocumentID=309.

Merga, Margaret, and Saiyida Mat Roni. 2017. "The Influence of Access to e-Readers, Computers, and Mobile Phones on Children's Book Reading Frequency." *Computers and Education* 109:187–196. http://www.sciencedirect.com/science/article/pii/S0360131517300489.

Melville, Herman. 1851. *Moby Dick*. New York: Harper Brothers.

Miller, Debbie. 2007. *Teaching with Intention: Defining Beliefs, Aligning Practice, Taking Action*. Portland, ME: Stenhouse.

———. 2012. *Reading with Meaning: Teaching Comprehension in the Primary Grades*. 2nd ed. Portland, ME: Stenhouse.

———. 2013. "Not So Gradual Release." In *Comprehension Going Forward*, ed. Harvey "Smokey" Daniels. Portsmouth, NH: Heinemann.

———. 2017. Keynote address at Hong Kong International School Literacy Institute. Hong Kong. January 21–22.

Milliot, Jim. 2016. "As E-Book Sales Decline, Digital Fatigue Grows." *Publisher's Weekly*. June 17. http://www.publishersweekly.com/pw/by-topic/digital/retailing/article/70696-as-e-book-sales-decline-digital-fatigue-grows.html.

Mooney, Chris, and Brady Dennis. 2017. "On Climate Change, Scott Pruitt Causes and Uproar—and Contradicts the EPA's Own Website." *Washington Post*, March 9. https://www.washingtonpost.com/news/energy-environment/wp/2017/03/09/on-climate-change-scott-pruitt-contradicts-the-epas-own-website/?utm_term=.8fcbd5b38ed6.

Muhtaris, Katie, and Kristin Ziemke. 2015. *Amplify: Digital Teaching and Learning in the K–6 Classroom*. Portsmouth, NH: Heinemann.

Newkirk, Tom. 2016. "Research and Policy: Unbalanced Literacy: Reflections on the Common Core." *Language Arts* 93 (4):304.

NGSS Lead States. 2013. *Next Generation Science Standards: For States by States*. Washington DC: The National Academies Press.

Palincsar, Annemarie S., and A. L. Brown. 1984. "Reciprocal Teaching of Comprehension-Fostering and Monitoring Activities." *Cognition and Instruction* 1: 117–175.

Paris, S. G., M. Y. Lipson, and K. K. Wixon. 1983. "Becoming a Strategic Reader." *Contemporary Educational Psychology* 8:293–316.

Paterson, Katherine. 1995. *A Sense of Wonder: On Reading and Writing Books for Children*. New York: Penguin.

Pearson, P. David. 1995. Personal Interview.

———. 2006a. "Roots of Reading/Seeds of Science." Presented at the National Geographic Literacy Institute, Washington, DC.

———. 2006b. Letter to the Editor. *New York Times*. March 28.

———. 2010. Keynote. International Reading Association World Congress. Auckland, New Zealand. July 14.

———. 2014. "Vocabulary: Its Role in Comprehension, Knowledge Acquisition, and Disciplinary Learning." Keynote. Colorado Council of the International Reading Association. Denver. February 7.

———. 2015. "Reading Research Policy and Practice: Why It Is Essential to Keep Them in Alignment." Keynote. Wisconsin State Reading Association. Milwaukee. February 5.

Pearson, P. David, and Linda Fielding. 1994. "Synthesis of Research/Reading Comprehension: What Works." *Educational Leadership* 51 (5): 62–68.

Pearson, P. David, and M. C. Gallagher. 1983. "The Instruction of Reading Comprehension." *Contemporary Educational Psychology* 8:317–344.

Pearson, P. David, J. A. Dole, G. G. Duffy, and L. R. Roehler. 1992. "Developing Expertise in Reading Comprehension: What Should Be Taught and How Should It Be Taught?" In *What Research Has to Say to the Teacher of Reading*, ed. J. Farstup and S. J. Samuels, 2nd ed. Newark, DE: International Reading Association.

Perkins, David. 1992. *Smart Schools: Better Thinking and Learning for Every Child*. New York: Free Press.

Pink, Daniel. 2011. *Drive: The Surprising Truth About What Motivates Us*. New York: Penguin.

Plimpton, George. 1988. *Writers at Work*. Eighth Series. New York: Penguin.

Ravitch, Diane. 2010. *The Death and Life of the Great American School System: How Testing and Choice Are Undermining Education*. New York: Basic Books.

Reutzel, D. R., J. A. Smith, and P. C. Fawson. 2005. "An Evaluation of Two Approaches for Teaching Reading Comprehension Strategies in the Primary Years Using Science Information Texts." *Early Childhood Research Quarterly* 20:276–305.

Ribons, Hilary. 2014. "Why These Successful Boston Coffee Shops Don't Offer Free Wi-Fi." *BostInno*. April 15. http://bostinno.streetwise.co/2014/04/15/why-these-successful-boston-coffee-shops-dont-offer-free-wifi/.

Ritchhart, Ron. 2002. *Intellectual Character: What It Is, Why It Matters and How to Get It*. San Francisco: Jossey-Bass.

———. 2015. *Creating Cultures of Thinking: The Eight Forces We Must Master to Truly Transform Our Schools*. San Francisco: Jossey-Bass.

Rosenblatt, Louise. [1938] 1996. *Literature as Exploration*. New York: Modern Language Association of America.

Schmidt, Eric. 2009. Interview with Fareed Zakaria. "Global Public Square." CNN. November 29.

Schwarz, Patrick. 2006. *From Disability to Possibility: The Power of Inclusive Classrooms*. Portsmouth, NH: Heinemann.

Sibberson, Franki, and Karen Szymusiak. 2008. *Beyond Leveled Books*. 2nd ed. Portland, ME: Stenhouse.

Sparks, Sarah. 2016. "Screen vs. Print: Does Digital Reading Change How Students Get the Big Picture?" Inside School Research. *Education Week*. May 16. http://blogs.edweek.org/edweek/inside-school-research/2016/05/does_digital_reading_change_comprehension.html?cmp=eml-contshr-shr.

Stanovich, Keith E. 2000. *Progress in Understanding Reading: Scientific Foundations and New Frontiers*. New York: Guilford.

Stead, Tony. 2005. *Reality Checks: Teaching Reading Comprehension with Nonfiction K–5*. Portland, ME: Stenhouse.

Tatum, Alfred W. 2005. *Teaching Reading to Black Adolescent Males: Closing the Achievement Gap*. Portland, ME: Stenhouse.

Tishman, Shari, David N. Perkins, and Eileen Jay. 1994. *The Thinking Classroom: Learning and Teaching in a Culture of Thinking*. Boston: Allyn and Bacon.

Tovani, Cris. 2000. *I Read It, but I Don't Get It: Comprehension Strategies for Adolescent Readers*. Portland, ME: Stenhouse.

———. 2003. *Do I Really Have to Teach Reading? Content Comprehension, Grades 6–12*. Portland, ME: Stenhouse.

———. 2011. *So What Do They Really Know?* Portland, ME: Stenhouse.

Trabasso, Tom, and Edward Bouchard. 2002. "Teaching Readers How to Comprehend Text Strategically." In *Comprehension Instruction: Research-Based Best Practices*, ed. Cathy Collins Block and Michael Pressley. New York: Guilford.

Trelease, Jim. 2013. *The Read-Aloud Handbook*. 7th ed. New York: Penguin.

Webster's New World Dictionary. 1991. New York: Simon and Schuster.

Wiggins, Grant, and Jay McTighe. 2005. *Understanding by Design*. 2nd ed. Englewood Cliffs, NJ: Prentice Hall.

Wikipedia, s.v. "Close reading," last modified December 13, 2016, https://en.wikipedia.org/wiki/Close_reading.

Wilkinson, I. A. G., and E. H. Son. 2011. "A Dialogic Turn in Research on Learning and Teaching to Comprehend." In *Handbook of Reading Research*, vol. 4, eds. M. L. Kamil, P. D. Pearson, E. B. Moje, and P. P. Afflerbach. New York: Routledge.

Willingham, Daniel. 2016. In "Response: Reading Digitally vs. Reading on Paper" by Larry Ferlazzo. *Education Week*. May 28. http://blogs.edweek.org/teachers/classroom_qa_with_larry_ferlazzo/2016/05/response_reading_digitally_vs_reading_paper.html?_ga=1.48223847.1398758869.1490925461.

Wolf, Maryanne. *Proust and the Squid: The Story and Science of the Reading Brain*. New York: HarperCollins.

Page numbers followed by *f* indicate figures.

A

Abercrombie, Barbara, 128

acquiring knowledge, 28*f*, 29. *See also* knowledge

Action questions, 251. *See also* questioning

activating knowledge. *See also* background knowledge; knowledge

  comprehension and, 8–9, 9*f*

  inquiry approach and, 259

  thinking aloud and, 76

active learning, 238–239. *See also* learning

active reading, 9–10. *See also* reading

active use of knowledge, 28*f*, 29. *See also* knowledge

aesthetic reading, 10–11. *See also* reading

agency, 6–7, 36

Allen, James, 172

Allington, Richard, 20, 61–62

All the Light We Cannot See (Doerr), 127

Amonte, Arlene, 165–166

Amos and Boris (Steig), 105–106

analyzing, 32, 37

An Angel for Solomon Singer (Rylant), 220–221

anchor charts

  learning from video clips and, 112–113, 113*f*

  monitoring comprehension and, 93

  overview, 74

  questioning and, 147

  tips for, 80

  vocabulary and, 172

Anning, Mary, 260–262

annotating text

  assessment and, 101, 104

  connections, 122–124

  inferring and visualizing with poetry and, 168, 168*f*, 169*f*

  interactive reading aloud and, 78

  learning from video clips and, 112–113, 113*f*

  monitoring comprehension and, 96, 96*f*, 97, 98*f*

  overview, 74, 85, 188

  tips for, 79

  website reading and, 99

application of strategies, 61. *See also* strategy instruction

artistic responses to reading. *See also* responding to texts

  content instruction and, 243, 243*f*

  Facts/Questions/Responses (FQR) think sheet, 248–249, 248*f*, 249*f*

  overview, 84–85

  picture books and, 158–159, 159*f*

  visualization and, 154, 155*f*, 158–159, 159*f*

Art of Miss Chew, The (Polacco), 29

assessment. *See also* evaluation

  comprehension instruction, 66–68

  connections and, 120–124

  determining importance and, 208–210

  inferences and visualization and, 179–183

  monitoring comprehension, 101–104

  questioning and, 145–146, 146*f*, 147–150

  technology and, 48

  video summaries and, 225

audience, 42, 48

audiobooks, 49, 56

Audiobooks for Youth (Burkey), 49

authentic questions, 37, 145–146, 146*f*. *See also* questioning

authentic response, 65. *See also* responding to texts

Avalanche (Kramer), 113–114, 122

awareness, 6–7, 7*f*, 14

B

background knowledge. *See also* activating knowledge; building knowledge; connections; knowledge

  assessment and, 120–124

  big ideas and, 107–108

  close reading and, 32

  content knowledge and, 110–111

  inferences and, 143–144, 153, 153*f*, 177–178